A
MICHIGAN
READER

Happy 30th Anniversary, Joe!

Love,

Mary

April 7, 1975

A MICHIGAN READER

11,000 B.C.
to
A.D. 1865

Edited by

George S. May
Herbert J. Brinks

William B. Eerdmans
Publishing Company   Grand Rapids, Michigan

Library of Congress Cataloging in Publication Data

May, George Smith, 1924-   comp.
    A Michigan reader: 11,000 B. C. to A. D. 1865.

    Companion vol. to A Michigan reader: 1865 to the
present, edited by R. M. Warner and C. W. Vander Hill.
    1. Michigan—History—Addresses, essays, lectures.
I. Brinks, Herbert, 1935-   joint comp. II. Title.
F566.M155   917.74'03'1   73-20211
ISBN 0-8028-7029-5

For the memory of
Willis F. Dunbar, 1902-1970
Teacher, Scholar, and Friend

Contents

Preface

Teachers of United States history have the problem of selecting supplemental readings for their classes from large numbers of monographs and articles of potential usefulness to their students and to the structure of their classes. Teachers of state and local history have a contrary problem. The reading materials useful as supplements to their classes are not nearly so plentiful, so varied, or so skillfully written. What exists is frequently not easily available, and inexpensive paperbacks are virtually nonexistent. This reader has been assembled with no pretenses of solving this problem for students of Michigan history, but it does provide in convenient form a modest selection of articles from a wide variety of sources on the history of Michigan from prehistory to the Civil War. A companion volume, edited by Robert M. Warner and C. Warren Vander Hill, provides readings in the state's history from the Civil War to the present.

The reader does not present material on all major themes or events in the history of the state during the period covered. The selection of articles was frankly subjective, reflecting as much the interests and approaches to history of its individual compilers as it does the importance of the events and periods covered. The editors of both volumes agreed that each would have a large amount of freedom in the selection process. This wise decision saved much time and probably disputes among the writers. We all reviewed each contributor's selection, however. As a result, all of us made modifications of our original choices.

The earliest period in Michigan history was compiled by George S. May, professor of history at Eastern Michigan University and a well-known writer on all aspects of Michigan history, including his splendid pictorial history of the state. May notes the prehistoric origins of the state and gives us examples of the historiography of Michigan's original inhabitants, the Indians. His articles trace the impact of the coming of Europeans on Indian civilization as these outsiders sought to extend the empire of their native lands—first France, then Britain, and finally the newly emerging United States.

Herbert Brinks, formerly Director of the Historical Society of Michigan and presently Professor of History at Calvin College, completed the section covering the Michigan territorial and early statehood period through the 1860s. This was a period, bracketed by the War of 1812 and the Civil War, of economic crises, rapid settlement, self-discovery, and establishment of the social, economic, and political foundations for later developments.

In sum, we have given you a potpourri of writings that will, we hope, add a useful, interesting, and stimulating dimension to classes in Michigan history.

Robert M. Warner
Director, Michigan Historical Collections
Professor of History, University of Michigan

Part I

THE REAL MICHIGAN

Introduction

The state of Michigan has meant many things to many people during the past four centuries. Indeed, a fair number of people, particularly native sons, travelers, immigrants, and foreign observers, have written accounts of how they viewed the state and what it meant to them. Among the most noteworthy of these reflections is that of Bruce Catton, the noted historian of the Civil War, and a native of Benzonia. In the following article Catton, while not pretending to be an authority on the history of Michigan, captures the unique flavor of life in the state as only a native son with his extraordinary literary skills could do. It is also a view of the Wolverine State that is "pre-expressway," of a time not so long ago when automobile travel was a journey from town to town at a much more leisurely pace than most of us are accustomed to today. Those interested in learning more about Catton's views of his early years in Michigan should read his autobiographical work, *Waiting for the Morning Train* (Garden City, N.Y., 1972).

The Real Michigan

BRUCE CATTON

Michigan is perhaps the strangest state in the Union, a place where the past, the present and the future are all tied up together in a hard knot. It is the 20th Century incarnate, and if you look closely you can also see the twenty-first coming in; but it is also the 19th Century, the backward glance and the authentic feel and taste of a day that is gone forever. It killed the past and it is the past; it is the skyscraper, the mass-production line and the frantic rush into what the machine will some day make of all of us, and at the same time it is golden sand, blue water, green pine trees on empty hills, and a wind that comes down from the cold spaces, scented with the forests that were butchered by hard-handed men in checked flannel shirts and floppy pants. It is the North Country wedded to the force that destroyed it.

You enter Michigan, mostly, by way of Detroit, which is something special. It is a profound weight on the land; an enormous city, with great skyscrapers taking the light from Canada, automobile factories and used-car lots scattered across the flat prairies, enough business strewn along the Detroit River to make a Russian's eyes pop; and in the old days, which lasted until World War II, you came into Detroit, usually, by steamboat, which was an experience in itself.

The boats came up from the Lake Erie ports, Cleveland and Buffalo and Sandusky, and they gave a theatrical touch to the whole business. Lake Erie is beautiful and shallow and treacherous, with a capacity for whipping up unexpected storms that would bother any mariner who ever lived, although mostly it is pleasant enough; and the old side-wheelers came paddling down its length, usually in the middle of the night—it was nice sleeping, in a snug stateroom on one of those boats, with an air-conditioned wind coming in at the open porthole, and the wash of the paddle wheels

Reprinted from *Holiday* (August, 1957), pp. 26-39, by permission of the author.

beating a quiet rhythm in the darkness—and in the morning the boat came up the Detroit River, and the factories and pumping stations on the bank suddenly made you realize that man had taken over Nature and was trying to make something out of it. Then, a little after breakfast time, the boat docked along the Detroit water front, and no city in America offered a more thrilling or exciting entrance.

The boats are mostly gone, and this is really Detroit's fault. Detroit did not exactly invent the automobile, but it picked the thing up when it was nothing better than a costly and unreliable toy for the rich and made it a necessity for everybody in America, and the automobile—getting slightly out of hand—killed the Great Lakes passenger boats, except for a few cruise ships. You come into Detroit nowadays in your own car, or perhaps by train, and the old impact is gone. The place dawns on you gradually now; it used to hit you between the eyes, with the early light slanting in from beyond Ontario. But even now Detroit clamors at you, arrogantly, with all the confidence that comes to men who know they are really in charge of things and who don't mind enjoying the feeling, and there is something overwhelming about it all.

For here is a foretaste of what the machine is doing to us. Here men picked up the Industrial Revolution and swung it; this place, with its infinite genius for making any sort of contrivance men have ever dreamed of, and making it more cheaply and better than anyone else, is the doorway to the future. Everything goes in a rush, everybody is busy—and the place is big and sprawling and grimy and pulsing with life. Here is where we are going, make no mistake about it, and the big financial centers down East can say what they like and be hanged. Detroit sets the pace because this is where the muscle and the knowledge are; and if you don't think the future belongs to America, you should come here and breathe the air for a while.

Detroit makes its bow to the past, of course. It has such a place as Greenfield Village, in Dearborn, and here the past that Detroit killed forever—the past of wayside inns, one-man machine shops, quiet country villages snuggling by the route of stagecoaches, and rural dancers moving to the wheezy tunes scraped out by self-taught fiddlers—is preserved like a fly in amber, and it is very much worth visiting. But this, after all, is only a gesture. Detroit has been taking us away from that for half a century, and if it shows you Greenfield Village it also shows you the machine-age pace which turned every-thing Dearborn has on exhibit into museum pieces. Dearborn houses both this fragment of the past and also the Ford Motor

Company, which did as much as any one organism could do to put the past in its place.

Detroit's streets come in like the spokes of a wheel, the other half of the wheel having been cut off by the Detroit River. Because the pace has been uneven there are vast skyscrapers standing beside parking lots, with rummy old brick buildings from the Civil War era snuggling up against twenty-story hotels and elongated office buildings; burlesque theaters and sleazy secondhand-book stores rub elbows with the most up-to-date, chromium-and-cutstone buildings that America can build, and the river drifts by, down in front, bearing the iron ore and coal and petroleum on which modern America is built; and whether you like it or not you can feel the hard pulse of America beating up and down these automobile-clogged streets.

Some years ago a civic-minded booster dreamed up the phrase, "dynamic Detroit," to express the essence of this city. He hit it off perfectly. Detroit *is* dynamic. Here is where they call the tune, and it is not a tune the Greenfield Village fiddlers ever quite managed to express.

But Detroit, after all, is not really Michigan. Its industrial empire spraddles over a good part of the state, to be sure—with Flint, and Pontiac, and Jackson and Lansing and Grand Rapids and all the rest—but the tremendous industrial nexus centered here is only half of the story. The other half is something very different—old times, the breath of bygone days and memories that went out of date before the men who remembered them were old—and as a man born out of his proper time I love this other Michigan a good deal more than I love Detroit.

The map of the Lower Peninsula is shaped like a fat old-fashioned mitten—a left-hand mitten, placed palm down, with a bulky thumb sticking out into the cold blue of Lake Huron. Detroit is down in the lower right-hand margin, below where the thumb begins, and the great industrial network lies across the lower part of the state: across the upper part of the wrist. But if you will take the map, and draw a line from Bay City—at the bottom of the gap between the bulbous thumb and the rest of the hand—straight west across the state, you will have cut Michigan into its two distinctive parts. Everything below the line is 20th Century; everything above it is North Country—old, half empty, touched by the cold winds that drift down from the Arctic, with trees and sand and crystal-clear water and drowsy small towns as its distinguishing marks. It is a country that will put its seal on you if you are not careful, because it offers a lonely beauty and an escape from almost everything Detroit stands for.

The present falls away, when you go up into this part of the state. Suppose you drive up from Detroit, along U. S. Route 10; it goes through places like Flint and Saginaw and Midland, any one of which would be world-famous if it were in some other country—and then, suddenly, it takes you into the empty cut-over land, where ghost towns cluster by the road, where the rivers flow cold and clear past hills that furnished lumber for half the world a generation or two ago, where cabins nestle down by quiet lakes and where the air drifts straight through you as if nobody had ever soiled it with smoke or grime or gas fumes. From here on north there are not so many farms, the soil is very sandy, excellent for growing pine trees, not often so good for growing anything else, and if it amuses you to count abandoned farms (unpainted shacks going peacefully to ruin amid fields nobody has tilled for a quarter century or more) you can make quite a list in an afternoon's drive. The road leads you out of ambition into peace and contentment; the deceptive light of an eternal summer afternoon lies on the rolling country; the innumerable lakes glitter brightly blue in the fading light, and when you stop your car and listen you hear a blessed quiet.

This part of the state must have been quite a sight, a hundred years ago. Over an area of better than 25,000 square miles there was a magnificent forest—great pines, mostly, with a healthy sprinkling of hardwoods like maples and beeches—like nothing you can find in America today. From lake to lake and for 250 miles from north to south there was an eternal green twilight, with open spaces where the lakes and rivers were; twilight, with the wind forever making an unobtrusive noise in the branches overhead, brown matted needles and leaves underfoot—everything just about as it was shortly after the last ice age.

There is one tiny fragment of it left. If you will go to the little town of Kalkaska, in the northwest part of the state's Lower Peninsula, and drive thirty miles or so to the east, you will reach Hartwick Pines State Park; and here, running down to the bank of the Au Sable River, is an eighty-five-acre tract of virgin timber, the last that remains, preserved for tourists. You leave your car by the park-administration building and suddenly you are in the middle of it, with trees rising 150 feet overhead, and a shaded coolness all about that is proof against the summer's worst heat wave. Walking through it is not unlike walking through a cathedral. It has that effect on people. It is even more moving in the dead of winter, with the big trees coming up out of a white silence that is all but absolute; the trouble is that then you have to use skis or snowshoes to get there.

Anyway, Michigan a century ago was one magnificent forest, and even as recently as the Civil War it had hardly been touched. But then the lumberjacks went to work, and they shaved the countryside the way a razor shaves a man's chin. Where there had been wilderness, boom lumber towns sprang up, with rickety railroad lines threading their way back into the hills. In the springtime, every stream was clogged with logs, with lumberjacks scampering across the treacherous shifting carpet with peavy and cant hook, mounds of sawdust rising beside the busy mills, and a mill town with 1200 inhabitants normally supported from twelve to twenty saloons. Michigan voted for prohibition before the Federal prohibition amendment went into effect in 1920, and anyone who remembers what those saloons did to small-town life can easily understand why. For a time Saginaw was the greatest lumber city in the world, then Muskegon had the title, and then some other place; fresh-cut boards were stacked in endless piles by the railroad sidings or the lakeside wharves . . . and then, all of a sudden, it was all over. The lumber was gone, the mills were dismantled, the booming cities and towns lapsed into drowsiness, store-fronts were boarded up—and the razor which had done all of this shaving had left a stubble of stumps like a frowsy three-day beard across thousands of square miles. Some towns died entirely, some almost died, and the endless whine of the gang saws became quiet forever.

All of which put its mark on a whole generation of people. Here was a region half the size of Ireland which, after only fifty years of history, suddenly found itself at a dead end. A society began to decay before it had matured. Towns dwindled and died before the eyes of the very men who had founded them. Boys who grew to manhood in these dying towns moved off to the city, leaving behind the old folks and the girls—half a century ago it was not so simple for an untrained girl to make a place for herself in a far-off city, and thousands upon thousands of these girls were condemned to lives of unwanted loneliness. They were strong and healthy and they had dreams and high hopes, and these came to very little because life had shoved them off into a side alley, since marriage was just about the only career a girl could hope for in those days. The human cost of a dying boom can be pretty high.

So they killed the infinite forest, once and for all. But there was still the land itself, rolling in vast gentle waves under a clear blue sky; there were the hundreds and hundreds of lakes, blue and cold and sparkling with imitation whitecaps; there was the great stretch of sand, putting a golden border on the water; there were the rivers, so clear you could count bits of gravel ten feet deep, so cold they turned your feet numb if you tried to wade; and there was the air, filtered by its eternal drift down from the ultimate edge of icy nowhere, fresh enough to revive a Peruvian mummy, odorous with the scent of jack pines.

All of this adds up to an earthly paradise for people from the hot cities who want to get away from asphalt and noise and muggy heat when they have a chance and touch base with Mother Nature; and today the tourist trade is the second industry in the entire state, topped only by the exalted automobile industry itself. This place where the wilderness used to be may indeed be the North Country, but it is only a hop-skip-and-jump from enormous centers of population. From Detroit or Chicago, it is a handy one-day drive to any spot in the Lower Peninsula, but at the end of the drive you feel that you have left the city and all of its works in another world.

So the old lumber area has had a rebirth, and the air of defeat and decline has vanished. This change has gone hand in hand with others. For one thing, the trees are coming back; huge state and national forests lie across vast stretches of empty land. In addition, there is a belt of cherry and peach orchards twenty miles wide and 200 miles long down the western side of the state. In spring, when the blossoms are out, the rolling hillsides near Lake Michigan offer a spectacle of breath-taking beauty, and many a town that used to live on its sawmills now lives on its cannery-and-packing plant. Every July they have a big "cherry festival" at Traverse City—a bright, bustling little city which has made full recovery from the death of the lumber boom—and a pretty girl is named Cherry Queen; her function, usually in addition to posing for photographs, is to take a cherry pie to Washington and present it to the President. This makes a nice trip for the girl, nets the President a first-rate pie, and presumably makes everybody happy.

But under everything there is this strange, beautiful, lonely land itself, this land of blue sky and clear water, where puff-ball clouds drift lazily overhead, trailing pleasant shadows over water and forest and bright little towns as if nobody ever had to be in a hurry about anything and time had come to a standstill just because what is here and now is too pleasant to leave. This is good country to come from and it is even better to go back to. It is a land of memories and also a land of escape: a place where you can be utterly idle in more pleasant ways than any other place I know.

I was born in Michigan and I grew up there, and not long ago I went back to see what it is like today. I came in through the industrial network in the lower right-hand corner of the state, and after a while I was driving northwest on U.S. Route 10—a fine road which goes for many miles at a stretch without touching a town, and which cannot in any case touch a real, full-dress city because in all of Michigan, north of that east-west line from Bay City, there is not a single place with as many as 20,000 permanent residents.

Beyond Clare, which calls itself the gateway to the northland, I turned right on M 115, which goes on past pleasant little lakes dotted with summer cottages, past a sprinkling of drowsy farms, and past uncounted miles of unused land. Yet a road, after all, takes you where you yourself are going, and not where the road goes, and what you see depends mostly on what's inside of you; and when you go back to re-explore your own country you are likely to find memories and dreams all mixed up with solid reality. I was heading for my own particular corner of the state, where I spent my boyhood, because I wanted to see what the years had done to it; and if in the end I learned more about what the years had done to me—well, that is what usually happens when you go on a pilgrimage.

My own land is mostly Benzie County, which has fewer inhabitants now than it had half a century ago but which has lost its old backwoods isolation and is a homey, friendly sort of country. There is a tiny town with the improbable name of Benzonia, which was founded by some eager folk from Oberlin College just before the Civil War when all of this land was new. The air was so clear and good that they wanted a name that would tell about it, so they dipped into their erudition and came up with a Latin-Greek hybrid which means, roughly, fragrant air. They built a little college, and for fifty years it struggled along, graduating eight or ten people a year; then it was turned into a preparatory school, and my father was principal of it when I was a boy, and just after World War I there was no longer any need for this school because the state's high schools had improved, and it quietly died. Nothing is left of it now except a brick building which has been turned into a village community house, but the little town drowses under the long sunlight, with a special flavor that other little towns don't have, touched by the memory of the old-timers who wanted to bring education to the lumber country.

Every man makes his own state—or maybe his state makes him; it is hard to be certain about such things. But you grow up with something on your mind, and it comes out of the place where you were born and reared, and you never can get away from it no matter where you go. And if you go back, long afterward, to the place you knew when you were young, you see it through eyes that were specially conditioned; you cannot be objective about it; you try to write about your background and find that you are really writing about yourself.

I remember, forty years ago, a January night when the thermometer registered five below and there was a brilliant full moon, and I went to the front door, late at night, to lock up. I stood in the doorway for a moment, looking out at the moonlit landscape, the little grove of trees across the street and the three feet of snow that covered everything. There is not in all America today anything quite as still and quiet as a Michigan small town could be, late on a moon-swept night, in January, in the days before World War I. Nobody in all the earth was making a sound, nothing was moving, there was only the white snow, the black trees, the blue shadows lying on the whiteness, and the big moon in a cloudless sky; and to stand there and look out at it was, inexplicably, to be in touch with the Infinite—and, somehow, the Infinite was good, it was lonely but friendly, it meant something you did not have to be afraid of if you understood it. So Michigan means that to me—along with much else—and coldness and loneliness and shattering loveliness go hand in hand, so that while you will always be awed and abashed when you come up against the Infinite you do not really need to be afraid. And maybe that is a fairly good idea to get and take with you.

I can remember another night, in summer time, much earlier, when as a rather small boy my family took me across Lake Michigan on a steamboat from Milwaukee. It was dark and cool and windy, and we came out of the river and out past the breakwater, and the steamer began to rise and fall on the waves of the big lake. For a small child it was quite scary—nothing but water and the dark, with big waves coming in from nowhere and making foaming noises under the bow, and the Michigan shore seemed an unimaginable distance away and the dark sea ahead was what all adventurers have always seen when they pitted themselves against the great emptiness and its wonder and peril, and life itself is an enormous gamble played by people who are eager and frightened at the same time, with nothingness before and above and the chance of a dawn-swept landfall in the morning lying there, insubstantial and improbable beyond the night, as the possible reward. That is really the truth of it, and that too is good to know.

I am well aware, of course, that, as the world's seas go, Lake Michigan is not really a very large body of water. To cross it by steamer is to spend no more than half a dozen hours afloat, and when the trip is over you have reached only the state of Michigan, which actually is as prosaic a bit of land as you can find. Yet the thoughts of a small boy can be lonely, frightening and touched with unfathomable wonder, and the borders of an unattainable land can glimmer, insubstantial but genuine, over the most matter-of-fact horizon. What you owe the land where you were born and reared is something you can never quite pin down; but if that land can stir dreams and fears and the hints of a completely illogical but convincing promise, you are that much ahead of the game. For what you think and feel when you are very small never quite leaves you, and if it always lures you on to something that the visible landscape does not quite make explicit you are immeasurably the gainer.

All of this means very little, probably, by any rational scheme of things. Yet somehow it is part of the color and the flavor which this strange, light-struck, improbable country gave to me when I was too young to know any better, and it has had its own queer effect on everything I have thought or done ever since. So I bring it in here, along with the pine trees and the cold winds and the everlasting golden sands, to try to explain why I like to go back to Michigan. I am probably trying to recapture something unattainable, but that does not matter; so long as the feel and the gleam of it still lie on the edge of my subconscious it is real, for me, and the only value in any dream consists in the fact that you have to keep pursuing it even though you know that you can never quite reach it. If the real Michigan keeps getting overlaid with the Michigan I thought I saw in the old days, I can only say that I am that much better off—for what I thought I saw then was worth a lifetime's quest.

There is plenty to see up here. Half a mile from this hilltop village is one of America's loveliest lakes—Crystal Lake, named with an utter literalness; it is so clear you can see the bottom where it is twenty feet deep—nine miles long by three miles wide, with wooded hills all around and a fringe of pleasant summer cottages along its sandy shores.

Crystal Lake itself will always be something special for me, because it symbolizes an emotion that goes beyond time and space. When I was very small the minister of the one church in my town of Benzonia took some months off, and—by dint of what patient frugality I do not know: the pastor of a country church at that time earned precious little money—made a trip to the Holy Land. When he returned he made his report, and of it I remember just one thing. The magical Sea of Galilee, he said, the sea where our Lord walked and taught and performed miracles, was just about the size and shape of our Crystal Lake. To be sure, the hills which bordered Galilee were dun-colored, barren of trees, a bleak and impoverished landscape; while our hills, green as the heart of a maple leaf, were ringed with clear water, set about with pleasant little towns, cool and pleasant, inviting people to linger on their long journey from one mystery to another. But the resemblance was there, and the lake in which I caught diminutive perch was very like the lake on which Peter tried to walk dry-shod; and for some reason my life is richer because a saintlike little pastor, half a century ago, saw Galilee through innocent eyes which could interpret any lake in terms of Michigan's pine trees and green open valleys. I have never been to Palestine, but somehow I have seen the Sea of Galilee and the Word that was preached by that Near-Eastern sea has a special sound for me.

. . . .

From Frankfort you swing up toward Traverse City on route M 22, which cuts up across what is known as the Leelenau Peninsula. Once this was lumber country and now it is cherry country, but mostly it is a region for summer vacationers. Every little town has its lake (Glen Lake, which lies back of Sleeping Bear Point, is a show place) and there are other lakes with no towns at all, locked in by ice and snow for four or five months of the year.

Sleeping Bear Point is an enormous sand dune, five miles long by 500 feet high, jutting out into Lake Michigan. A road of sorts leads to the top, but your car would stall in the deep, fine sand, so you go to the town of Glen Haven and take passage in one of the special low-gear cars with oversized, half-inflated tires, which waddle through the sand as if they were made for it. On the crest there is nothing at all to see but this golden empty ridge and the great blue plain of Lake Michigan far below, with white surf curling on the beach at the foot of the bluff, yet it is one of the finest sights in the Middle West. There is no noise except the lake wind ruffling the spare trees: there is just nothing except a feeling of infinite space and brightness, and utter freedom from the smoke and the rush and the racket of ordinary 20th Century life.

The country north of Traverse City is high and open, with Lake Michigan nearly always in view off to the left, and the little towns and villages along the way reflect the past in a curious manner. First there was the lumber era, in which today's sleepy hamlet was a rip-roaring little city with a solid mile of sawmills along the water front. Then, when the lumber was gone, there was the early summer-resort trade: passenger boats coming up from Chicago or around from Detroit; imposing but flimsy frame hotels, all veranda and white pillars, overlooking every beach; Pullman cars unloading a new consignment of vacationers at the railroad depot every morning . . . and after a while the automobiles came and killed boat lines, passenger trains and most of the hotels, so that these towns which had made one readjustment had to make another. The result is odd.

Every town contains echoes of those two vanished eras, and seems to be looking back regretfully to the past; and yet most of them are brighter and more hopeful than they ever were before, the old feeling of backwoods isolation is gone, the people who live here are having a better time of it than ever before and the general level of prosperity is higher and more stable. Yet the feeling of the past does linger, so that in this area which has hardly been settled more than a century there are haunting echoes of antiquity.

Your memory can play queer tricks on you. At Charlevoix I drove east, skirting the south shore of beautiful Lake Charlevoix to reach Boyne City. Boyne City was perhaps the last lumber boom town in the Lower Peninsula. We lived there, for a year or so, when I was about six years old, and it was a lively place then. There were four immense sawmills along the lake front, and a big "chemical plant"—I suppose it was a place where they extracted turpentine and other by-products from the pines—and there was even a blast furnace, although what it may have been doing there I have never been able to understand. Anyway, Boyne City was bustling and exciting, and our back yard ran down to the Boyne River, where the log drives came down in the spring. To my six-year-old eyes that river was immense; it was, I realized, probably smaller than the Mississippi, but it was fascinating, wide, turbulent, somehow menacing—a dangerous river which easily could (and, two or three times, very nearly did) drown a small boy who incautiously tried to play on its treacherous carpet of moving logs. So I returned to the old back yard and took another look at the river—and realized that either the river had shrunk or I had stretched considerably. The river is charming—gentle, crystal-clear, friendly, no more hostile than a brook. Along the lake front there is an uncommonly pleasant park, where the sawmills used to be. A rusted remnant of the old blast furnace still survives, but everything else seems to be gone; and this is not the exciting town where I used to live, it is just a bright, friendly little community where old memories are held in suspension in the sunlight.

Another of my favorite towns in this part of the state is Petoskey, where I was born. No man ever breaks completely away from his birthplace; you carry the mark of your home town with you. I remember it as a sleepy sort of place, built on a spectacular side hill that slants up steeply from the cold blue of Little Traverse Bay, with funny little tourist-bait shops at the bottom where Indian wares and other trinkets were offered for sale to the "summer people." These shops always smelled pleasantly of birch bark—there were baskets, and toy canoes, and other contrivances—and to this day the odor of birch bark takes me back to tiny stores which must have gone out of existence a whole generation ago.

Petoskey has grown up to date and prosperous. It is no longer a lumber center, and the great trains of flatcars piled high with pine logs no longer go rumbling past what used to be the Grand Rapids & Indiana depot, and the sprawling summer hotels I remember so well are not there any more; but because the hill is so high and because so much of the big lake lies open at the foot of the hill Petoskey gives you what so much of this part of Michigan always gives—the strange feeling that you are at an immense altitude, on some sort of ridge where you can look down on half of the Middle West and where the wind that never quite dies down has come to you without touching anything at all along the way from wherever it is that winds are born.

Even though it always speaks of the past, and seems to look back toward it in a dreamy sort of way, most of this part of Michigan has no particular history. But when you go north from Petoskey you step far back into legend and the distant past. Things were going on here when the eastern seaboard colonies were still young. La Salle, Jolliet and Marquette were here nearly three centuries ago. At Mackinaw City, at the very tip of Michigan's Lower Peninsula, and an hour's easy drive from Petoskey, there is a lake-front park with a rebuilt stockade which marks the site of one of early America's most significant strong points—Fort Michilimackinac. Here, around 1681, missionaries and fur traders and French soldiers and a scattering of just plain adventurers built an outpost of French civilization in a spot which was more remote and isolated than any spot on earth can be today.

After the French left Canada the British took over, and in 1763 Pontiac's painted warriors broke in, seized stockade and fort, and massacred the British garrison. Then the fort was abandoned, to be rebuilt on Mackinac Island, which lies in the center of the straits. The Americans took it over after the Revolution, and the British recaptured it in the War of 1812, and then it was returned to American possession again. Now it stands empty, a tourists' show place, looking out at the unending procession of freighters that cruise slowly past on their way to and from the lower lakes.

Mackinac Island is a delightful spot, and it is unusual in two ways. In the first place, although it is spelled Mackinac it is, for some incomprehensible reason, pronounced Mackinaw; and in the second place it is the one spot in the whole state of Michigan—one of the very few spots in all the United States—where you never see an automobile. Automobiles are not allowed on the island, and to come to this place, with its hotels and boardinghouses and curio shops lining the quiet streets, and the old-fashioned horse-drawn surreys leisurely wheeling their way in and out, is to step straight back into the Victorian era. To get about the island you walk, or ride behind a horse, or get on a bicycle. More so than any other place in the state, this is a refuge from the present.

Big changes are coming to Upper Michigan and the symbol of their approach is the stupendous five-mile-long bridge being built across the straits to connect the Lower and Upper Peninsula. The bridge will cost around $100,000,000; it is expected to be completed this fall, and it will at last tie the two halves of the state firmly together. At present, you cross the straits by one of a fleet of state-owned ferry boats.

Michigan's Upper Peninsula is an immense finger of land running 300 miles from west to east, with cold, steely-blue Lake Superior, the largest lake in the world, lying all along its northern flank. Eighty-five per cent of this area is forested and lumbering is still going on, the Marquette iron range still turns out iron ore, and some copper is still being mined; but comparatively speaking the Upper Peninsula is almost empty, with fewer than 300,000 inhabitants. If the northern half of the Lower Peninsula is North Country the Upper Peninsula is the same thing at treble strength. It is traversed by excellent concrete roads, and you can drive for two hours without seeing a town, or anything that looks like permanent human habitation. For mile after mile there is nothing except clear blue lakes, vast areas of cut-over timber, forests which look as if nobody had ever taken an ax into them, and outcroppings of bleak rock. With Lake Superior so close this country has its own built-in air-conditioning; there is a sharp edge to the air, a feeling of unlimited space and quiet and peace, and that strange quality of half-ominous, half-friendly loneliness is with you all of the time. Once the bridge is finished, all of this will probably be watered down, but it can never be wholly destroyed. After all, up in this country there is nothing between you and the North Pole except a few thousand miles of totally empty land and water.

One of the interesting things to see up here is the canal at Sault Ste. Marie, whose big locks connect Lake Superior with the lower lakes. The Soo, as everybody calls it, is a lively little city during the eight months of the navigation season; it boasts that its canal handles more traffic than Panama and Suez combined. All day and all night the ships—enormous things, 500 and 600 feet in length—come majestically in from the upper lake, floating high above your head, sinking slowly as the water burbles out of the locks, and then gliding off for the great industrial region hundreds of miles to the south. In an average day, eighty or ninety of them will go through. Day and night, you are forever hearing the deep, haunting bass of their whistles—the inescapable, wholly characteristic and somehow deeply romantic noise of the Soo region. (Progress is taking a hand here, these immense boats are being equipped with air horns, which emit a blatting which carries a great deal farther than the traditional steam whistle but which is pure discord and nothing more.)

Driving west from the Soo, on the broad highway that leads to Marquette and the iron-range country, you pass Seney, a drowsy little country town so unobtrusive that you can go all the way through it before you realize you have reached it. It's quiet and orderly today, but half a century ago Seney was a hell-roaring lumber town, with a reputation for unrestrained misconduct that did not need to take second place to any Western cattle town or mining camp. There is a myth, formerly given wide circulation in the Sunday supplements, about a log stockade that once adorned the town. In it, according to one version, dance-hall girls were kept when not dancing; according to another, captive lumberjacks were immured here between spells in the backwoods. There is one odd thing about these fancy yarns of the high-wide-and-handsome days of the lumber towns; the sins which were committed in these places were never really attractive. It is very hard to glamorize a village rowdy, and the lumberjack tough mugs were at bottom village rowdies and nothing better. Seney's most notorious character, for instance, was a loafer who used to win free drinks in bars by biting the heads off frogs, mice and other vermin. He finally came to a well-merited end, according to the story, when he bit the head off a small owl which was the particular pet of a burly lumberjack, who promptly brought this unattractive character's career to a close by smiting him vigorously over the head with the handle of a peavy.

Marquette is the metropolis of the Upper Peninsula. It is a solid industrial town, with red ore from the great ridges behind it coming down to the docks in red hopper cars, and if it is not the most lovely city in the United States it occupies one of the nation's most beautiful sites. The south shore of Lake Superior curves in and out, along here, with deep bays and jutting, pine-crowned headlands; the old primeval rock breaks through the crust of the land to remind you that this is the backbone of the continent, where rocks so ancient they even lack fossils lie bare under the long summer sunlight, grim and lonely and desolate. Just at sunset, from east of Marquette, you can see the city with the opaque blue panel of Lake Superior silent in front of it and a flaming red sky behind it, lying in the evening stillness like a dream of the city that never was; it is transfigured, a strange light lies on its towers and parapets, and this place that for so long was a Mecca for Cornish miners (the roadside stands still peddle Cornish pasties instead of hot dogs, and very good they are too) becomes an unattainable no-place out of fable, dropping long dark shadows on a silent cold sea.

If you are well advised, you will head west from Marquette for the copper country. Do it, if possible, early in October when the lonely road will take you through forests aflame with scarlet and gold and bronze, and a wild, doomed beauty that belongs beyond the farthest edge of the world lies on all the landscape; the touch of everlasting winter is in the air and yet for an hour or so the sunlight is still warm, and nothing you will ever see will move you more or linger with you longer. You come out, at last, onto the long spine of the Keweenaw Peninsula—an outcrop of rock and wild trees, reaching far up into Lake Superior, perhaps the oldest land in the new world. The copper mines which caused men to come here in the first place go deep under the lake—some of the shafts go down for more than a mile. You get the feeling of a land that has been passed by, a hard, forbidding and strangely charming bit of country that had a short hectic history and does not especially want any more; and all about is the cold steely blue of the greatest of lakes, and the picturesque little settlements that manage to be both friendly and forsaken at the same moment.

It would be possible, of course, to drive on, noting the points of interest in the Upper Peninsula, mentioning the more unusual towns—like Eagle Harbor, one of the most completely beautiful villages I ever expect to see, with two long headlands enclosing a quiet strip of water and the great angry lake piling destructive surging waves against the rocks outside—but my state is half reality and half the dim, enchanted memories of a long-lost boyhood, and anyway I did not live in the entire state of Michigan. I knew only selected parts of it, and these parts stay in my memory and call back unforgettable things which were born of the cold emptiness and the inviting, menacing beauty of this North Country.

They are Upper Michigan, the part that lies north of the automobile belt, the doomed, bewitched country which presently will surrender to the Mackinac bridge and to the superhighway and which, ultimately, will undoubtedly become just another part of the sprawling, industrialized Middle West. But while today's light lasts it is still a land apart, there is a pleasantly melancholy flavor of a lost past to it, and although men murdered the forests with a passionate ferocity the forests somehow still live and put their strange touch on the countryside. There are cool shadows under the trees and a timeless peace lies on the cutover tracts and the fields where the young second growth is hiding the stumps.

It is a strange country: lonely enough, even in summer, and cold as the far side of the moon when winter comes, with the far-off hills rising pale blue from the frozen white landscape. It offers a chance to draw a deep breath, to turn around and look back at the traveled path, to stand on a high hill and be alone with the fresh air and the sunlight. It is wood and water, golden sand and blue lakes, emptiness and memories and the sort of isolation which it is hard for a city man to come by, these days. All in all, it is quite a state.

Part II

11,000 B.C.
to A.D. 1800

Introduction

Michigan as it is known today is of quite recent origins. It was only in 1805 that Michigan as a distinct area, bearing that name, emerged with the creation of Michigan Territory. Even then, it was many years before Michigan was populous enough to become a state. To be sure, men, women, and children had been living in the area for about thirteen thousand years prior to that time, but their life and the conditions governing that life were very simple, compared to those which developed later. During most of those many millennia, Michigan was inhabited by a few thousand people, scattered over the two peninsulas along the lake shores or rivers. They differed somewhat in their cultures but they were all members of the group that would later be called American Indians. For most of the time they lived off the food they could find on the land or in the surrounding waters. Agriculture was introduced about the time of Christ, but for most Michigan residents, hunting, fishing, and gathering activities remained the principal means used in trying to meet their food requirements. Saplings and bark from Michigan's vast timber resources were used in constructing their dwellings, and wood, of course, was also used for their fires. For a time, some of them also engaged in a primitive form of mining to obtain chunks of pure copper found in the Upper Peninsula, which they then shaped into artifacts. This was the earliest such use of metals in the New World, virtually the only mining in Michigan until well into the nineteenth century.

The coming of the first European peoples early in the seventeenth century after Christ did not change the age-old patterns of life in Michigan as much as some have assumed. Culturally, it is true, the Indians adopted much from the white man—clothing, tools and other utensils, and weapons, among other items that the Indian quickly saw were superior to anything he had. But he resisted efforts to Europeanize his outlook on life, and most of the Frenchmen who came to Michigan, and also most of the British and the few Americans who had arrived by the end of the eighteenth century, were not interested in seeing the Indian displaced or his way of life radically changed. They were interested in Michigan as a source of furs, and the Indians were the ones they depended on to get those furs for them. Thus, for over two centuries, until the decline of the fur trade in the late 1820s, the Indian was encouraged to continue his hunting activities on a greater scale than ever before, and the wilderness character of Michigan was carefully preserved in order not to destroy the opportunity for the pursuance of those activities.

As for the white man, and the few score blacks, slaves and freemen (the latter sharing the white man's interest in the fur trade), they, like the Indians, lived in a few settlements along the main waterways, the only practical travel routes at that time. The wooden houses they constructed were more substantial than the Indian dwellings, but they proved only slightly more enduring. Pre-nineteenth-century buildings are virtually nonexistent in Michigan today. The farming that took place around these settlements was no more successful in eliminating the residents' dependence on other sources of food than had been the earlier gardening endeavors of the Indians.

As long as the wildlife of the Great Lakes area remained the dominant interest, therefore, life in Michigan during the first two centuries under the white man's rule remained, with certain obvious differences, essentially as it had been since the first hunters arrived sometime around 11,000 B.C., in the midst of the last Ice Age. All this changed with astounding rapidity when the main emphasis switched to agriculture, lumbering, mining, and finally manufacturing. Until recently, at least, it was almost universally accepted that the changes represented progress and improvement. Whether they have been or not, it is probable that most of the people of that earlier age, if they had had the opportunity, would have gladly traded their hard life for the greater material comforts of life in the twentieth century. They never had that opportunity, and in today's Michigan, it is probably just as impossible that anyone, should he wish to do so, will ever again have the opportunity to live in the ways of that earlier time.

1: Michigan's Prehistoric Inhabitants

Almost from the start of Michigan's historic period in the early 1600's there has been much curiosity and speculation about the peoples that were found in the area in the earlier prehistoric days. Bela Hubbard's *Memorials of a Half-Century in Michigan and the Lake Region* (New York, 1888) includes an early attempt to evaluate the archaeological evidence uncovered by Hubbard and other nineteenth-century pioneer settlers. By the 1930s, archaeologists from the University of Michigan and a few other institutions were beginning the accumulation of information along more scientific and systematic lines. One of the first full-scale attempts to synthesize this new body of knowledge was made by George Irving Quimby in his *Indian Life in the Upper Great Lakes, 11,000 B.C. to A.D. 1800* (Chicago, 1960), from which the following selection, dealing with the Hopewell Indians, the most culturally advanced of the prehistoric inhabitants of Michigan, is taken. Quimby, a native of Grand Rapids, has engaged in work at numerous archaeological sites, chiefly in Michigan and the Great Lakes area, since 1935. He is currently director of the Thomas Burke Memorial Washington State Museum in Seattle. In 1966 he published a companion volume to his earlier study, entitled *Indian Culture and European Trade Goods: The Archaeology of the Historic Period in the Western Great Lakes Region* (Madison, 1966). See also James E. Fitting, *The Archaeology of Michigan: A Guide to the Prehistory of the Great Lakes Region* (Garden City, N.Y., 1970). Alexis A. Praus's *Bibliography of Michigan Archaeology* (Ann Arbor, 1964) is a useful guide to the literature.

The Hopewell Indians

GEORGE I. QUIMBY

The Hopewell Indians were a prehistoric mound-building people who occupied parts of the eastern United States for more than a thousand years beginning around 500 B.C. Their primary cultural centers were in the central Mississippi, Ohio, and Illinois river valleys. These Indians were farmers, traders, and artists of exceptional ability.

About 100 B.C. some groups of Hopewell Indians entered the Upper Great Lakes region from their cultural center in the Illinois River Valley. Being a riverine people, they traveled up the Illinois River to the Kankakee, then they followed the Kankakee River to its headwaters in northwestern Indiana and crossed the portage to the St. Joseph River Valley of southwestern Michigan.

After establishing their settlements and ceremonial centers along the upper Kankakee and lower St. Joseph rivers, the Hopewell Indians went northward in western Michigan, probably first to the Kalamazoo Valley, then to the lower Grand River Valley where they established an important ceremonial center at the present site of Grand Rapids.

Somewhat later, groups of Grand River Hopewellians settled in the valley of the Muskegon River. This was the northernmost occupancy of the Upper Great Lakes region by Hopewell Indians, although in the Upper Mississippi region of western Wisconsin other groups of Hopewell Indians had settled even farther north.

In either case the northernmost occupancy of each region by Hopewell Indians was within a deciduous forest zone which at that time probably was dominated by oak and hickory, but which in historic times was composed principally of maple, beech, birch, and hemlock.

The northernmost occupancy of Hopewell Indians in both the Upper Great Lakes and Upper Mississippi regions was also limited by climate. They favored a relatively warm climate and did not settle north of the line that in modern times designates a frost-free season of at least 150 days. . . .

This climatic limitation on the Hopewell Indians must have been related to their agricultural pursuits. They made their living by farming and supplemented their food production by hunting and fishing. They raised corn, squash, perhaps beans, and probably tobacco. But corn-growing most likely was limited by the climate. It seems probable that in Hopewell times, the tropical flint corn had not yet been adapted to growth in cooler regions. Yet by A.D. 1700 a hardier Indian corn was being raised on the south side of Lake Superior, well north of the zone of Hopewell occupancy and in an era of cooler world climate. But the Hopewell Indians seem to have been the first farmers in the region, and their habitat was limited to the areas where the somewhat delicate tropical flint corn of that period could be grown.

The Hopewell Indians seem to have hunted all of the available animals, particularly deer. These animals included all or nearly all of those still found in the region when the first Europeans arrived nearly 1,000 years after the end of Hopewell culture. The only domesticated animal of the Hopewell Indians was the dog.

The physical appearance of the Hopewell Indians can be reconstructed from their skeletons and some small sculptured figures found in their burial places. These Indians were of medium height and longheaded or medium longheaded. The figurines suggest that they were stocky or plump, particularly the women, with oval faces and "slant" eyes.

The men wore breech cloths of animal skin or woven fabric and the women wore wrap-around skirts of woven cloth or skin. Both men and women wore slipper-like moccasins, probably made of animal skin.

Women seem to have worn their hair long in back but parted in the middle on top of the head and drawn back above the ears. Men removed some of their hair leaving a forelock in front and long hair gathered into a knot at the back of the head.

Their dwellings probably were types of wigwams, round or oval in plan with dome-shaped roofs, made of saplings covered with bark, mats, or skins.

Their villages and ceremonial centers were always along rivers. They erected large conical or dome-shaped mounds of earth over the dead and built earthen walls inclosing large areas that were circular, oval, or rectangular.

The largest Hopewell ceremonial center in the Upper Great Lakes region was at the present site of Grand Rapids, Michigan. Near the center of the city on the west side of the Grand River there formerly stood a group of about thirty to forty mounds, the largest of which was at least 30 feet high and 200 feet in circumference. On the opposite side of the river, about two miles south of the city, there is a group of fifteen mounds, the largest of which is 15 feet high and about 100 feet in diameter. There once seems to have been associated with this mound group a large rectangular inclosure with low walls of earth.

A Hopewell site in the St. Joseph River Valley at which there was a group of nine mounds was associated with an inclosure about 80 feet wide and 110 feet long, shaped like a horseshoe. The walls of earth have disappeared but the outline of the inclosure still shows in aerial photographs. In the Ohio Hopewell center there are many very elaborate earth wall inclosures constructed by the Indians.

During a part of each summer, some groups of Hopewell Indians left their settlements on the rivers and moved to the shore of Lake

Michigan. These summer campsites were always located in sheltered hollows among sand dunes, usually in areas of land between Lake Michigan and an inland lake or river estuary. Food refuse collected from one of these sites included remains of bear, beaver, deer, wolf, muskrat, rabbit, large-mouth bass, channel catfish, sheepshead, painted turtle, and mussels.

The Hopewell Indians made great use of exotic raw materials for the manufacture of tools, weapons, ornaments, and objects used in religious ceremonies. To obtain these raw materials they engaged in widespread trade and commerce.

From the Rocky Mountain region of the far West they obtained obsidian for their ceremonial blades and grizzly bear teeth for ornaments. Large marine shells came from the south Atlantic coast and the Gulf of Mexico. Copper and silver came from the mines in the western Lake Superior area, and mica sheets came from the middle Atlantic coastal region. Galena, or lead, was brought into the Upper Great Lakes region from Missouri and northwestern Illinois.

Tools and weapons were made of copper, stone, and bone. There were ungrooved axes of copper and polished stone; awls of bone, antler, and copper; corner-notched projectile points of chipped flint; knives of chipped flint and obsidian; needles of bone and copper; small flake knives; large ceremonial blades of chipped flint of unusual coloring; graving tools of stone, beaver incisors, and copper; and scrapers and drills of chipped flint.

The Hopewell Indians had musical instruments. Most characteristic were panpipes consisting of three or four conjoined tubes of bone or reed, graduated in length, and bound together with a broad, flat, encircling band of silver or copper. They also had rattles of various kinds, including some made of turtle shell, and probably they had drums.

Tobacco pipes made of polished stone were of the platform-type with a bowl centered on a platform and a stem hole from one end of the platform to the bowl. Most such pipes were simple, symmetrical, curved-base platforms with spool or barrel-shaped bowls. Some were elaborate effigy forms with bowls carved realistically in the form of animals and humans.

One such pipe had a bowl carved in the form of a bear, another had a bowl in the form of a nude woman seated on the platform, her cradled baby in front of her. Still another pipe with two bowls had a platform carved to represent an alligator.

The Hopewell Indians had fine pottery and utensils. There were spoons made of notched mussel shells and probably of wood. Large dippers or containers were made of imported marine shells.

Pottery was of several styles. There was a utilitarian ware consisting of round- or conoidal-based jars made of fired clay tempered with particles of granitic stone and covered on the exterior with the imprints of a cord-wrapped paddle.

A characteristic Hopewellian ware similar in paste and form to the ware just described differed in that the exterior surface was smoothed and then decorated with bands and zones of rather thick dentate stamp impressions.

The finest pottery ever found in the prehistoric Upper Great Lakes region was the Hopewell ceremonial ware made of fired clay tempered with small particles of limestone. Characteristic of this type were small quadrilobate jars with flat bottoms. The smooth, gray surfaces of such vessels were decorated with contrasting body zones filled with closely spaced impressions of a fine-toothed dentate stamp rocked back and forth, and the rims were decorated with a band of fine cross-hatching. This pottery probably was made only for burial with the dead.

Some other Hopewell pottery types seem to have been copies of this fine ceremonial ware. These types, represented by jars with round or flat bottoms and bodies that frequently were quadrilobate, were made of fired clay tempered with particles of granitic stone. Some of this pottery was relatively plain, but most of it was decorated with curvilinear zones filled with curved zigzag lines or punctate impressions.

Ornaments of the Hopewell Indians were made of metal, shell, bone, and stone. Beads for necklaces were made of copper, river pearls, marine shell, and the canine teeth of bears. Spool-shaped ear ornaments of copper were on some occasions worn at the wrists. There were armbands of silver and probably of copper. Pendants and breast ornaments included those of polished stone, copper, perforated and cut animal jaws, bone and copper effigies of animal teeth, perforated eagle claws, and bear canine teeth inlaid with river pearls. Pieces of imported sheet mica may have been used as ornaments or mirrors.

The Hopewell Indians wove cloth by means of finger techniques rather than on a loom. Twining was the most common method of weaving. Thread was twisted by hand from bast fiber—the soft inner bark of certain trees.

The Hopewell Indians were the outstanding artists of the Upper Great Lakes region and their products were never surpassed by the Indians who lived in the region in later times.

The elaborate effigy forms made of sheet copper and mica, the complicated geometric forms in copper made probably from folded patterns, and the delicate engraving on bone, shell, and wood so characteristic of the Ohio Hopewell center were lacking in the Upper Great Lakes region. But the other art forms were present, particularly sculpture in stone and bone portraying humans, animals, birds, fishes, reptiles, and insects. Probably all of Hopewell art had religious and ceremonial significance.

Hopewell art and material wealth were lavished on the dead, probably with elaborate ceremonies. Deceased people of high rank were placed in subfloor pits or tombs sometimes lined with bark or logs. Tools, weapons, utensils, pottery, pipes, and ceremonial objects, all of excellent quality, were placed in the grave. Bodies were placed in an extended or a flexed position. Bundles of bones, probably from partly decomposed bodies that had been placed on burial scaffolds, were also placed in grave pits.

When the burials were completed large mounds of earth were erected over the grave pits. These mounds were conical or dome-shaped. It is likely that only individuals of high social position, such as priests and chiefs or members of ruling families, were given mound burial.

The Hopewell Indians must have had a social organization that included class structures; hereditary ranks and privileges; divisions of labor; ways of organizing co-operative work projects, such as the building of mounds and inclosures; and means for individuals to become specialized as artists, traders, metal workers, and the like. This social organization, whatever its actual details, was much more elaborate than that of any of the earlier prehistoric groups of Indians in the Upper Great Lakes region.

The period of Hopewell culture in this region was from about 100 B.C. to A.D. 700. This dating is derived from cross-ties between the ceramic stratigraphy in the Upper Great Lakes region and that of the Illinois Valley Hopewell center, where there is an adequate number of radiocarbon-dated sites.

Hopewell culture in the Upper Great Lakes region, as well as elsewhere in the eastern United States, represents a climax of culture—a kind of classical period, the like of which was never achieved again.

Hopewell culture was based on agriculture, which was sufficiently developed to permit a stable mode of life. Agriculture originated in tropical America some thousands of years prior to its introduction into the Upper Great Lakes region. From its centers in the nucleus of America, agriculture based on the cultivation of corn, squash, and beans gradually diffused to various parts of North America, but not all of the crops in this tropical assemblage diffused at the same time or to the same places. However, by about

100 B.C., the probable time of its introduction into the Upper Great Lakes region, agriculture was well established elsewhere in North America and most likely squash and beans, as well as tropical flint corn, were brought into the Upper Great Lakes region from the Illinois River Valley by migrating Hopewell Indians.

There were other Indians living in the Upper Great Lakes at the same time as the Hopewell Indians. These neighbors of the Hopewell people had a much simpler culture. Some of them made their living by farming and hunting—others only by hunting and fishing.

They used stemmed and notched arrows and spearpoints of chipped flint, ungrooved axes or celts of ground stone or copper, stemmed and notched knives of chipped flint, awls of bone and copper, chipped flint drills, bone harpoon points with barbs, antler flaking-tools, and various kinds of flint scrapers.

There were beads of shell or small beads of rolled sheet copper and breast ornaments or gorgets of ground slate.

They had elbow pipes of fired clay and sometimes effigy pipes of clay and stone.

Their pottery consisted of jars with rather straight rims and round or semi-conoidal bottoms. These were made of clay tempered with particles of granitic stone. Exterior vessel surfaces were frequently covered completely with impressions of a cord-wrapped paddle, but in some eastern areas of the region there was a ware with smooth surfaces and rim and upper body decorations of a simple geometric pattern produced by rather crude stamping with dentate stamps or punching with a pointed tool.

Dwellings probably were circular or oval in ground plan, conical or dome-shaped, made of large saplings, and covered with bark, skins, or woven mats.

The dead, often accompanied by grave offerings, were buried in cemeteries or in subfloor pits beneath small mounds. Bodies were flexed or extended. There were also bundle burials and sometimes cremations.

In addition to burial mounds, some of these neighbors of the Hopewell Indians constructed large circular inclosures—embankments of earth inclosing a circular area. Either they or the Hopewell Indians also seem to have been responsible for the so-called garden beds in southern Michigan.

Garden beds were low earth ridges about 18 inches high arranged in precise geometric forms, somewhat like an old-fashioned formal garden. Most were of rectilinear patterns of varying complexity, but some were shaped like wagon wheels. The largest of these garden beds embraced an area of 120 acres. Such garden beds seem to be related to inclosures and should not be confused with the Indian cornfields of protohistoric times.

After about A.D. 700 the glory that was Hopewell was gone. The subsequent cultures of the Upper Great Lakes region seem to have been diversified outgrowths of a generalized Early Woodland and Middle Woodland base to which from time to time were added some exotic elements introduced from other regions.

2: The Indians of Michigan: An Indian's and a White Man's View

With the arrival of the French in the seventeenth century, an abundance of written information began to become available on the native inhabitants found in Michigan at that time. Most of the literature on these Indians that has appeared in print since that time has been written by white men. A notable exception is Andrew J. Blackbird's *History of the Ottawa and Chippewa Indians of Michigan* . . . (Ypsilanti, 1887), from which the first of the following two selections is taken. Blackbird, a Michigan Ottawa, spent two and a half years at what is now Eastern Michigan University before lack of funds compelled him to return to his home in northern Michigan where he became a government Indian interpreter in 1861 and later served as postmaster at Harbor Springs for eleven years. His *History of the Ottawa and Chippewa Indians* is partly an account of Indian life as he had experienced it and partly an attempt to write the history of these Indians, based on their folk traditions, in order to correct the errors he found in accounts written by white men.

One white man who was a contemporary of Blackbird and who pioneered in trying to achieve a more realistic and objective view of the Indian than that presented by earlier writers was Francis Parkman. The selection that follows from his work *The Conspiracy of Pontiac*, first published in 1851, revised in 1870, and reprinted in numerous editions since that date, is a classic example not only of Parkman's renowned mastery of the language, but also of how one's own background can interfere with even the most sincere efforts to look at others as they might look at themselves.

An adequate history of the Michigan Indians remains to be written, but Emerson F. Greenman's pamphlet, *The Indians of Michigan* (Lansing, 1961); W. Vernon Kinietz, *The Indians of the Western Great Lakes, 1615-1760* (Ann Arbor, 1940); and W. B. Hinsdale, *The First People of Michigan* (Ann Arbor, 1930) are good examples of the studies that have been published, most of which have had an anthropological, rather than a historical orientation.

Ottawa and Chippewa Indians

ANDREW J. BLACKBIRD

I have seen a number of writings by different men who attempted to give an account of the Indians who formerly occupied the Straits of Mackinac and Mackinac Island, . . . also giving an account of the Indians who lived and are yet living in Michigan, scattered through the counties of Emmet, Cheboygan, Charlevoix, Antrim, Grand Traverse, and in the region of Thunder Bay, on the west shore of Lake Huron. But I see no very correct account of the Ottawa and Chippewa tribes of Indians, according to our knowledge of ourselves, past and present. Many points are far from being credible. They are either misstated by persons who were not versed in the traditions of these Indians, or exaggerated. . . .

In my first recollection of the country of Arbor Croche, which is sixty years ago, there was nothing but small shrubbery here and there in small patches, such as wild cherry trees, but the most of it was grassy plain; and such an abundance of wild strawberries, raspberries and blackberries that they fairly perfumed the air of the whole coast with fragrant scent of ripe fruit. The wild pigeons and every variety of feathered songsters filled all the groves, warbling their songs joyfully and feasting upon these wild fruits of nature; and in these waters the fishes were so plentiful that as you lifted up the anchor-stone of your net in the morning, your net would be so loaded with delicious whitefish as to fairly float with all its weight of the sinkers. As you look towards the course of your net, you see the fins of the fishes sticking out of the water in every way. Then I never knew my people to want for anything to eat or to wear, as we always had plenty of wild meat and plenty of fish, corn, vegetables, and wild fruits. I thought (and yet I may be mistaken) that my people were very happy in those days, at least I was as happy myself as a lark, or as the brown thrush that sat daily on the uppermost branches of the stubby growth of a basswood tree which stood near by upon the hill where we often played under its shade, lodging our little arrows among the thick branches of the tree and then shooting them down again for sport.

Early in the morning as the sun peeped from the east, as I would yet be lying close to my mother's bosom, this brown thrush would begin his warbling songs perched upon the uppermost branches of the basswood tree that stood close to our lodge. I would then say to

From *History of the Ottawa and Chippewa Indians of Michigan; A Grammar of Their Language, and Personal and Family History of the Author* (Ypsilanti: The Ypsilantian Job Printing House, 1887), pp. 9-23. Footnotes in the original have been omitted.

myself, as I listened to him, "here comes again my little orator," and I used to try to understand what he had to say; and sometimes thought I understood some of its utterances as follows: "Good morning, good morning! arise, arise! shoot, shoot! come along, come along!" etc., every word repeated twice. Even then, and so young as I was, I used to think that little bird had a language which God or the Great Spirit had given him, and every bird of the forest understood what he had to say, and that he was appointed to preach to other birds, to tell them to be happy, to be thankful for the blessings they enjoy among the summer green branches of the forest, and the plenty of wild fruits to eat. The larger boys used to amuse themselves by playing a ball called Paw-baw-do-way, foot-racing, wrestling, bow-arrow shooting, and trying to beat one another shooting the greatest number of chipmunks and squirrels in a day, etc.

I never heard any boy or any grown person utter any bad language, even if they were out of patience with anything. Swearing or profanity was never heard among the Ottawa and Chippewa tribes of Indians, and not even found in their language. Scarcely any drunkenness, only once in a great while the old folks used to have a kind of short spree, particularly when there was any special occasion or a great feast going on. But all the young folks did not drink intoxicating liquors as a beverage in those days. And we always rested in perfect safety at night in our dwellings, and the doorways of our lodges had no fastenings to them, but simply a frail mat or a blanket was hung over our doorways which might be easily pushed or thrown one side without any noise if theft or any other mischief was intended. But we were not afraid for any such thing to happen [to] us, because we knew that every child of the forest was observing and living under the precepts which their forefathers taught them, and the children were taught almost daily by their parents from infancy unto manhood and womanhood, or until they were separated from their families.

These precepts or moral commandments by which the Ottawa and Chippewa nations of Indians were governed in their primitive state, were almost the same as the ten commandments which the God Almighty himself delivered to Moses on Mount Sinai on tables of stone. Very few of these divine precepts are not found among the precepts of the Ottawa and Chippewa Indians, except with regard to the Sabbath day to keep it holy; almost every other commandment can be found, only there are more, as there were about twenty of these "uncivilized" precepts. They also believed, in their primitive state, that the eye of this Great Being is the sun by day, and by night the moon and stars, and, therefore, that God or the

Great Spirit sees all things everywhere, night and day, and it would be impossible to hide our actions, either good or bad, from the eye of this Great Being. Even the very threshold or crevice of your wigwam will be a witness against you, if you should commit any criminal action when no human eye could observe your criminal doings, but surely your criminal actions will be revealed in some future time to your disgrace and shame. These were continual inculcations to the children by their parents, and in every feast and council, by the "Instructors of the Precepts" to the people or to the audience of the council. For these reasons the Ottawas and Chippewas in their primitive state were strictly honest and upright in their dealings with their fellow-beings. Their word of promise was as good as a promissory note, even better, as these notes sometimes are neglected and not performed according to their promises; but the Indian promise was very sure and punctual, although, as they had no timepieces, they measured their time by the sun. If an Indian promised to execute a certain obligation at such time, at so many days, and at such height of the sun, when that time comes he would be there punctually to fulfill this obligation. This was formerly the character of the Ottawa and Chippewa Indians of Michigan. . . .

According to my recollection of the mode of living in our village, so soon as darkness came in the evening, the young boys and girls were not allowed to be out of their lodges. Every one of them must be called in to his own lodge for the rest of the night. And this rule of the Indians in their wild state was implicitly observed.

Ottawa and Chippewa Indians were not what we would call entirely infidels and idolaters; for they believed that there is a Supreme Ruler of the Universe, the Creator of all things, the Great Spirit, to which they offer worship and sacrifices in a certain form. It was customary among them, every spring of the year, to gather all the cast off garments that had been worn during the winter and rear them up on a long pole while they were having festivals and jubilees to the Great Spirit. The object of doing this was that the Great Spirit might look down from heaven and have compassion on his red children. Only this, that they foolishly believe that there are certain deities all over the lands who to a certain extent govern or preside over certain places, as a deity who presides over this river, over this lake, or this mountain, or island, or country, and they were careful not to express anything which might displease such deities; but that they were not supreme rulers, only to a certain extent they had power over the land where they presided. These deities were supposed to be governed by the Great Spirit above.

The murders in cold blood among the Ottawa and Chippewa nations of Indians in their primitive state were exceedingly few, at least there was only one account in our old tradition where a murder had been committed, a young Ottawa having stabbed a young Chippewa while in dispute over their nets when they were fishing for herrings on the Straits of Mackinac. This nearly caused a terrible bloody war between the two powerful tribes of Indians (as they were numerous then) so closely related. The tradition says they had council after council upon this subject, and many speeches were delivered on both sides. The Chippewas proposed war to settle the question of murder, while the Ottawas proposed compromise and restitution for the murder. Finally the Ottawas succeeded in settling the difficulty by ceding part of their country to the Chippewa nation, which is now known and distinguished as the Grand Traverse Region. A strip of land which I believe to have extended from a point near Sleeping Bear, down to the eastern shore of the Grand Traverse Bay, some thirty or forty miles wide, thence between two parallel lines running southeasterly until they strike the head waters of Muskegon River, which empties into Lake Michigan not very far below Grand Haven. They were also allowed access to all the rivers and streams in the Lower Peninsula of Michigan, to trap the beavers, minks, otters and muskrats. The Indians used their furs in former times for garments and blankets. This is the reason that to this day the Odjebwes (Chippewas) are found in that section of the country.

It may be said, this is not true; it is a mistake. We have known several cases of murders among the Ottawas and Chippewas. I admit it to be true that there have been cases of murders among the Ottawas and Chippewas since the white people knew them. But these cases of murders occurred sometime after they came in contact with the white races in their country; but I am speaking now of the primitive condition of Indians, particularly of the Ottawas and Chippewas, and I believe most of those cases of murders were brought on through the bad influence of white men, by introducing into the tribes this great destroyer of mankind, soul and body, intoxicating liquors! Yet, during sixty years of my existence among the Ottawas and Chippewas, I have never witnessed one case of murder of this kind, but I heard there were a few cases in other parts of the country, when in their fury from the influence of intoxicating liquors.

There was one case of sober murder happened about fifty years ago at Arbor Croche, where one young man disposed of his lover by killing, which no Indian ever knew the actual cause of. He was arrested and committed to the Council and tried according to the Indian style; and after a long council, or trial, it was determined the murderer should be banished from the tribe. Therefore, he was banished. Also, about this time, one case of sober murder transpired among the Chippewas of Sault Ste. Marie, committed by one of the young Chippewas whose name was Wau-bau-ne-me-kee (White-thunder), who might have been released if he had been properly tried and impartial judgment exercised over the case, but we believe it was not. This Indian killed a white man, when he was perfectly sober, by stabbing. He was arrested, of course, and tried and sentenced to be hung at the Island of Mackinac. I distinctly remember the time. This poor Indian was very happy when he was about to be hung on the gallows. He told the people that he was very happy to die, for he felt that he was innocent. He did not deny killing the man, but he thought he was justifiable in the sight of the Great Spirit, as such wicked monsters ought to be killed from off the earth; as this white man came to the Indian's wigwam in the dead of night, and dragged the mother of his children from his very bosom for licentious purpose. He remonstrated, but his remonstrances were not heeded, as this ruffian was encouraged by others who stood around his wigwam, and ready to fall upon this poor Indian and help their fellow-ruffian; and he therefore stabbed the principal party, in defence of his beloved wife, for which cause the white man died. If an Indian should go to the white man's house and commit that crime, he would be killed; and what man is there who would say that is too bad, this Indian to be killed in that manner? But every man will say amen, only he ought to have been tortured before he was killed; and let the man who killed this bad and wicked Indian be rewarded! This is what would be the result if the Indian would have done the same thing as this white man did.

The Ottawas and Chippewas were quite virtuous in their primitive state, as there were no illegitimate children reported in our old traditions. But very lately this evil came to exist among the Ottawas—so lately that the second case among the Ottawas of Arbor Croche is yet living. And from that time this evil came to be quite frequent, for immorality has been introduced among these people by evil white persons who bring their vices into the tribes.

In the former times or before the Indians were christianized, when a young man came to be a fit age to get married, he did not trouble himself about what girl he should have for his wife; but the parents of the young man did this part of the business. When the parents thought best that their son should be separated from their family by marriage, it was their business to decide what woman their son should have as his wife; and after selecting some particular girl among their neighbors, they would make up quite large package of presents and then go to the parents of the girl and demand the daughter for their son's wife, at the same time delivering the presents to the parents of the girl. If the old folks say yes, then they would fetch the girl right along to their son and tell him, We have brought this girl as your wife so long as you live; now take her, cherish her, and be kind to her so long as you live. The young man and girl did not dare to say aught against it, as it was the law and custom amongst their people, but all they had to do was to take each other as man and wife. This was all the rules and ceremony of getting married in former times among the Ottawas and Chippewas of Michigan: they must not marry their cousins nor second cousins.

Again, most every historian, or annalist so-called, who writes about the Island of Mackinac and the Straits and vicinity, tells us that the definition or the meaning of the word "Michilimackinac" in the Ottawa and Chippewa language, is "large turtle," derived from the word Mi-she-mi-ki-nock in the Chippewa language. That is, "Mi-she" as one of the adnominals or adjectives in the Ottawa and Chippewa languages, which would signify tremendous in size; and "Mikinock" is the name of mud turtle—meaning, therefore, "monstrous large turtle," as the historians would have it. But we consider this to be a clear error. Wherever those annalists, or those who write about the Island of Mackinac, obtain their information as to the definition of the word Michilimackinac, I don't know, when our tradition is so direct and so clear with regard to the historical definition of that word, and is far from being derived from the word "Michimikinock," as the historians have told us. Our tradition says that when the Island was first discovered by the Ottawas, which was some time before America was known as an existing country by the white man, there was a small independent tribe, a remnant race of Indians who occupied this island, who became confederated with the Ottawas when the Ottawas were living at Manitoulin, formerly called Ottawa Island, which is situated north of Lake Huron. The Ottawas thought a good deal of this unfortunate race of people, as they were kind of an interesting sort of people; but, unfortunately, they had most powerful enemies, who every now and then would come among them to make war with them. Their enemies were of the Iroquois of New York. Therefore, once in the dead of the winter while the Ottawas were having a great jubilee and war dances at their island, now Manitoulin, on account of their great conquest over the We-ne-be-goes of Wisconsin . . . during which time the Senecas of New York, of the Iroquois family of Indians, came upon the remnant race and fought them, and almost entirely annihilated them. But two escaped to tell the story, who effected their escape by flight and by hiding in one of the natural caves at the island, and therefore that was the end of this race. And according to our understanding and traditions the tribal name of those disastrous people was "Mi-shi-ne-macki naw-go," which is still existing to this day as a monument of their former existence; for the Ottawas and Chippewas named this little island "Mi-shi-ne-macki-nong" for memorial sake of those their former confederates, which word is the locative case of the Indian noun "Michinemackinawgo." Therefore, we contend, this is properly where the name Michilimackinac is originated.

This is the earliest possible history of this little Island, as I have related, according to the Ottawa traditions; and from that time forward there have been many changes in its history, as other tribes of Indians took possession of the island, such as the Hurons and Chippewas; and still later by the whites—French, English, and Americans; and numbers of battles have been fought from time to time there, by both Indians and whites, of which I need not relate as other historians have already given us the accounts of them. But only this I would relate, because I have never yet seen the account of it: It is related in our traditions that at the time when the Chippewas occupied the island they ceded it to the United States Government, but reserved a strip of land all around the island as far as a stone throw from its water's edge as their encampment grounds when they might come to the island to trade or for other business.

Perhaps the reader would like to know what became of those two persons who escaped from the lamented tribe Mishinemackinaw-goes. I will here give it just as it is related in our traditions, although this may be considered, at this age, as a fictitious story; but every Ottawa and Chippewa to this day believes it to be positively so. It is related that the two persons escaped were two young people, male and female, and they were lovers. After everything got quieted down, they fixed their snow-shoes inverted and crossed the lake on the ice, as snow was quite deep on the ice, and they went towards the north shore of Lake Huron. The object of inverting their snow-shoes was that in case any person should happen to come across their track on the ice, their track would appear as if going towards the island. They became so disgusted with human nature, it is related, that they shunned every mortal being, and just lived by themselves, selecting the wildest part of the country. Therefore, the Ottawas and Chippewas called them "Paw-gwa-tchaw-nish-naw-boy." The last time they were seen by the Ottawas, they had ten children—all boys, and all living and well. And every Ottawa and Chippewa believes to this day that they are still in existence and roaming in the wildest part of the land, but as supernatural beings—that is, they can be seen or unseen, just as they see fit to be; and sometimes they simply manifested themselves as being present by throwing a club or a stone at a person walking in a solitude, or by striking a dog belonging to the person walking; and sometimes by throwing a club at the lodge, night or day, or hearing their footsteps walking around the wigwam when the Indians would be camping out in an unsettled part of the country, and the dogs would bark, just as they would bark at any strange person approaching the door. And sometimes they would be tracked on snow by hunters, and if followed on their track, however recently passed, they never could be overtaken. Sometimes when an Indian would be hunting or walking in solitude, he would suddenly be seized with an unearthly fright, terribly awe stricken, apprehending some great evil. He feels a very peculiar sensation from head to foot—the hair of his head standing and feeling stiff like a porcupine quill. He feels almost benumbed with fright, and yet he does not know what it is; and looking in every direction to see something, but nothing to be seen which might cause sensation of terror. Collecting himself, he would then say, "Pshaw! it's nothing here to be afraid of. It's nobody else but Paw-gwa-tchaw-nish-naw-boy that is approaching me. Perhaps he wanted something of me." They would then leave something on their tracks—tobacco, powder, or something else. Once in a great while they would appear, and approach the person to talk with him, and in this case, it is said, they would always begin with the sad story of their great catastrophe at the Island of Mackinac. And whoever would be so fortunate as to meet and see them and to talk with them, such person would always become a prophet to his people, either Ottawa or Chippewa. Therefore, Ottawas and Chippewas called these supernatural beings "Paw-gwa-tchaw-nish-naw-boy," which is, strictly, "Wild roaming supernatural being."

Pine river country, in Charlevoix County, Michigan, when this country was all wild, especially near Pine Lake, was once considered as the most famous resort of these kind of unnatural beings. I was once conversing with one of the first white settlers of that portion of the country, who settled near to the place now called Boyne City, at the extreme end of the east arm of Pine Lake. In the conversation he told me that many times they had been frightened, particularly during the nights, by hearing what sounded like human footsteps around outside of their cabin; and their dog would be terrified, crouching at the doorway, snarling and growling, and sometimes fearfully barking. When daylight came, the old man would go out in order to discover what it was or if he could track anything around his cabin, but he never could discover a track of any kind. These remarkable, mischievous, audible, fanciful, appalling apprehensions were of very frequent occurrence before any other inhabitants or settlers came near to his place; but now, they do not have such apprehensions since many settlers came.

That massacre of Mishinemackinawgoes by Seneca Indians of New York happened probably more than five or six hundred years ago. I could say much more which would be contradictory of other writers of the history of the Indians in this country. . . .

Some Comments on Indians

FRANCIS PARKMAN

Except the detached nation of the Tuscaroras, and a few smaller tribes adhering to them, the Iroquois family was confined to the region south of the Lakes Erie and Ontario, and the peninsula east of Lake Huron. They formed, as it were, an island in the vast expanse of Algonquin population, extending from Hudson's Bay on the north to the Carolinas on the south; from the Atlantic on the east to the Mississippi and Lake Winnipeg on the west. They were Algonquins who greeted Jacques Cartier, as his ships ascended the St. Lawrence. The first British colonists found savages of the same race hunting and fishing along the coasts and inlets of Virginia; and it was the daughter of an Algonquin chief who interceded with her father for the life of the adventurous Englishman. They were Algonquins who, under Sassacus the Pequot, and Philip of Mount Hope, waged war against the Puritans of New England; who dwelt at Penacook, under the rule of the great magician, Passaconaway, and trembled before the evil spirits of the White Hills; and who sang *aves* and told their beads in the forest chapel of Father Rasle, by the banks of the Kennebec. They were Algonquins who, under the great tree at Kensington, made the covenant of peace with William Penn; and when French Jesuits and fur-traders explored the Wabash and the Ohio, they found their valleys tenanted by the same far-

From *The Conspiracy of Pontiac and the Indian Wars after the Conquest of Canada* (Boston: Little, Brown and Company, 1903), I, 32-49. Footnotes in the original have been omitted.

extended race. At the present day, the traveller, perchance, may find them pitching their bark lodges along the beach at Mackinaw, spearing fish among the rapids of St. Mary's, or skimming the waves of Lake Superior in their birch canoes.

. . . .

Of the tribes which, single and detached, or cohering in loose confederacies, dwelt within the limits of Lower Canada, Acadia, and New England, it is needless to speak; for they offered no distinctive traits demanding notice. Passing the country of the Lenape and the Shawanoes, and descending the Ohio, the traveller would have found its valley chiefly occupied by two nations, the Miamis or Twightwees, on the Wabash and its branches, and the Illinois, who dwelt in the neighborhood of the river to which they have given their name, while portions of them extended beyond the Mississippi. . . .

Turning his course northward, traversing Lakes Michigan and Superior, and skirting the western margin of Lake Huron, the voyager would have found the solitudes of the wild waste around him broken by scattered lodges of the Ojibwas, Pottawattamies, and Ottawas. About the bays and rivers west of Lake Michigan, he would have seen the Sacs, the Foxes, and the Menominies; and penetrating the frozen wilderness of the north, he would have been welcomed by the rude hospitality of the wandering Crees. . . .

The Ojibwas, with their kindred, the Pottawattamies, and their friends the Ottawas,—the latter of whom were fugitives from the eastward, whence they had fled from the wrath of the Iroquois,— were banded into a sort of confederacy. They were closely allied in blood, language, manners, and character. The Ojibwas, by far the most numerous of the three, occupied the basin of Lake Superior, and extensive adjacent regions. In their boundaries, the career of Iroquois conquest found at length a check. The fugitive Wyandots sought refuge in the Ojibwa hunting-grounds; and tradition relates that, at the outlet of Lake Superior, an Iroquois war-party once encountered a disastrous repulse.

In their mode of life, they were far more rude than the Iroquois, or even the southern Algonquin tribes. The totemic system is found among them in its most imperfect state. The original clans have become broken into fragments, and indefinitely multiplied; and many of the ancient customs of the institution are but loosely regarded. Agriculture is little known, and, through summer and winter, they range the wilderness with restless wandering, now gorged to repletion, and now perishing with want. In the calm days of summer, the Ojibwa fisherman pushes out his birch canoe upon the great inland ocean of the north; and, as he gazes down into the pellucid depths, he seems like one balanced between earth and sky. The watchful fish-hawk circles above his head, and below, farther than his line will reach, he sees the trout glide shadowy and silent over the glimmering pebbles. The little islands on the verge of the horizon seem now starting into spires, now melting from the sight, now shaping themselves into a thousand fantastic forms, with the strange mirage of the waters; and he fancies that the evil spirits of the lake lie basking their serpent forms on those unhallowed shores. Again, he explores the watery labyrinths where the stream sweeps among pine-tufted islands, or runs, black and deep, beneath the shadows of moss-bearded firs; or he drags his canoe upon the sandy beach, and, while his camp-fire crackles on the grass-plat, reclines beneath the trees, and smokes and laughs away the sultry hours in a lazy luxury of enjoyment.

But when winter descends upon the north, sealing up the fountains, fettering the streams, and turning the green-robed forests to shivering nakedness, then, bearing their frail dwellings on their backs, the Ojibwa family wander forth into the wilderness, cheered only on their dreary track by the whistling of the north wind and the hungry howl of wolves. By the banks of some frozen stream, women and children, men and dogs, lie crouched together around the fire. They spread their benumbed fingers over the embers, while the wind shrieks through the fir trees like the gale through the rigging of a frigate, and the narrow concave of the wigwam sparkles with the frostwork of their congealed breath. In vain they beat the magic drum, and call upon their guardian manitoes; the wary moose keeps aloof, the bear lies close in his hollow tree, and famine stares them in the face. And now the hunter can fight no more against the nipping cold and blinding sleet. Stiff and stark, with haggard cheek and shrivelled lip, he lies among the snowdrifts; till, with tooth and claw, the famished wildcat strives in vain to pierce the frigid marble of his limbs. Such harsh schooling is thrown away on the incorrigible mind of the northern Algonquin. He lives in misery, as his fathers lived before him. Still, in the brief hour of plenty he forgets the season of want; and still the sleet and the snow descend upon his houseless head.

I have thus passed in brief review the more prominent of the Algonquin tribes; those whose struggles and sufferings form the theme of the ensuing History. In speaking of the Iroquois, some of the distinctive peculiarities of the Algonquins have already been hinted at. It must be admitted that, in moral stability and intellectual vigor, they are inferior to the former; though some of the most conspicuous offspring of the wilderness, Metacom, Tecumseh, and Pontiac himself, owned their blood and language.

The fireside stories of every primitive people are faithful reflections of the form and coloring of the national mind; and it is no proof of sound philosophy to turn with contempt from the study of a fairy tale. The legendary lore of the Iroquois, black as the midnight forests, awful in its gloomy strength, is but another manifestation of that spirit of mastery which uprooted whole tribes from the earth, and deluged the wilderness with blood. The traditionary tales of the Algonquins wear a different aspect. The credulous circle around an Ojibwa lodge-fire listened to wild recitals of necromancy and witchcraft,—men transformed to beasts, and beasts transformed to men, animated trees, and birds who spoke with human tongue. They heard of malignant sorcerers dwelling among the lonely islands of spell-bound lakes; of grisly *weendigoes,* and bloodless *geebi*; of evil *manitoes* lurking in the dens and fastnesses of the woods; of pygmy champions, diminutive in stature but mighty in soul, who, by the potency of charm and talisman, subdued the direst monsters of the waste; and of heroes, who not by downright force and open onset, but by subtle strategy, tricks, or magic art, achieved marvellous triumphs over the brute force of their assailants. Sometimes the tale will breathe a different spirit, and tell of orphan children abandoned in the heart of a hideous wilderness, beset with fiends and cannibals. Some enamoured maiden, scornful of earthly suitors, plights her troth to the graceful manito of the grove; or bright aerial beings, dwellers of the sky, descend to tantalize the gaze of mortals with evanescent forms of loveliness.

The mighty giant, the God of the Thunder, who made his home among the caverns, beneath the cataract of Niagara, was a characteristic conception of Iroquois imagination. The Algonquins held a simpler faith, and maintained that the thunder was a bird who built his nest on the pinnacle of towering mountains. Two daring boys once scaled the height, and thrust sticks into the eyes of the portentous nestlings; which hereupon flashed forth such wrathful scintillations that the sticks were shivered to atoms.

The religious belief of the Algonquins—and the remark holds good, not of the Algonquins only, but of all the hunting tribes of America—is a cloudy bewilderment, where we seek in vain for system or coherency. Among a primitive and savage people, there were no poets to vivify its images, and no priests to give distinctness and harmony to its rites and symbols. To the Indian mind, all nature was instinct with deity. A spirit was embodied in every mountain, lake, and cataract; every bird, beast, or reptile, every tree, shrub, or grass-blade was endued with mystic influence; yet this untutored pantheism did not exclude the conception of certain divinities, of incongruous and ever-shifting attributes. The sun, too, was a god, and the moon was a goddess. Conflicting powers of good and evil divided the universe: but if, before the arrival of Europeans, the Indian recognized the existence of one, almighty, self-existent Being, the Great Spirit, the Lord of Heaven and Earth, the belief was so vague and dubious as scarcely to deserve the name. His perceptions of moral good and evil were perplexed and shadowy; and the belief in a state of future reward and punishment was by no means universal.

Of the Indian character, much has been written foolishly, and credulously believed. By the rhapsodies of poets, the cant of senti-mentalists, and the extravagance of some who should have known better, a counterfeit image has been tricked out, which might seek in vain for its likeness through every corner of the habitable earth; an image bearing no more resemblance to its original than the monarch of the tragedy and the hero of the epic poem bear to their living prototypes in the palace and the camp. The shadows of his wilderness home, and the darker mantle of his own inscrutable reserve, have made the Indian warrior a wonder and a mystery. Yet to the eye of rational observation there is nothing unintelligible in him. He is full, it is true, of contradiction. He deems himself the centre of greatness and renown; his pride is proof against the fiercest torments of fire and steel; and yet the same man would beg for a dram of whiskey, or pick up a crust of bread thrown to him like a dog, from the tent door of the traveller. At one moment, he is wary and cautious to the verge of cowardice; at the next, he abandons himself to a very insanity of recklessness; and the habitual self-restraint which throws an impenetrable veil over emotion is joined to the unbridled passions of a madman or a beast.

Such inconsistencies, strange as they seem in our eyes, when viewed under a novel aspect, are but the ordinary incidents of humanity. The qualities of the mind are not uniform in their action through all the relations of life. With different men, and different races of men, pride, valor, prudence, have different forms of mani-festation, and where in one instance they lie dormant, in another they are keenly awake. The conjunction of greatness and littleness, meanness and pride, is older than the days of the patriarchs; and such antiquated phenomena, displayed under a new form in the unreflecting, undisciplined mind of a savage, call for no special wonder, but should rather be classed with the other enigmas of the fathomless human heart. The dissecting knife of a Rochefoucault might lay bare matters of no less curious observation in the breast of every man.

Nature has stamped the Indian with a hard and stern physiognomy. Ambition, revenge, envy, jealousy, are his ruling passions; and his cold temperament is little exposed to those effeminate vices which are the bane of milder races. With him revenge is an overpowering instinct; nay, more, it is a point of honor and a duty. His pride sets all language at defiance. He loathes the thought of coercion; and few of his race have ever stooped to discharge a menial office. A wild love of liberty, an utter intolerance of control, lie at the basis of his character, and fire his whole existence. Yet, in spite of this haughty independence, he is a devout hero-worshipper; and high achievement in war or policy touches a chord to which his nature never fails to respond. He looks up with admiring reverence to the sages and heroes of his tribe; and it is this principle, joined to the respect for age springing from the patriarchal element in his social system, which, beyond all others, contributes union and harmony to the erratic members of an Indian community. With him the love of glory kindles into a burning passion; and to allay its cravings, he will dare cold and famine, fire, tempest, torture, and death itself.

These generous traits are overcast by much that is dark, cold, and sinister, by sleepless distrust, and rankling jealousy. Treacherous himself, he is always suspicious of treachery in others. Brave as he is,—and few of mankind are braver,—he will vent his passion by a secret stab rather than an open blow. His warfare is full of ambuscade and stratagem; and he never rushes into battle with that joyous self-abandonment with which the warriors of the Gothic races flung themselves into the ranks of their enemies. In his feasts and his drinking bouts we find none of that robust and full-toned mirth which reigned at the rude carousals of our barbaric ancestry. He is never jovial in his cups, and maudlin sorrow or maniacal rage is the sole result of his potations.

Over all emotion he throws the veil of an iron self-control, originating in a peculiar form of pride, and fostered by rigorous discipline from childhood upward. He is trained to conceal passion, and not to subdue it. The inscrutable warrior is aptly imaged by the hackneyed figure of a volcano covered with snow; and no man can say when or where the wild-fire will burst forth. This shallow self-mastery serves to give dignity to public deliberation, and harmony to social life. Wrangling and quarrel are strangers to an Indian dwelling; and while an assembly of the ancient Gauls was garrulous as a convocation of magpies, a Roman senate might have taken a lesson from the grave solemnity of an Indian council. In the midst of his family and friends, he hides affections, by nature none of the most tender, under a mask of icy coldness; and in the torturing fires of his enemy, the haughty sufferer maintains to the last his look of grim defiance.

His intellect is as peculiar as his moral organization. Among all savages, the powers of perception preponderate over those of reason and analysis; but this is more especially the case with the Indian. An acute judge of character, at least of such parts of it as his experience enables him to comprehend; keen to a proverb in all exercises of war and the chase, he seldom traces effects to their causes, or follows out actions to their remote results. Though a close observer of external nature, he no sooner attempts to account for her phenomena than he involves himself in the most ridiculous absurdities; and quite content with these puerilities, he has not the least desire to push his inquiries further. His curiosity, abundantly active within its own narrow circle, is dead to all things else; and to attempt rousing it from its torpor is but a bootless task. He seldom takes cognizance of general or abstract ideas; and his language has scarcely the power to express them, except through the medium of figures drawn from the external world, and often highly picturesque and forcible. The absence of reflection makes him grossly improvident, and unfits him for pursuing any complicated scheme of war or policy.

Some races of men seem moulded in wax, soft and melting, at once plastic and feeble. Some races, like some metals, combine the greatest flexibility with the greatest strength. But the Indian is hewn out of a rock. You can rarely change the form without destruction of the substance. Races of inferior energy have possessed a power of expansion and assimilation to which he is a stranger; and it is this fixed and rigid quality which has proved his ruin. He will not learn the arts of civilization, and he and his forest must perish together. The stern, unchanging features of his mind excite our admiration from their very immutability; and we look with deep interest on the fate of this irreclaimable son of the wilderness, the child who will not be weaned from the breast of his rugged mother. And our interest increases when we discern in the unhappy wanderer the germs of heroic virtues mingled among his vices,—a hand bountiful to bestow as it is rapacious to seize, and even in extremest famine, imparting its last morsel to a fellow-sufferer; a heart which, strong in friendship as in hate, thinks it not too much to lay down life for its chosen comrade; a soul true to its own idea of honor, and burning with an unquenchable thirst for greatness and renown.

The imprisoned lion in the showman's cage differs not more widely from the lord of the desert than the beggarly frequenter of frontier garrisons and dramshops differs from the proud denizen of the woods. It is in his native wilds alone that the Indian must be seen and studied. . . .

3: The Era of the Explorer and the Priest

Our principal sources of information for the early decades of French activities in the Michigan area come from the reports of Catholic priests who were in the region looking for potential missionary subjects. Most of these reports come from the series known as the *Jesuit Relations*, which was published annually in France from 1632 to 1673. The reprinting and translation of these volumes, together with other documents, in the seventy-three-volume set, *The Jesuit Relations and Allied Documents, 1610-1791*, edited by Reuben G. Thwaites (Cleveland, 1896-1903), provided students of Michigan history with a treasure trove of source material, principally on seventeenth-century developments. It also led to a tendency on the part of some to believe that all French explorers during these years were priests. Actually, Etienne Brule and Jean Nicolet, the first Frenchmen who are known to have penetrated the interior to Michigan in the 1620s and 1630s, were laymen. In 1641, however, two Jesuits, Isaac Jogues and Charles Raymbault, visited Sault Ste. Marie, where, in 1668, Father Jacques Marquette, the most famous of these missionaries, established the first of several Jesuit Indian missions in Michigan. It was also at the Sault in 1671 that French governmental authority began to be asserted when a ceremony was held at which France took formal possession of the area and the period of Jesuit dominance began to come to an end.

In the following selections, extracted from a documentary publication in 1917, edited by Louise Phelps Kellogg, all but one of which came from the *Jesuit Relations*, Jean Nicolet's expedition in 1634 from Ontario to Green Bay is described by Father Barthélemy Vimont, the report having originally appeared in the *Jesuit Relation* of 1642. The same annual volume also carried Father Jerome Lalemant's report of the visit to the Sault of Jogues and Raymbault. The Jesuit mission that was later established at the Sault is described by a Sulpician, Father René de Bréhant de Galinée, who, with Father Francois Dollier de Casson, visited the site at the conclusion of a pioneering exploration of the route from Lake Ontario through Lake Erie northward into Lake Huron. The Pageant of 1671 was described in the *Jesuit Relation* of 1670-71. Concluding this section is an account by Father Claude Dablon of the death and final burial of Father Marquette, an account that provides an insight into the religious motivation of these missionaries that is often overshadowed by the emphasis on their other activities.

Marquette, after his return from his exploration of the Mississippi with Louis Jolliet, had spent some time among the Illinois Indians, but early in 1675, sensing that he was near death, he set out in the company of two French canoemen up the eastern shore of Lake Michigan, in an effort to reach his mission at St. Ignace. The circumstances of his death and the subsequent disposal of his remains have led to a rather unseemly controversy in recent years between Ludington and Frankfort as to which can claim to be Marquette's death site, while others have argued as to whether fragments of bones found in St. Ignace in 1877 are those of the Jesuit missionary. These controversies, together with a full account of what Marquette accomplished while he was alive, are discussed in Joseph P. Donnelly, *Jacques Marquette, S.J., 1637-1675* (Chicago, 1968). Raphael N. Hamilton's *Father Marquette*, published in 1970 as part of the William B. Eerdmans Publishing Company's *Great Men of Michigan* series, is an excellent brief interpretive study.

Early Narratives of the Northwest

LOUISE P. KELLOGG (ED.)

The Journey of Jean Nicolet, 1634

I will now speak of the life and death of Monsieur Nicollet, interpreter and agent for the Gentlemen of the Company of New France. He . . . had lived in this region twenty-five years. What I shall say of him will aid to a better understanding of the country. He came to New France in the year 1618; and forasmuch as his nature and excellent memory inspired good hopes of him, he was sent to winter with the Island Algonquins, in order to learn their language. He tarried with them two years, alone of the French, and always joined the barbarians in their excursions and journeys, undergoing such fatigues as none but eyewitnesses can conceive; he often passed seven or eight days without food, and once, full seven weeks with no other nourishment than a little bark from the trees. He accompanied four hundred Algonquins, who went during that time to make peace with the Hyroquois [Iroquois], which he successfully accomplished; and would to God that it had never been broken, for then we should not now be suffering the calamities which move us to groans, and which must be an extraordinary impediment in the way of converting these tribes. After this treaty

From *Early Narratives of the Northwest, 1634-1699* (New York: Charles Scribner's Sons, 1917), pp. 15-16, 23-24, 204-207, 217-220, 272-278. Footnotes in the original have been omitted.

of peace, he went to live eight or nine years with the Algonquin Nipissiriniens, where he passed for one of that nation, taking part in the very frequent councils of those tribes, having his own separate cabin and household, and fishing and trading for himself. He was finally recalled, and appointed agent and interpreter. While in the exercise of this office, he was delegated to make a journey to the nation called People of the Sea [Winnebago Indians], and arrange peace between them and the Hurons, from whom they are distant about three hundred leagues westward. He embarked in the Huron country, with seven savages; and they passed by many small nations, both going and returning. When they arrived at their destination, they fastened two sticks in the earth, and hung gifts thereon, so as to relieve these tribes from the notion of mistaking them for enemies to be massacred. When he was two days' journey from that nation, he sent one of those savages to bear tidings of the peace, which word was especially well received when they heard that it was a European who carried the message; they despatched several young men to meet the Manitouiriniou—that is to say, "the wonderful man." They meet him; they escort him, and carry all his baggage. He wore a grand robe of China damask, all strewn with flowers and birds of many colors. No sooner did they perceive him than the women and children fled, at the sight of a man who carried thunder in both hands—for thus they called the two pistols that he held. The news of his coming quickly spread to the places round about, and there assembled four or five thousand men. Each of the chief men made a feast for him, and at one of these banquets they served at least sixscore beavers. The peace was concluded; he returned to the Hurons, and some time later to the Three Rivers [in Canada], where he continued his employment as agent and interpreter, to the great satisfaction of both the French and the savages, by whom he was equally and singularly loved.

The Journey of Raymbault and Jogues to the Sault, 1641

In this gathering of so many assembled nations, we strove to win the affections of the chief personages by means of feasts and presents. In consequence of this, the Pauoitigoueieuhak [Chippewa Indians] invited us to go and see them in their own country. (They are a nation of the Algonquin language, distant from the Hurons a hundred or a hundred and twenty leagues towards the west, whom we call the inhabitants of the Sault.) We promised to pay them a visit, to see how they might be disposed, in order to labor for their conversion, especially as we learned that a more remote nation whom they call Pouteatami [Potawatomi Indians] had abandoned their own country and taken refuge with the inhabitants of the Sault, in order to remove from some other hostile nation who persecuted them with endless wars. We selected Father Charles Raymbault to undertake this journey; and as, at the same time, some Hurons were to be of the party, Father Isaac Jogues was chosen, that he might deal with them.

They started from our house of Ste. Marie, about the end of September, and after seventeen days of navigation on the great lake or fresh-water sea that bathes the land of the Hurons, they reached the Sault, where they found about two thousand souls, and obtained information about a great many other sedentary nations, who have never known Europeans and have never heard of God—among others, of a certain nation, the Nadouessis [Sioux Indians], situated to the northwest or west of the Sault, eighteen days' journey farther away. The first nine days are occupied in crossing another great lake that commences above the Sault; during the last nine days one has to ascend a river that traverses those lands. These peoples till the soil in the manner of our Hurons, and harvest Indian corn and tobacco. Their villages are larger, and in a better state of defense, owing to their continual wars with the Kiristinons, the Irinions, and other great nations who inhabit the same country. Their language differs from the Algonquin and Huron tongues.

The captains of this nation of the Sault invited our Fathers to take up their abode among them. They were given to understand that this was not impossible, provided that they were well disposed to receive our instruction. After having held a council, they replied that they greatly desired that good fortune—that they would embrace us as their Brothers, and would profit by our words. But we need laborers for that purpose; we must first try to win the peoples that are nearest to us, and meanwhile pray Heaven to hasten the moment of their conversion.

. . . .

The Journey of Dollier and Galinée

. . . At length, after ten or twelve leagues, we entered the largest lake in all America, called the Fresh Water Sea of the Hurons, . . . It is 660 or 700 leagues in circumference. We travelled about 200 leagues on this lake, and were really afraid of being in want of provisions because the animals of this lake appear very unprolific. However, God did not will that we should lack in His service; for we were never more than a day without food. It is true that we happened several times to have nothing left, and to pass an evening and a morning without having anything whatever to put in the kettle; but I did not see that anyone became discouraged or troubled on that account. For we were so accustomed to see God aiding us mightily on these occasions, that we awaited with tranquility the effects of His bounty, in the thought that He who nourished so many barbarians in these woods would not abandon His servants.

Although this lake is as large as the Caspian Sea, and much larger than Lake Erie, storms do not arise in it either so violent or so long, because it is not very deep. Thus in many places, after the wind has gone down, it does not require more than five or six hours, whilst it will be necessary sometimes to wait one or two days until Lake Erie is calmed down.

. . . At last we arrived on the 25th May, the Day of Pentecost, at Sainte-Marie of the Sault, the place where the Reverend Jesuit Fathers have made their principal establishment for the missions of the Ottawas and neighboring tribes. They have had two men in their service since last year, who have built them a pretty fort, that is to say, a square of cedar posts twelve feet high, with a chapel and house inside the fort so that now they see themselves in the condition of not being dependent in any way on the Indians. They have a large clearing well planted, from which they ought to gather a good part of their sustenance; they are even hoping to eat bread there within two years from now. Before arriving here, we fell in with three canoes of Indians, with whom we arrived at the fort of the Fathers. These men informed us of the custom they had when they reached the fort, of saluting it with several gunshots, which we also did very gladly.

We were received at this place with all possible charity. We were present at a portion of vespers on the day of Pentecost, and the two following days. We received the communion with so much the more joy, inasmuch as for nearly a month and a half we had not been able to enjoy this blessing.

The fruit these Fathers are producing here is more for the French, who are here often to the number of 20 or 25, than for the Indians; for although there are some who have been baptized, there are none yet that are good enough Catholics to be able to attend divine service, which is held for the French, who sing high mass and vespers on saints' days and Sundays. The Fathers have, in this connection, a practice which seems to me rather extraordinary, which is, that they baptize adults not in danger of death, when they have manifested any good-will toward Christianity, before they are capable either of confessing or of attending holy mass, or keeping the other commandments of the Church; so that at Pointe du Saint-Esprit, a place at the head of Lake Superior, where the remnant of the Hurons retired after the burning of their villages, the

Father who passed the winter with them told me that although there was a large portion of them who had been baptized when the Fathers had been amongst the Hurons, he had never yet ventured to say mass before them, because these people regard this service as jugglery or witchcraft.

I saw no particular sign of Christianity amongst the Indians of this place, nor in any other country of the Ottawas, except one woman of the nation of the Amikoues, who had been instructed formerly at the French settlements, and who, being as she thought in danger of death, begged M. Dollier to have pity on her. He reminded her of her old instructions and the obligation she was under of confessing herself, if she had offended God since her last confession, a very long time before, and he confessed her with great testimonies of joy on both sides.

When we were with the Fathers we were still more than 300 leagues from Montreal, to which, however, we wished to proceed at once, in order to be able to return at an early day to some of the Ottawa tribes and winter there, and in the following spring to go in search of the River Ohio and the races settled there, in order to carry the Gospel to them.

We learned that two days previously a fleet of 30 Ottawa canoes had set out for Montreal, and that there was still another of Kilistinons which was to leave shortly. As we were not certain at what time the latter were to come, and knew, besides, the trouble there is in being obliged to follow Indians, we judged it more convenient to look out for a guide to conduct us to Montreal, because the routes are more difficult and toilsome than can be imagined. We succeeded in finding one at an expense of 25 or 30 crowns' worth of goods, which we simply had to promise, so we took leave of Fathers d'Ablon and Marquette, who were then at this place, it being the 28th of May.

Hitherto the country of the Ottawas had passed in my mind, and in the minds of all those in Canada, as a place where there was a great deal of suffering for want of food. But I am so well persuaded of the contrary that I know of no region in all Canada where they are less in want of it. The nation of the Saulteaux, or in Algonkin Waoüitiköungka Entaöuakk or Ojibways, amongst whom the Fathers are established, live from the melting of the snows until the beginning of winter on the bank of a river nearly half a league wide and three leagues long, by which Lake Superior falls into the Lake of the Hurons. This river forms at this place a rapid so teeming with fish, called white fish, or in Algonkin *attikamegue*, that the Indians could easily catch enough to feed 10,000 men. It is true the fishing is so difficult that only Indians can carry it on. No Frenchman has hitherto been able to succeed in it, nor any other Indian than those of this tribe, who are used to this kind of fishing from an early age. But, in short, this fish is so cheap that they give ten or twelve of them for four fingers of tobacco. Each weighs six or seven pounds, but it is so big and so delicate that I know of no fish that approaches it. Sturgeon is caught in this small river, close by, in abundance. Meat is so cheap here that for a pound of glass beads I had four minots of fat entrails of moose, which is the best morsel of the animal. This shows how many these people kill. It is at these places that one gets a beaver robe for a fathom of tobacco, sometimes for a quarter of a pound of powder, sometimes for six knives, sometimes for a fathom of small blue beads, etc. This is the reason why the French go there, notwithstanding the frightful difficulties that are encountered.

. . . .

The Pageant of 1671

It is not our present purpose to describe this ceremony in detail, but merely to touch on matters relating to Christianity and the welfare of our missions, which are going to be more flourishing than ever after what occurred to their advantage on this occasion.

. . . Monsieur Talon, our intendant, . . . was commanded by the King to return to this country; and at the same time received his Majesty's orders to exert himself strenuously for the establishment of Christianity here, by aiding our missions, and to cause the name and the sovereignty of our invincible monarch to be acknowledged by even the least known and the most remote nations. These commands, reinforced by the designs of the minister, who is ever equally alert to extend God's glory, and to promote that of his King in every land, were obeyed as speedily as possible. Monsieur Talon had no sooner landed than he considered means for insuring the success of these plans, choosing, to that end, Sieur de Saint Lusson, whom he commissioned to take possession, in his place and in his Majesty's name, of the territories lying between the east and the west, from Montreal as far as the South Sea, covering the utmost extent and range possible.

For this purpose, after wintering on the Lake of the Hurons, Monsieur de Saint Lusson repaired to Sainte Marie du Sault early in May of this year, 1671. First, he summoned the surrounding tribes living within a radius of a hundred leagues, and even more; and they responded through their ambassadors, to the number of fourteen nations. After making all necessary preparations for the successful issue of the whole undertaking to the honor of France, he began, on June fourth [actually June 14] of the same year, with the most solemn ceremony ever observed in these regions.

For, when all had assembled in a great public council, and a height had been chosen well adapted to his purpose, overlooking, as it did, the village of the people of the Sault, he caused the Cross to be planted there, and then the King's standard to be raised, with all the pomp that he could devise.

The Cross was publicly blessed, with all the ceremonies of the Church, by the superior of these missions; and then, when it had been raised from the ground for the purpose of planting it, the *Vexilla* was sung. Many Frenchmen there present at the time joined in this hymn, to the wonder and delight of the assembled savages; while the whole company was filled with a common joy at the sight of this glorious standard of Jesus Christ, which seemed to have been raised so high only to rule over the hearts of all these poor peoples.

Then the French escutcheon, fixed to a cedar pole, was also erected, above the Cross; while the *Exaudiat* was sung, and prayer for his Majesty's sacred person was offered in that far-away corner of the world. After this, Monsieur de Saint Lusson, observing all the forms customary on such occasions, took possession of those regions, while the air resounded with repeated shouts of "Long live the King!" and with the discharge of musketry, to the delight and astonishment of all those peoples, who had never seen anything of the kind.

After this confused uproar of voices and muskets had ceased, perfect silence was imposed upon the whole assemblage; and Father Claude Allouez began to eulogize the King, in order to make all those nations understand what sort of a man he was whose standard they beheld, and to whose sovereignty they were that day submitting. Being well versed in their tongue and in their ways, he was so successful in adapting himself to their comprehension as to give them such an opinion of our incomparable monarch's greatness that they have no words with which to express their thoughts upon the subject.

"Here is an excellent matter brought to your attention, my brothers," said he to them, "a great and important matter, which is the cause of this council. Cast your eyes upon the Cross raised so high above your heads: there it was that Jesus Christ, the Son of God, making himself man for the love of men, was pleased to be fastened and to die, in atonement to his Eternal Father for our sins. He is the master of our lives, of Heaven, of Earth, and of Hell. Of Him I have always spoken to you, and His name and word I have borne into all these countries. But look likewise at that other post, to which are affixed the armorial bearings of the great captain of France whom we call King. He lives beyond the sea; he is the captain of the greatest captains, and has not his equal in the world. All the captains you have ever seen, or of whom you have ever heard, are mere children compared with him. He is like a great tree, and they, only like little plants that we tread under foot in walking. You know about Onnontio, that famous captain of Quebec. You know and feel that he is the terror of the Iroquois, and that his very name makes them tremble, now that he has laid waste their country and set fire to their villages. Beyond the sea there are ten thousand Onnontios like him, who are only the soldiers of that great captain, our Great King, of whom I am speaking. When he says, 'I am going to war,' all obey him; and those ten thousand captains raise companies of a hundred soldiers each, both on sea and on land. Some embark in ships, one or two hundred in number, like those that you have seen at Quebec. Your canoes hold only four or five men, or, at the very most, ten or twelve. Our ships in France hold four or five hundred, and even as many as a thousand. Other men make war by land, but in such vast numbers that, if drawn up in a double file, they would extend farther than from here to Mississaquenk [the Straits of Mackinac], although the distance exceeds twenty leagues. When he attacks, he is more terrible than the thunder: the earth trembles, the air and the sea are set on fire by the discharge of his cannon; while he has been seen amid his squadrons, all covered with the blood of his foes, of whom he has slain so many with his sword that he does not count their scalps, but the rivers of blood which he sets flowing. So many prisoners of war does he lead away that he makes no account of them, letting them go about whither they will, to show that he does not fear them. No one now dares make war upon him, all nations beyond the sea having most submissively sued for peace. From all parts of the world people go to listen to his words and to admire him, and he alone decides all the affairs of the world. What shall I say of his wealth? You count yourselves rich when you have ten or twelve sacks of corn, some hatchets, glass beads, kettles, or other things of that sort. He has towns of his own, more in number than you have people in all these countries five hundred leagues around; while in each town there are warehouses containing enough hatchets to cut down all your forests, kettles to cook all your moose, and glass beads to fill all your cabins. His house is longer than from here to the head of the Sault," that is, more than half a league, "and higher than the tallest of your trees; and it contains more families than the largest of your villages can hold."

The Father added much more of this sort, which was received with wonder by those people, who were all astonished to hear that there was any man on earth so great, rich, and powerful.

Following this speech, Monsieur de Saint Lusson took the word, and stated to them in martial and eloquent language the reasons for which he had summoned them, and especially that he was sent to take possession of that region, to receive them under the protection of the great King whose panegyric they had just heard, and to form thenceforth but one land of their territories and ours. The whole ceremony was closed with a fine bonfire, which was lighted toward evening, and around which the *Te Deum* was sung to thank God, on behalf of those poor peoples, that they were now the subjects of so great and powerful a monarch.

The Death of Father Marquette

After the Ilinois, filled with great esteem for the Gospel, had taken leave of the Father, he continued his journey, and shortly after reached the Lake of the Ilinois [Lake Michigan], upon whose waters he had to journey nearly a hundred leagues, by an unknown route, whereon he had never before travelled; for he was obliged to coast along the southern shore of the lake, having come by the northern. But his strength was so rapidly diminishing that his two men despaired of being able to bring him alive to the end of their journey. Indeed, he became so feeble and exhausted that he was unable to assist or even to move himself, and had to be handled and carried about like a child.

Meanwhile, he preserved in that condition an admirable equanimity, resignation, joy, and gentleness, consoling his dear companions and encouraging them to suffer patiently all the hardships of that voyage, in the assurance that God would not abandon them after his death. It was during this voyage that he began to make more special preparation for death. He held communion, sometimes with our Lord, sometimes with his holy Mother, or with his guardian angel, or with all Paradise. He was often overheard repeating these words, *Credo quod redemptor meus vivit*; or *Maria, Mater Gratiae, Mater Dei, memento mei.* In addition to the spiritual exercise, which was read to him every day, he requested toward the close that they would read to him his meditation preparatory for death, which he carried about with him. He recited every day his breviary; and although he was so low that his sight and strength were greatly enfeebled, he continued to do so to the last day of his life, despite the remonstrance of his companions.

Eight days before his death, he was thoughtful enough to prepare the holy water for use during the rest of his illness, in his agony, and at his burial; and he instructed his companions how it should be used.

The evening before his death, which was a Friday, he told them, very joyously, that it would take place on the morrow. He conversed with them during the whole day as to what would need to be done for his burial: about the manner in which they should inter him; of the spot that should be chosen for his grave; how his feet, his hands, and his face should be arranged; how they should erect a Cross over his grave. He even went so far as to counsel them, three hours before he expired, that as soon as he was dead they should take the little hand-bell of his chapel, and sound it while he was being put under ground. He spoke of all these things with so great tranquillity and presence of mind that one might have supposed that he was concerned with the death and funeral of some other person, and not with his own.

Thus did he converse with them as they made their way upon the lake, until, having perceived a river, on the shore of which stood an eminence that he deemed well suited to be the place of his interment, he told them that that was the place of his last repose. They wished, however, to proceed farther, as the weather was favorable, and the day was not far advanced; but God raised a contrary wind, which compelled them to return, and enter the river which the Father had pointed out. They accordingly brought him to the land, lighted a little fire for him, and prepared for him a wretched cabin of bark. They laid him down therein, in the least uncomfortable way that they could; but they were so stricken with sorrow that, as they have since said, they hardly knew what they were doing.

The Father, being thus stretched on the ground in much the same way as was St. Francis Xavier, as he had always so passionately desired, and finding himself alone in the midst of these forests, for his companions were occupied with the disembarkation, he had leisure to repeat all the acts in which he had continued during these last days.

His dear companions having afterward rejoined him, all disconsolate, he comforted them, and inspired them with the confidence that God would take care of them after his death, in these new and unknown countries. He gave them the last instructions, thanked them for all the charities which they had exercised in his behalf during the whole journey, and entreated pardon for the trouble that he had given them. He charged them to ask pardon for him also, from all our Fathers and brethren who live in the country of the Outaouacs [Ottawas]. Then he undertook to prepare them for the sacrament of penance, which he administered to them for the last time. He gave them also a paper on which he had written all his faults since his own last confession, that they might place it in the hands of the Father Superior, that the latter might be enabled to pray to God for him in a more special manner. Finally, he promised not to forget them in Paradise. And, as he was very considerate, knowing that they were much fatigued with the hardships of the preceding days, he bade them go and take a little repose. He assured them that his hour was not yet so very near, and that he would awaken them when the time should come, as, in fact, two or three hours afterward he did summon them, being ready to enter into the agony.

They drew near to him, and he embraced them once again, while they burst into tears at his feet. Then he asked for holy water and his reliquary; and having himself removed his crucifix, which he carried always suspended round his neck, he placed it in the hands of one of his companions, begging him to hold it before his eyes. Then, feeling that he had but a short time to live, he made a last effort, clasped his hands, and, with a steady and fond look upon his crucifix, he uttered aloud his profession of faith, and gave thanks to the Divine Majesty for the great favor which he had accorded him of dying in the Society, of dying in it as a missionary of Jesus Christ, and, above all, of dying in it, as he had always prayed, in a wretched cabin in the midst of the forests and bereft of all human succor.

After that, he was silent, communing within himself with God. Nevertheless, he let escape from time to time these words, *Sustinuit anima mea in verbo ejus;* or these, *Mater Dei, memento mei*—which were the last words that he uttered before entering his agony, which was, however, very mild and peaceful.

He had prayed his companions to put him in mind, when they should see him about to expire, to repeat frequently the names of Jesus and Mary, if he could not himself do so. They did as they were bidden; and, when they believed him to be near his end, one of them called aloud, "Jesus, Mary!" The dying man repeated the words, distinctly, several times; and as if, at these sacred names, something presented itself to him, he suddenly raised his eyes above his crucifix, holding them riveted on that object, which he appeared to regard with pleasure. And so, with a countenance beaming and all aglow, he expired without any struggle, and so gently that it might have been regarded as a pleasant sleep.

His two poor companions, shedding many tears over him, composed his body in the manner which he had prescribed to them. Then they carried him devoutly to burial, ringing the while the little bell as he had bidden them; and planted a large Cross near to his grave, as a sign to passers-by.

When it became a question of embarking, to proceed on their journey, one of the two, who for some days had been so heartsick with sorrow, and so greatly prostrated with an internal malady, that he could no longer eat or breathe except with difficulty, bethought himself, while the other was making all preparations for embarking, to visit the grave of his good Father, and ask his intercession with the glorious Virgin, as he had promised, not doubting in the least that he was in Heaven. He fell, then, upon his knees, made a short prayer, and having reverently taken some earth from the tomb, he pressed it to his breast. Immediately his sickness abated, and his sorrow was changed into a joy which did not forsake him during the remainder of his journey.

God did not permit that a deposit so precious should remain in the midst of the forest, unhonored and forgotten. The savages named Kiskakons, who have been making public profession of Christianity for nearly ten years, and who were instructed by Father Marquette when he lived at the Point of St. Esprit, at the extremity of Lake Superior, carried on their last winter's hunting in the vicinity of the Lake of the Ilinois. As they were returning in the spring, they were greatly pleased to pass near the grave of their good Father, whom they tenderly loved; and God also put it into their hearts to remove his bones and bring them to our church at the mission of St. Ignace at Missilimakinac, where those savages make their abode.

They repaired, then, to the spot, and resolved among themselves to act in regard to the Father as they are wont to do toward those for whom they profess great respect. Accordingly, they opened the grave, and uncovered the body; and, although the flesh and internal organs were all dried up, they found it entire, so that not even the skin was in any way injured. This did not prevent them from proceeding to dissect it, as is their custom. They cleaned the bones and exposed them to the sun to dry; then, carefully laying them in a box of birch-bark, they set out to bring them to our mission of St. Ignace.

There were nearly thirty canoes which formed, in excellent order, that funeral procession. There were also a goodly number of Iroquois, who united with our Algonquin savages to lend more honor to the ceremonial. When they drew near our house, Father Nouvel, who is its Superior, with Father Piercon, went out to meet them, accompanied by the Frenchmen and savages who were there; and having halted the procession, he put the usual question to them, to make sure that it was really the Father's body which they were bringing. Before conveying it to land, they intoned the *De profundis* in the presence of the thirty canoes, which were still on the water, and of the people who were on the shore. After that, the body was carried to the church, care being taken to observe all that the ritual appoints in such ceremonies. It remained exposed under the pall, all that day, which was Whit-monday, the 8th of June; and on the morrow, after having rendered to it all the funeral rites, it was lowered into a small vault in the middle of the church, where it rests as the guardian angel of our Outaouas missions. The savages often come to pray over his tomb. Not to mention more than this instance, a young girl, aged nineteen or twenty years, whom the late Father had instructed, and who had been baptized in the past year, fell sick, and applied to Father Nouvel to be bled and to take certain remedies. The Father prescribed to her, as sole medicine, to come for three days and say a *pater* and three *ave's* at the tomb of Father Marquette. She did so, and before the third day was cured, without bleeding or any other remedies.

Father Jaques Marquette, of the province of Champagne, died at the age of thirty-eight years, of which twenty-one were passed in the Society—namely, twelve in France and nine in Canada. He was sent to the missions of the upper Algonquins, who are called Outaouacs; and labored therein with the zeal that might be expected from a man who had proposed to himself St. Francis Xavier as the model of his life and death. He resembled that great saint, not only in the variety of barbarian languages which he mastered, but also by the range of his zeal, which made him carry the faith to the ends of this new world, and nearly 800 leagues from here into the forests, where the name of Jesus Christ had never been proclaimed.

He always entreated God that he might end his life in these laborious missions, and that, like his dear St. Xavier, he might die in the midst of the woods, bereft of everything. Every day, he interposed for that end both the merits of Jesus Christ and the intercession of the Virgin Immaculate, for whom he entertained a singular tenderness.

Accordingly, he obtained through such powerful mediators that which he solicited with so much earnestness; since he had, like the apostle of the Indies, the happiness to die in a wretched cabin on the shore of Lake Ilinois [Michigan], forsaken by all the world.

4: The French Voyageur

Although it was the Indian as a possible convert to Catholicism that attracted the missionary to the Michigan area, it was the Indian as a source of furs that interested most Frenchmen who came to North America. The fur trade remained the backbone of the French colonial economy, and the search for new sources of furs inevitably led the French to Michigan, not only because of the furs found there but also because it commanded the water routes that led to even greater resources of furs to the west, south, and north. The few who enjoyed the full profits of this trade depended on the strength and courage of the men they hired to transport the trade goods to the Indians in the west and then to bring back the furs for which these goods were traded. These employees—Michigan's first workingmen in the modern sense of the term—were most commonly referred to as voyageurs, or canoemen. They are described in Grace Lee Nute's modern historical classic, *The Voyageur*, published in 1931. Miss Nute, long associated with the Minnesota Historical Society and one of the most respected twentieth-century historians of the Great Lakes region, also wrote the volume on Lake Superior for the excellent *American Lakes Series* of the 1940s.

No one as yet has done justice to the Michigan fur trade, a topic for a major historical study. Ida A. Johnson's *The Michigan Fur Trade* (Lansing, 1919) is an amateurish work. Two works that are essential to an understanding of the fur trade and how it operated are Harold A. Innis, *The Fur Trade in Canada* (New Haven, 1930), a fine book, although rather difficult reading, and Paul C. Phillips' two-volume study, *The Fur Trade* (Norman, Oklahoma, 1961).

The Voyageur

GRACE LEE NUTE

The term *voyageur*, a French word meaning "traveler," was applied originally in Canadian history to all explorers, fur-traders,

From *The Voyageur*, pp. 3-7, 13-20. © Copyright and first published in 1931, reprinted in 1955 by the Minnesota Historical Society, St. Paul, Minnesota. Reprinted by permission of the author and the society. Footnotes in the original have been omitted.

and travelers. It came in time to be restricted to the men who operated the canoes and batteaux of fur-traders, and who, if serving at all as traders, labored as subordinates to a clerk or proprietor. Even as late as 1807, however, the famous Beaver Club of Montreal, a group of prominent and, usually, successful fur-merchants or traders, balloted to determine whether its name should be changed to the Voyageur Club. Thus the term was somewhat vague, though always referring to men who had had actual experience in the fur trade among the Indians. . . .

The French *régime* was responsible for the rise of this unique group of men. From the days of earliest exploration until 1763 a large part of what is now Canada and much of the rest of the continent west of the Appalachian Mountains was French territory. In this vast region lived the several tribes of Indians with whom the French settlers about Quebec and Montreal were not slow to barter furs. Beaver, marten, fox, lynx, bear, otter, wolf, muskrat, and many other furs were obtained. Furs were in great demand in Europe and Asia, and both the English colonists along the Atlantic seaboard and the French in New France supported themselves in large part by means of a very flourishing fur trade.

At first the Indians took their skins and furs down the St. Lawrence to Quebec and Montreal, whither annual fairs attracted them; but in the process of time ambitious traders intercepted the natives and purchased their furs in the interior, thus gaining an advantage over fellow traders. The enmity between the Iroquois and the Algonquin also tended to prevent the Indians from making their annual trips to the lower St. Lawrence, since the western tribes, who brought most of the furs, feared to pass down the river through enemy territory.

When traders began to enter the Indian country, the voyageur may be said to have been born. Farther and farther up the St. Lawrence, up the Ottawa River, into lakes Huron and Michigan, the traders ventured. Erie and Ontario were explored, and finally Lake Superior. From these lakes more venturesome traders entered the rivers emptying into them and reached the Ohio and Illinois countries and the region about the Mississippi. They even found the rivers emptying into Lake Superior from the west and marked out the route by way of Rainy Lake into Lake Winnipeg. When Canada was lost to the English in 1763, French posts were established far up the Saskatchewan, and French traders had seen the Rocky Mountains and knew the "Oregon" River. On these trips westward the birch-bark canoe was almost the sole vehicle of transportation, and men from the hamlets on the lower St. Lawrence were the canoemen.

Naturally the French Government found it necessary as time went on to establish rules and regulations for this lucrative business. Licenses (congés) to enter the Indian country were required; certain articles were prohibited in the trade; and only a specified number of traders might be licensed in one year. A man with sufficient capital to purchase a season's outfit acquired a license and hired men of his neighborhood to take the goods in canoes to the point at which the trader wished to sell his wares to the Indians. After bartering knives, beads, wampum, blankets, vermilion, and numberless trinkets and other articles for furs worth infinitely more in monetary value, these subtraders returned to their proprietor with the results of their transactions. The French term for the proprietor was bourgeois, and for the subtrader voyageur. The latter in time became a general term covering the mangeur de lard ("pork-eater") and the hivernant ("winterer"). The former were the novices, the men who could be entrusted only with the management of the canoes and who for that reason returned home each season. The hivernants were experienced voyageurs who spent the winters at posts in the interior, exchanging trade goods for furs under the direction of a commis. The latter was a clerk who was training to become a bourgeois and who was frequently a son or a near relative of a bourgeois. These terms came into use in the French period, but they and the system described were retained by the British after 1763 and by the Americans after 1816, when the British abandoned their posts in the American Northwest. French remained the "official" language as long as the fur trade flourished. Some of the terms are still in use in the forts of the Hudson's Bay Company in northern and western Canada.

Because this system developed under the French régime and about Quebec and Montreal, the fur trade continued to its last breath to be dependent to a great degree for canoemen and winterers upon the French Canadians in the country about these two cities. Just as the sailing vessel could be managed best by men in whose families was the seafaring tradition, so the fur-trading expeditions into the Northwest proved most lucrative when carried out by men from Sorel, Three Rivers, L'Orignal, and other Quebec hamlets, where babes grew into manhood with the almost certain knowledge that they would some day paddle canoes for the Northwest Company, the Hudson's Bay Company, the American Fur Company, or a rival firm or trader. John Jacob Astor, the prince of American fur-traders and the organizer of the largest American fur company, is said to have remarked that he would rather have one voyageur than three American canoemen.

Though the voyageurs were usually unlettered men and unambitious as well, Fate has decreed that even their individual names should not be lost. When a trader made application for a license, he was required to state the names of all his men. Hundreds of these licenses are extant, especially in Montreal, Quebec, and Ottawa, and from them one learns to recognize whole families of voyageurs who were enrolled year after year in official records. Doubtless many of these visitors to the West in the seventeenth, eighteenth, and early nineteenth centuries will remain forever unknown, but hundreds of others are becoming better known year by year as these old records are investigated.

The number of voyageurs in any given year is truly surprising. The West was not the unknown, uninhabited region that the imagination of writers has pictured. To dispel any doubt on this point one has only to refer to the lists of licenses already mentioned. In the year 1777, for example, 2,431 voyageurs are recorded in the licenses obtained at Montreal and Detroit. Add to this number the men already in the interior as *hivernants,* the employees of the Hudson's Bay Company, and the traders from the new states on the coast, and five thousand is a conservative estimate of the men who were sprinkled from Montreal to the Rocky Mountains, from Hudson Bay to the Gulf of Mexico.

Voyageurs formed a class as distinct in dress, customs, and traditions as sailors or lumberjacks. They had the further unifying characteristic of speaking a language which was not the native tongue either of their employers or of the people with whom they did business. They were termed voyageurs by all who had occasion to speak of them, and the word was used with the implication that a distinct and easily recognizable group of men was meant. Later writers have sometimes confused the terms *voyageur* and *coureur de bois.* The latter term was used in referring to illicit traders of the French *régime,* men who ventured into the wilderness without licenses. It is incorrect, therefore, to make it synonymous with *voyaguer.* The only other term by which voyageurs were commonly known was *engagés,* a loose expression which might be translated as "employees."

. . . .

"My man dressed himself in the habit of a voyageur, that is, a short shirt, a red woolen cap, a pair of deer skin leggins which reach from the ancles a little above the knees, and are held up by a string secured to a belt about the waist, the aziōn ['breech cloth'] of the Indians, and a pair of deer skin moccasins without stockings on the feet. The thighs are left bare. This is the dress of voyageurs in summer and winter." Add a few items which the worthy missionary, Sherman Hall, neglected to mention—a blue capote, the inevitable pipe, a gaudy sash, and a gay beaded bag or pouch hung from the sash—and you have the voyageur as he appeared speeding over lakes, advancing cautiously up narrow creeks, toiling over portages, cracking his whip over the heads of his dogs, laughing down rapids, fiddling in log forts, and singing wherever he was.

One would expect voyageurs to be men of heroic proportions, but usually they were not. The average voyageur was five feet six inches in height. Few were more than five feet eight inches. Had they been taller, they would have occupied too much of the precious space in a canoe already overcrowded with cargo. But though the voyageur was short, he was strong. He could paddle fifteen—yes, if necessary, eighteen—hours per day for weeks on end and joke beside the camp fire at the close of each day's toil. He could carry from 200 to 450 pounds of merchandise on his back over rocky portage trails at a pace which made unburdened travelers pant for breath in their endeavor not to be left behind. A distinguished traveler on the Great Lakes in 1826, Thomas L. McKenney, later of the United States Bureau of Indian Affairs, wrote how his men took the canoe out of the water, mended a breach in it, reloaded, cooked breakfast, shaved, washed, ate, and reëmbarked—all in *fifty-seven* minutes! "Some estimate may be formed from this," says McKenney, "of the celerity of the movements of these voyageurs. I can liken them to nothing but their own ponies. They are short, thick set, and active, and never tire. A Canadian, if born to be a labourer, deems himself to be very unfortunate if he should chance to grow over five feet five, or six inches;—and if he shall reach five feet ten or eleven, it forever excludes him from the privilege of becoming voyageur. There is no room for the legs of such people, in these canoes. But if he shall stop growing at about five feet four inches, and be gifted with a good voice, and lungs that never tire, he is considered as having been born under a most favourable star."

One result of the voyageur's mode of life was the overdevelopment of arms and shoulders at the expense of other parts of the body. This fact is brought out in a description by Dr. John J. Bigsby, the secretary of the commission that marked out the international boundary between Canada and the United States according to the provisions of the Treaty of Ghent of 1814. His portraits of the canoemen of his party as he saw them first at Lachine are probably more realistic than those of any other contemporary writer.

"I was disappointed and not a little surprised at the appearance of the *voyageurs*. On Sundays, as they stand round the door of the village churches, they are proud dressy fellows in their particoloured sashes and ostrich-feathers; but here they were a motley set to the eye: but the truth was that all of them were picked men, with extra wages as serving in a light canoe.

"Some were well made, but all looked weak in the legs, and were of light weight. A Falstaff would have put his foot through the canoe to the 'yellow sands' beneath. The collection of faces among them chanced to be extraordinary, as they squatted, paddle in hand, in two rows, each on his slender bag of necessaries. By the bye, all their finery (and they love it) was left at home. One man's face, with a large Jewish nose, seemed to have been squeezed in a vice, or to have passed through a flattening machine. It was like a cheese-cutter,—all edge. Another had one nostril bitten off. He proved the buffoon of the party. He had the extraordinary faculty of untying the strings of his face, as it were, at pleasure, when his features fell into confusion—into a crazed chaos almost frightful; his eye, too, lost its usual significance; but no man's countenance . . . was fuller of fun and fancies than his, when he liked. A third man had his features wrenched to the right—exceedingly little, it is true; but the effect was remarkable. He had been slapped on the face by a grisly bear. Another was a short, paunchy old man, with vast features, but no forehead—the last man I should have selected; but he was a hard-working creature, usually called 'Passe-partout,' because he had been everywhere, and was famous for the weight of fish he could devour at a meal. . . . Except the younger men, their faces were short, thin, quick in their expression, and mapped out in furrows, like those of the sunday-less Parisians."

Now and again one found a giant among these dwarfs. Nicholas Garry, deputy-governor of the Hudson's Bay Company from 1822 to 1835, mentions as one of his voyageurs "a Man six Feet high and of herculean make, who was called in consequence 'La Petite Vierge.'" Nicknames were common among these men. Frequently, too, as in the case of Garry's "little maiden," the nickname was in exact contradiction of some characteristic of the man. Stephen H. Long, an explorer in the valley of the Red River of the North in 1823, gives an example of this trait in describing how his men had no sooner seen his black man Andrew "than they immediately agreed among themselves to apply to him the term Wapishka . . . which means white."

McKenney, in the letter already quoted, points out an essential characteristic of the voyageur—his pride of profession. He was class conscious; he considered himself favored by fortune to belong to his group; he took a happy pride in doing his work in such a way as to bring credit to his fellow workers; and he considered the toil and hardships of his chosen work incidental to the profession and was seldom known to pity himself. An example of this attitude is given by McKenney in describing a man on Lake Superior whose business it was at the time to catch fish. He was sixty-nine years of age and active as a boy, though radically diseased. "On his legs, and arms, and breast," writes McKenney, "are tatooed, the marks of superiority in his profession, which has been that of a voyageur, and it seems he excelled in carrying packages across the portages, both on account of their weight and the celerity of his movement. He is now sallow, and dropsical, but active as stated. On questioning him as to his former life, he said, with a slap of the hands, 'he had been the greatest man in the northwest.' It is questionable whether Bonaparte ever felt his superiority in all the departments of mind which so distinguished him, or in his achievements, to an extent of greater excitement, than does this poor man on Michael's island, in the animating and single belief in his supremacy as a *north-western voyageur.*"

The voyageurs gave proof of this joy and pride in their work by decking themselves and their canoes in color. "The voyageurs," again to quote McKenney, "are engaged, and on the spot, each with a red feather in his hat, and two others, in possession of the steersman, one for the bow, and the other for the stern of the canoe. These plumes in the canoe are intended to indicate that she has been tried, and found worthy."

The young Chicago scientist, Robert Kennicott, who made a study of flora and fauna of the Canadian Northwest in the fifties and sixties, describing his guide as one of the best runners in America, remarks that he "seemed to feel much more pride in being a good voyageur than a famous runner." And to show how seriously these men took their work he relates that once on the voyage his canoe grazed a rock by accident. "Then, though not the least harm was done, and it was not altogether his fault, old Baptiste our guide was cross till the day after, when he recovered his good humor in the pleasure of running some difficult rapids."

Whether in canoes or with dog trains the voyageurs were ever trying to outdo one another in speed and endurance. Kennicott relates how the agreeable change from working against the current to moving with it put his voyageurs in excellent humor: "the canoes were constantly contending for the lead, the relative cleverness of the bowsmen in cutting off bends in the river . . . causing much excitement and sport." Canoe racing was, indeed, one of the chief delights of voyageurs.

With pride in their own ability went its usual concomitant, ridicule of lesser powers in others. To have the laugh on a greenhorn or to be able to taunt a fellow voyageur of weakness or slowness was to relish life thoroughly. "In an hour we were in still water," writes McKenney, "when our voyageurs, all wet . . . began to chatter again, and pass their jokes upon the bowsman, in whose face many a swell had broken in making this traverse." With dog trains fear of this ridicule showed itself characteristically. Many a warming did Kennicott's dog No-gah get because he would not *mouche* ("go fast") when it was his spell ahead. When a sled could not keep up and take its proper place in the brigade at each spell, it was said to be *planted,* "which is considered something very disgraceful; and a good voyageur will push (i.e. help his dogs by pushing with a long pole always attached to the top of a loaded sled) till he is nearly knocked up, rather than be planted, even though his dogs are known to be weak, or his load extra heavy." When the advance party with Kennicott arrived at Peel's River, they gave the dogs a *festin,* ate two suppers themselves, sat comfortably before the fire, and "boasted of our dogs; while the three unfortunate owners of poor trains lay in their windy camp that night and the next." When the laggards came up, the fortunate owners of good dogs laughed at them, much to their indignation. "Anyone who expects much sympathy for such trifling misery in this country," observes the author, "will be left to wipe his own eyes. If one gets frozen, starved, . . . he may expect ridicule, not condolence. . . . It is very comical, sometimes, to see the pains taken by the old voyageurs to cache a frost bite, or any fatigue."

The boasting of which Kennicott makes mention was characteristic of the voyageurs. The speed of their dogs, the lines of their canoes, the heaviness of their burdens on portages, their skill in shooting rapids, and similar topics were points discussed soon and late before blazing camp fires. Pulling the long bow did not arise when the first Paul Bunyan story was told. For a century and more its counterparts had made animated many an encampment of gesticulating French-Canadian voyageurs. The difference lies in the fact that the hero of every voyageur's yarn was himself instead of a mythical giant embodying the same exaggerated traits and abilities as those of which he boasted.

One of the most interesting traits of the voyageur was his extreme courtesy. His Gallic ancestry was nowhere so evident as in the deferential ease with which he addressed his superiors, the Indians, ladies, or men of his own class. The French language came to his aid here, for though he could neither read nor write, his by birthright were the graceful French phrases and expressions which mean little and yet are so effectual in establishing cordial relations. Many of the vulgar, beastly phases of the voyageur's life are offset by the refinement of his bearing and his speech.

5: The Voyage of the *Griffin*

A new era in Michigan's history began in the 1670s. The era of exploration, typified by the efforts of men such as Nicolet and Marquette, was over, and was now to be succeeded by the era of empire-building, as other men moved in to establish outposts where the region's resources might be exploited. The Pageant at the Sault in the summer of 1671 had signaled the start of this era. Then later in the decade Robert Cavelier de la Salle developed his elaborate schemes to establish French settlements in the west—in Illinois and down the Mississippi to the Gulf of Mexico. On August 7, 1679, he set sail from Niagara in the *Griffin*, the first sailing vessel on the upper Great Lakes. On board was yet another French priest, Father Louis Hennepin, a member of the Recollect order, whose books describing his adventures in the west as he carried out various tasks assigned him by La Salle, became best sellers in Europe, going through numerous editions and translations. Historians have expressed grave reservations regarding the truth of some of his narratives, but his account of the voyage of the *Griffin* is our principal source of information on this ill-fated vessel, whose disappearance on the return leg of her maiden voyage has since caused endless speculation as to the ship's fate. For the Michigan reader one of the most interesting such speculative efforts is that of George I. Quimby in "The Voyage of the *Griffin*: 1679," in *Michigan History*, 49 (June, 1965), 97-107, an article that also appears in Quimby's book *Indian Culture and European Trade Goods*.

The Voyage of the *Griffin*

FATHER LOUIS HENNEPIN

We made sail the 7th of the month of August, in the same year 1679, steering west by south. After the "Te Deum" we fired all the cannon and wall pieces, in presence of several Iroquois warriors who

From *Description of Louisiana*, translated from the edition of 1683 . . . by John Gilmary Shea (New York: John G. Shea, 1880), pp. 90-107. Footnotes in the original have been omitted.

were bringing in prisoners from the nations on the prairies, situated more than five hundred leagues from their country, and these savages did not neglect to give a description of the size of our vessel to the Dutch of New York, with whom the Iroquois carry on a great trade in furs, which they carry to them in order to obtain fire arms and goods to clothe themselves.

Our voyage was so fortunate that on the morning of the tenth day, the feast of Saint Lawrence, we reached the entrance of the Detroit [strait] by which Lake Orleans [Huron] empties into Lake Conty [Erie], and which is one hundred leagues distant from Niagara river. This strait is thirty leagues long and almost everywhere a league wide, except in the middle where it expands and forms a lake of circular form, and ten leagues in diameter, which we called Lake St. Clare, on account of our passing through it, on that Saint's day.

The country on both sides of this beautiful strait is adorned with fine open plains, and you can see numbers of stags, does, deer, bears, by no means fierce and very good to eat, . . . and all kinds of game, swans in abundance. Our guys were loaded and decked with several wild animals cut up, which our Indian and our Frenchmen killed. The rest of the strait is covered with forests, fruit trees like walnuts, chestnuts, plum and apple trees, wild vines loaded with grapes, of which we made some little wine. There is timber fit for building. It is the place in which deer most delight.

We found the current at the entrance of this strait as strong as the tide is before Rouen. We ascended it nevertheless, steering north and northeast, as far as Lake Orleans. There is little depth as you enter and leave Lake St. Clare, especially as you leave it. The discharge from Lake Orleans divides at this place into several small channels, almost all barred by sandbanks. We were obliged to sound them all, and at last discovered a very fine one, with a depth of at least two or three fathoms of water, and almost a league wide at all points. Our bark was detained here several days by head winds and this difficulty having been surmounted, we encountered a still greater one at the entrance of Lake Orleans, the north wind which had been blowing some time rather violently, and which drives the waters of the three great lakes into the strait, had so increased the ordinary current there, that it was as furious as the bore is before Caudebec. We could not stem it under sail, although we were then aided by a strong south wind; but as the shore was very fine, we landed twelve of our men who towed it along the beach for half a quarter of an hour, at the end of which we entered Lake Orleans on the 23d of the month of August, and for the second time we chanted a Te Deum in thanksgiving, blessing God, who here brought us in sight of a great bay [Georgian Bay] in this lake, where our ancient Recollects had resided to instruct the Hurons in the faith, in the first landing of the French in Canada, and these Indians once very numerous have been for the most part destroyed by the Iroquois.

The same day the bark ran along the east coast of the lake, with a fair wind, heading north by east, till evening when the wind having shifted to southwest with great violence, we headed northwest, and the next day we found ourselves in sight of land, having crossed by night a great bay, called Sakinam [Saginaw], which sets in more than thirty leagues.

On the 24th we continued to head northwest till evening, when we were becalmed among some islands, where there was only a fathom and a half or two fathoms of water. We kept on with the lower sails a part of the night to seek an anchorage, but finding none where there was a good bottom and the wind beginning to blow from the west, we headed north so as to gain deep water and wait for day, and we spent the night in sounding before the bark, because we had noticed that our pilot was very negligent, and we continued to watch in this way during the rest of the voyage.

On the 25th the calm continued till noon, and we pursued our course to the northwest, favored by a good southerly wind, which soon changed to southwest. At midnight we were compelled to head north on account of a great Point which jutted out into the lake; but we had scarcely doubled it, when we were surprised by a furious gale, which forced us to ply windward with mainsail and foresail, then to lie to till daylight.

On the 26th the violence of the wind obliged us to lower the topmasts, to fasten the yards at the clew, to remain broadside to the shore. At noon the waves running too high, and the sea too rough, we were forced to seek a port in the evening, but found no anchorage or shelter. At this crisis, the Sieur de la Salle entered the cabin, and quite disheartened told us that he commended his enterprise to God. We had been accustomed all the voyage to induce all to say morning and evening prayers together on our knees, all singing some hymns of the church, but as we could not stay on the deck of the vessel, on account of the storm, all contented themselves with making an act of contrition. There was no one but our pilot alone, whom we were never able to persuade.

At this time the Sieur de la Salle adopted in union with us Saint Anthony of Padua as the protector of our enterprises and he promised God if He did us the grace to deliver us from the tempest, that the first chapel he should erect in Louisiana should be dedicated to that great Saint.

The wind having fallen a little we lay to all the night, and we drifted only a league or two at most.

On the morning of the 27th we sailed northwest with a southwest wind, which changed towards evening into a light southeast trade wind, by favor of which we arrived on the same day at Missilimakinac, where we anchored in six fathoms of water in a bay, where there was a good bottom of potter's clay. This bay is sheltered from southwest to north, a sand bank covers it a little on the northeast, but it is exposed to the south which is very violent.

Missilimakinac is a point of land at the entrance and north of the strait, by which Lake Dauphin [Michigan] empties into Lake Orleans. This strait is a league wide and three long, and runs west northwest. Fifteen leagues east of Missilimakinac you find another point which is at the entrance of the channel by which Lake Condé [Superior] empties into Lake Orleans. This channel has an opening of five leagues, and is fifteen in length. It is interspersed with several islands, and gradually narrows in down to Sault Sainte Marie, which is a rapid full of rocks, by which the waters of Lake Condé are discharged and are precipitated in a violent manner. . . .

There are Indian villages in these two places; those who are settled at Missilimakinac, on the day of our arrival, which was August 28th, 1679, were all amazed to see a ship in their country, and the sound of the cannon caused an extraordinary alarm. We went to the Outtaoüactz [Ottawas] to say mass and during the service, the Sieur de la Salle, very well dressed in his scarlet cloak trimmed with gold lace, ordered the arms to be stacked along the chapel and the sergeant left a sentry there to guard them. The chiefs of the Outtaoüactz paid us their civility in their fashion, on coming out of the church. And in this bay where the Griffin was riding at anchor, we looked with pleasure at this large well equipped vessel, amid a hundred or a hundred and twenty bark canoes coming and going from taking white fish, which these Indians catch with nets, which they stretch sometimes in fifteen or twenty fathoms of water, and without which they could not subsist.

The Hurons, who have their village surrounded by palisades twenty-five feet high and situated near a great point of land opposite the island of Missilimakinac, proved the next day that they were more French than the Outtaoüactz, but it was in show, for they gave a salute by discharging all their guns, and they all have them, and renewed it three times, to do honor to our ship, and to the French, but this salute had been suggested to them by some Frenchmen, who come there, and who often carry on a very considerable trade with these nations, and who designed to gain the Sieur de la Salle by this show, as he gave umbrage to them, only in order better to play their parts subsequently by making it known that the bark was going to be the cause of destruction to individuals, in order to render the one who had built her odious to the people.

The Hurons and the Outtaoüactz form alliances with one another in order to oppose with one accord the fury of the Iroquois, their sworn enemy. They cultivate Indian corn on which they live all the year, with the fish which they take to season their sagamity. This they make of water and meal of their corn which they crush with a pestle in a trunk of a tree hollowed out by fire.

. . . .

On the 2nd of the month of September, from Missilimakinac we entered Lake Dauphin, and arrived at an island situated at the entrance of the Lake or Bay of the Puants, forty leagues from Missilimakinac, and which is inhabited by Indians of the Poutouatami nation. We found some Frenchmen there, who had been sent among the Illinois in previous years, and who had brought back to the Sieur de la Salle a pretty fair amount of furs.

. . . .

Contrary to our opinion, the Sieur de la Salle, who never took any one's advice, resolved to send back his bark from this place, and to continue his route by canoe, but as he had only four, he was obliged to leave considerable merchandise in the bark, a quantity of utensils and tools he ordered the pilot to discharge every thing at Missilimakinac, where he could take them again on his return. He also put all the peltries in the bark with a clerk and five good sailors. Their orders were to proceed to the great fall of Niagara, where they were to leave the furs, and take on board other goods which another bark from Fort Frontenac . . . was to bring them, and that as soon as possible thereafter, they should sail back to Missilimakinac, where they would find instructions as to the place to which they should bring the bark to winter.

They set sail on the 18th of September, with a very favorable light west wind, making their adieu by firing a single cannon; and we were never afterwards able to learn what course they had taken, and though there is no doubt, but that she perished, we were never able to learn any other circumstances of their shipwreck than the following. The bark having anchored in the north of Lake Dauphin [Michigan], the pilot, against the opinion of some Indians, who assured him that there was a great storm in the middle of the lake, resolved to continue his voyage, without considering that the sheltered position where he lay, prevented his knowing the force of the wind. He had scarcely sailed a quarter of a league from the coast, when these Indians saw the bark tossing in an extraordinary manner, unable to resist the tempest, so that in a short time they lost sight of her, and they believe that she was either driven on some sandbank, or that she foundered.

6: Cadillac and the Founding of Detroit

La Salle's plans for settlements in the west did not encompass Michigan, but at the very end of the century another Frenchman who was much like La Salle in many respects prepared to establish the first truly permanent French settlement in Michigan. This man, Antoine de la Mothe Cadillac, is one of the immortals of Michigan history. Particularly in Detroit, the city he founded in 1701, he has long been treated with great reverence—a reverence not shared by other, possibly more objective observers, such as the Canadian historian W. J. Eccles, who, in his well-received work *Canada Under Louis XIV, 1663-1701* (Toronto, 1964), refers to Cadillac as "one of the worst scoundrels ever to set foot in North America." Cadillac was ultimately removed from Detroit in 1710 and assigned to Louisiana, as a result of the complaints of those whom he had antagonized. Nevertheless, he deserves credit for establishing the first white settlement in Michigan that was intended to be not a temporary haven for missionaries, traders, or soldiers, but instead was to be a home for French families—families whose descendants today are found throughout Detroit and southeastern Michigan.

Cadillac was a rather gifted writer. A military man, he had the ability to describe things in precise, understandable terms that sometimes seems to be brought out by military training. His long memoir on the Mackinac area, where he commanded the garrison at St. Ignace in the 1690s, is one of the best descriptions of that area and its inhabitants in that period. (See *The Western Country in the 17th Century*, by Lamothe Cadillac and Pierre Liette, edited by M. M. Quaife [Chicago, 1947].) Among the many letters and reports by or about Cadillac collected by Clarence M. Burton, the great Detroit historian, and published under the title "Cadillac Papers" in the *Michigan Pioneer and Historical Collections*, the following account, written by Cadillac in 1702, discusses the progress that had been made at Detroit. The seemingly idyllic conditions of the beautiful surroundings, as Cadillac describes them, present a rather poignant contrast to modern conditions on the same site. The unfavorable comments leveled at the "missionaries," that is, the Jesuits, reflect quite accurately the sharp animosity that always characterized Cadillac's relationships with this Catholic order.

Accounts of the founding of Detroit and its early slow development are legion, for no other community in Michigan has had its history written as often as Detroit's has been. However, for comprehensiveness it is still hard to beat one of the earliest of these works, Silas Farmer's *History of Detroit and Michigan* (Detroit, 1884), a local history masterpiece.

Reflections on the Founding of Detroit

ANTOINE DE LA MOTHE CADILLAC

Detroit is a river lying north-north-east towards Lake Huron and south-south-west to the entrance of Lake Erie. According to my reckoning it will be about 25 or 26 leagues in length and it is navigable throughout so that a vessel of 100 guns could pass through it safely.

Towards the middle there is a lake which has been called St. Claire, which is about 30 leagues in circumference and 10 leagues in length. This lake is scarcely noticed, on account of several large and fine islands which form various passages or channels which are no wider than the river. It is only for about four leagues that the channel is wider.

. . . .

All the surroundings of this lake are extensive pasture lands, and the grass on them is so high that a man can scarcely be seen in it.

This river or strait of the seas is scattered over, from one lake to the other, both on the mainland and on the islands there, in its plains and on its banks, with large clusters of trees surrounded by charming meadows; but these same trees are marvelously lofty, without nodes and almost without branches until near the top, except the great oak.

On the banks and round about the clusters of timber there is an infinite number of fruit trees, chiefly plums and apples. They are so well laid out that they might be taken for orchards planted by the hand of a gardener.

On all sides the vine is seen; there are some with bitter and rough grapes,—others whose berries are extremely large and plump. There are also white and red grapes, the skins of which are very thin, full of good juice. The latter are the best, and I have taken care to select some of these plants and have them planted near the fort. I have no

From *Michigan Pioneer and Historical Collections* (Lansing: Robert Smith Printing Company, 1904), XXXIII, 133-144. Footnotes in the original have been omitted.

doubt that, by cultivating it as they do in France, this vine will produce good grapes and consequently good wine.

I have observed there nearly twenty different kinds of plums. There are three or four kinds which are very good; the others are very large and pleasant to look at, but they have rather tough skins and mealy flesh. The apples are of medium size, too acid. There is also a number of cherry-trees, [but] their fruit is not very good. In places there are mulberry trees which bear big black mulberries; this fruit is excellent and refreshing. There is also a very large quantity of hazel nuts and filberts. There are six kinds of walnuts; [the timber of] these trees is good for furniture and gun-stocks. There are also stretches of chestnuts, chiefly towards Lake Erie. All the fruit trees in general are loaded with their fruit; there is reason to believe that if these trees were grafted, pruned and well cultivated, their fruit would be much better, and that it might be made good fruit.

In places the woods are mixed, as white oak, red, walnut, elm, white wood trees, mulberry trees, cottonwood, chestnuts, ash; and in others they are not.

. . . .

There is another tree which is well defended, the prickles of which are half a foot long and pierce the wood like a nail; it bears a fruit like kidney-beans. The leaf is like the capillary plant; neither man nor animal could climb it. That would be good for making fences, its grain is very hard; when it has arrived at maturity, the wood is so hard that is is very difficult to drive an axe into it.

There are also citron-trees which are the same in form and color as the citrons of Portugal, but they are sweeter and smaller; there is a very large number of them, they are good preserved. The root of this tree is a very subtle and deadly poison; and it is also a sovereign remedy against snake-bites. It is only necessary to pound it and to apply it to the wound, and you are instantly cured. There are but few snakes at Detroit; they are very common in the country of the Iroquois.

I have seen an herb, pointed out to me by the Iroquois, which renders the venom of snakes innocuous; perhaps it may have some other use.

It is certain that, on both sides of the river of Detroit, the lands are very fertile and extend in the same manner and with the same pleasing character about ten leagues into the interior, after which few fruit trees are to be found and fewer prairies seen. But 15 leagues from Detroit, at the entrance to Lake Erie, inclining to the south-south-west, are boundless prairies which stretch away for about 100 leagues. . . . Forty leagues from this lake, going straight towards the south, there is no winter; the French and the savages have reported that they have seen neither ice nor snow there.

I sent this spring to the Chevalier de Calliere some hides and wool of these animals [buffalo], and he sent both to the directors of the Company of the colony to make trial of them, and it has been found that this discovery will prove a valuable one; that the hides may be very usefully employed, and this wool used for stockings and cloth-making. There is a number of stags and hinds, they are seen in hundreds, [with] roebuck, black bears, otters and other smaller fur-bearing animals; the skins of these animals sell well. There are also numbers of beavers on this mainland and in the neighborhood.

Game is very common there, as wild geese and all kinds of wild ducks. There are swans everywhere; there are quails, woodcocks, pheasants, rabbits—it is the only place on the continent of America where any have been seen. There are so many turkeys that 20 or 30 could be killed at one shot every [time they are] met with. There are partridges, hazel-hens, and a stupendous number of turtle-doves.

As this place is well supplied with animals, the wolves, of which there are numbers, find abundant food there; but it often costs them their skins because they sell well also; and this aids in destroying them, because the savages hunt them.

There are wood rats which are as large as rabbits; most of them are grey, but there are some seen which are as white as snow. The female has a pouch under her belly which opens and shuts as she requires, so that, sometimes when her little ones are playing, if the mother finds herself pressed, she quickly shuts them up in her pouch and carries them all away with her at once and gains her retreat.

I have seen a number of different [kinds of] birds of rare beauty. Some have plumage of a beautiful red fire color, the most vivid it were possible to see; they have a few spots of black in the tail and at the tips of their wings, but that is only noticed when they are seen flying. I have seen others all yellow, with tails bigger than their bodies, and they spread out their tails as peacocks do. I have seen others of a sky blue color with red breasts; there are some which are curiously marked like those great butterflies. I have observed that a pleasant warbling proceeds from all these birds, especially from the red ones with large beaks.

There are many cranes, grey and white; they stand higher than a man. The savages value these latter greatly, on account of their plumage, with which they adorn themselves.

In the river of Detroit there are neither stones nor rocks, but in Lake Huron there are fine quarries, and it is a country wooded like

Canada, that is to say, with endless forests. Houses could be provided and buildings erected of bricks, for there is earth which is very suitable for that, and fortunately, [only] five leagues from the fort. There is an island which is very large, and is entirely composed of limestone.

We have fish in great abundance, and it could not be otherwise, for this river is inclosed and situated between two lakes, or rather between as many seas. A thing which is most convenient for navigation is that it does not wind at all; its two prevailing winds are the north-east and the south-west.

This country, so temperate, so fertile, and so beautiful that it may justly be called the earthly paradise of North America, deserves all the care of the King to keep it up and to attract inhabitants to it, so that a solid settlement may be formed there which shall not be liable to the usual vicissitudes of the other posts in which only a mere garrison is placed.

I could not send any of our oxen or calves to France until after barges have been built, on which I believe they are going to work at once. One of them will be on Lake Frontenac and the other at Detroit in order to facilitate the conveyance of hides and wool which could not be effected by canoe transport. These barges will serve also for the other large skins, for beaver skins, and other small furs which will be conveyed at less expense in this way. They will serve for everything in general that is included in trade; and, as they will be capable of sailing two thousand leagues in the surrounding districts, we shall not fail, in time, to make some discovery which perhaps will be no less lucrative than glorious to France.

It is necessary to have settlers, in order to develop the trade. We were nearly 100 years in Canada without thinking of prosecuting the porpoise-fishery, although we saw them every day before our eyes; as soon as there was no demand for the beaver, we began to think of something else. That is, My Lord, the account of the country of Detroit and all I can tell you of it as I have only been one year there, very busy in doing what follows, to which I beg you to give your attention.

. . . The houses there are of good timber, of white oak, which is even and hard and as heavy as iron. This fort is in no danger provided there are enough people there to defend it.

Its position is delightful and very advantageous; it is [at] the narrowest part of the river, where no one can pass by day without being seen.

You know that I set out from Montreal on the 2nd of June, 1701, with 100 men and three months' provisions; that I arrived at Detroit on the 24th of July, having gone by the ordinary route of the Utaüais [Ottawas], by which I made only 30 portages, in order to try it.

After the fort was built, and the dwellings, I had the land cleared there and some French wheat sown on the 7th of October, not having had time to prepare it well. This wheat, although sown hastily, came up very fine and was cut on the 21st of July.

I also had some sown this spring, as is done in Canada; it came up well enough, but not like that of the autumn. The land having thus shown its quality, and taught me that the French tillage must be followed, I left orders with M. de Tonty to take care to begin the sowing about the 20th of Sept., and I left him 20 arpents of land prepared. I have no doubt he has increased it somewhat since my departure.

I also had twelve arpents or more sown this spring, in the month of May, with Indian corn which came up eight feet high; it will have been harvested about the 20th of the month of August, and I hope there will be a good deal of it. All the soldiers have their own gardens.

I believe we shall have 60 arpents of land sown this next spring, hence I count on having a large quantity of corn; and I will have a mill built on the spot, so as to be absolutely independent of Canada for provisions. I have also a fine garden in which I have put some vines, and some ungrafted fruit trees. It is one arpent square, and we shall enlarge it if necessary. In all this I have only complied with the orders of the Governor-General.

All that is no easy task, especially as everything has to be carried on the shoulders, for we have no oxen or horses yet to draw [loads] nor to plough; and to accomplish it, it is necessary to be very active.

I have also had a boat of ten tons burden built which will be useful for many purposes in the river.

On the right of the fort, at a good distance, there is a village of the Hurons to which I have granted lands in the name of His Majesty, according to my order. The chief of this tribe, with four of the most important men, in accepting them shouted "Long Live the King" three times with me; and I have myself set up the landmarks, and marked out the place where I wished them to build their fort and their village. By this means I have set all the tribes on the track of asking me for lands, and for permission to settle there. Having shown the others the way, this tribe has cleared up to the present about 200 arpents of land, and will make a great harvest.

There is also, on the left of the fort, a village of Oppenago, that is, of Wolves, to whom I have likewise granted lands, on condition, however, of giving them up to me if I want them afterwards, on granting them others further off; the spot where they are might be useful for a common land hereafter. These are the most tractable and most peaceable of the savages. I am convinced that, if only a little care is taken of them, they will very soon become Christians. They dress like the French, as far as they can; they are very caressing; they even make rough attempts at our language as far as they can. They have also made fine fields of wheat.

Above this village, half a league higher up, there is a village made up of four tribes of the Oütavois, to whom I have likewise granted lands; they have made some very fine fields of Indian corn there. Thus, within the space of one league, there are four forts and four hundred men bearing arms, with their families, besides the garrison.

Before I set out from the fort, eighteen Miamis came, on behalf of their tribe, to ask me for lands and to beg the savages who are there to approve of their coming to settle there and joining them. Thus the settlements could not promise better; these having prepared the way, the others will not be long before they come there, especially as, before I left, we learnt that the corn at Missilimakinak had been killed this year by the frost as it was the preceding [year], a thing which very often happens at that place.

Last year, my wife and Mme. Tonty set out on the 10th of Sept. with our families to come and join us there. Their resolution in undertaking so long and laborious a journey seemed very extraordinary. It is certain that nothing [ever] astonished the Iroquois so greatly as when they saw them. You could not believe how many caresses they offered them, and particularly the Iroquois who kissed their hands and wept for joy, saying that French women had never been seen coming willingly to their country. It was that which made the Iroquois also say that they well knew that the general peace which the Chev. de Callière had just made was indeed sincere, and that they could no longer doubt it since women of this rank came amongst them with so much confidence. If these ladies gave favorable impressions regarding us to the Iroquois, those our allies received from them were no less so. They received them at Detroit under arms with many discharges of musketry. They looked upon this move as the most important that could be made to prove to them that we wished to settle there in earnest, and that we wished to make it a post to dwell in, and a flourishing settlement.

. . . .

There are at Detroit a good fort, good dwellings, [and] the means of living and subsisting. There are three villages of the savages; the rest will very soon come there. They are watching to see whether what was promised them is being carried out. It is for you to push this matter about the inhabitants (that deserves our attention, on account of the war) and to consider whether you will permit the inhabitants of Canada to settle there; to form a seminary to begin to instruct the savage children in piety, and in the French language; to allow the recollects to settle there in order to discharge their functions there. It is the Lord's vine; we must let it be cultivated by all sorts of good laborers. For nearly a hundred years, it has been labored at without success; have trial made, My Lord, whether the methods which I have had the honor to propose to you are not more sound.

. . . .

So large a volume could be made of all that the missionaries have said, preached, and written, since they have been in the lands of the Utavais, against the trade in brandy and the [trading] expeditions in the woods that a man's [whole] life would not suffice to get through the reading of it.

The trade in that drink in the backwoods, and notably at Missili-makinak, has always given them occasion for inveighing against all the French who go to trade among the savages; and the [trading] expeditions in the woods have equally served as a pretext for accusing and decrying those who did not conform to their wishes. They have maintained that the brandy trade was an insuperable obstacle to the propagation of the Faith because it made the savages incapable of being taught; and the lewdness, which they stated the French were guilty of with the savage women, was the second head of their discourse, [they] maintaining that it was an obstacle to the success of religion by reason of the bad impression with which the minds of the savages were filled at the sight of such debauchery.

They complained next of the bad custom the Congés [licenses] or permits which were granted to go and trade with the Utavais and with the other tribes. The governors who bestowed them were suspected of sharing with those who made use of them. Their secretaries were accused of taking payments from those who had the preference in [getting] them. It was asserted that their cupidity or avarice increased the number of them, through the readiness and influence they met with in the minds of their masters.

They have accused the officers and commandants who were at these posts of being continually guilty of malversation and of obstructing the Voyageurs, in order to favor their own trade.

Lastly, they complained, with reason, that the excessive hunting by the French in the woods produced a burdensome influx of beaver skins for which there was no demand.

They persisted so obstinately in these complaints, whether well or ill founded, that the Court, having been disposed to listen to them, desired to put an end to them by the suppression of the licenses ["congés"] and permits, by prohibiting the brandy trade, by the evacuation of the posts which had been occupied there, and by the recall of the officers who were there for the purpose of keeping our allies united and attached to our interests. The close connection which exists between the upper colony and the lower (which gives a framework to New France) did not allow of leaving it in this melancholy condition, to which the combined circumstances of the time had reduced it, with ruinous results.

. . . .

What follows goes to prove that all difficulties have been remedied at a stroke, and that this was done by establishing Detroit where there is no longer any trade in drinks carried on with the savages, and if by chance they are sold any at times, that is done without them being intoxicated for, as the drinks are handed over to the charge of the warehouse guards, they are responsible for any bad use which may be made of them.

By means of this post the licentiousness of the French with the savage women is practically abolished; for your intentions were to send some families there, or at least to let the soldiers get married, who, having their wives, do not trifle with indecency. Nor will the Voyageurs, who are intended for conveying goods, cause any scandalous disorder; for, finding themselves included within the inclosure of a fort, and under the superintendence of missionaries, and of a commandant with the power of [inflicting] punishment, they will not dare to expose themselves to disgrace and to the confusion of being severely punished for it.

As the commandant and officers of this post are absolutely excluded from trading, or only trade for the interests of the Company, according to their agreements, they silence all the complaints which could be made against them; for, as they are assembled in one and the same fort, exposed to the view of the public and of the guardians of the warehouse, they would very soon be informed against if they contravened their orders.

By means of this post, the suspicions of trading, which have been entertained against the governors and others, stand completely effaced; and the accusations which have been made against their secretaries remain equally confounded.

The trade of the country is relieved and increased by it; for I have employed the savages at this post in hunting stags, hinds, elks, roebucks, black bears, otters, sables and other small furs, so that, as they have found the means of supplying their wants by the trade they do in the skins of these animals, they have at the same time given up hunting the beaver; and consequently the excessive stock of that article, of which there have been such loud complaints, is diminished by the purchases of it which have been made in France. Since it is a fact that the beaver trade which has been done at Detroit has not exceeded ten thousand, as appears from the receipt of the warehouse keepers, the Company will only have to settle the quantity it will require in future, and I will try and satisfy it.

The post of Detroit is indisputably the most suitable as regards the security of the trade and the fertility of the land. If it remains the only one, with sufficient troops, there will be nothing now to be feared whether on the part of our allies or from the enemies of the State; for, if the French do not go about in the distant parts of the woods, and give up separating into small parties among the further tribes to transact their trade, they will no longer be exposed to the humiliations and insults which they have so often endured without being able to help it, such as being plundered and cruelly beaten, which has disgraced the name of France among these tribes. It is a very different matter when the savages come and trade under the bastion of a fort. There they take care to make no venture and offer no insult because they know well that they would be compelled to conduct themselves properly, and that a small number of Frenchmen united and inside a fort [lit. "shut up"] together are invincible to them.

7: Michigan at the End of the French Period

Over a half century after Cadillac wrote his report on Detroit, the progress that had been made toward the establishment of a substantial French colony in Michigan was at best slight. Conditions as they existed in 1757 are revealed in the following excerpts from a report written by the famous French soldier and explorer, Louis Antoine de Bougainville, after whom an island in the Solomon group in the Pacific is named, as well as the popular shrub, the Bougainvillea. In 1757 Bougainville was serving as aide-de-camp to the Marquis de Montcalm, commander of the French forces in the French and Indian War. Although Bougainville had no personal acquaintance with the posts in the west that he discussed, he recognized their importance, and particularly he saw the value of strengthening Detroit and by encouraging more settlement there to make it the supply point for much of the western part of the colony of New France. However, it was too late for his recommendations to have any effect. The constant emphasis on the fur trade that had always existed in Michigan under the French had failed to encourage a broader-based economy that would have attracted more settlers and might have helped at least to delay what was perhaps the inevitable loss of the French North American empire.

Detroit in 1757

LOUIS ANTOINE DE BOUGAINVILLE

Detroit.—Detroit is a post worthy of attention, it is the entrepôt of the southern forts which communicate with the Illinois. The lands there are rich and easy to cultivate, the sky beautiful and serene, the climate magnificent, almost no winter, very little snow, the beasts winter in the fields and feed there. There are already about two hundred habitants, who have abundant provisions and cattle, and who furnish flour to the different posts of the upper

From *Wisconsin Historical Collections* (Madison: State Historical Society of Wisconsin, 1908), XVIII, 167-175, 183, 192, 194-195. Footnotes in the original have been omitted.

countries. The fort is on the border of the river that separates Lake Erie from Lake Huron where there is only a gentle slope that forms a slight current. At twenty leagues from Lake Huron and six from Lake Erie, the river of detroit is twelve to fifteen arpents wide, all the waters of the upper lakes, Michigan and of Lake Huron pass there, and go to discharge themselves into Lake Erie.

It is then a question of encouraging this establishment, which is an important place because of all the nations around, and of the routes of communication with the Illinois. In order to accomplish this, the government should be arranged with a staff officer, five or six companies complete with officers and soldiers, and give to each captain, and even to the subalterns a seigniory of ninety arpents depth by a league in front, and oblige each soldier to take land on the seigniory of his captain or officer, who will give each a domain or fief, and then in order to establish and cultivate the lands more quickly, they should be divided into companies of a dozen soldiers with a sergeant to guide them, and make them work together a week on each plot of an arpent and a half by thirty in depth, so that they are near together. By this means the lazy will be obliged to employ themselves as the others, since they work in common, and this was formerly the method of the famous Republic of Sparta. The officers would be interested to follow closely their soldiers that they might not lose time, and even would have built for them small houses, and when each soldier married would give him a cow and a sheep, a pair of oxen with a plow and other necessary utensils for work, and cooking utensils. The oxen would be only lent to them, they would return them to the king when they had reared others, and the former were only fit for the butcher. For this purpose the companies must be permanent; for if they changed, the soldiers would not be attached to anything. Those who marry must be replaced, so that the companies may be full, and then, as much as possible in choosing among the other companies, with those willing to serve.

It should be remarked that the habitants of detroit can rear as many animals as they wish, because of the abundance of the pasturage, and the beauty of the climate. Thus in giving attention to the establishment of Detroit there would arise great advantages. This government would soon be in a condition to furnish the posts of Niagara, Frontenac, la Presentation, and others in the region of the Belle River with flour and meat, which would relieve the capital greatly, as well in the matter of provisions as of men who are occupied in transporting stores from Montreal to Fort Frontenac—a passage of seventy leagues with fearful rapids to mount, which wears out the best men diverting them from agriculture to the transportation of stores for the different posts of the south. Detroit being established, nothing would be easier than to bring all the succor necessary in provision and beasts to furnish the posts mentioned, and this by means of flat-bottom transports, or barks which would carry from sixty to seventy tons, and which crossing Lake Erie would bring the government produce to Point à Binot. There a small fort could be built for an entrepôt both for stores coming from Montreal for the southern posts, as well as for those coming from Detroit for the posts that the government provisions, and for the goods of commerce; this would greatly diminish the number of engagés used as voyageurs. And the transports going and coming to Point à Binot would be laden with different goods. One might go and return by bateau from the little fort at Niagara to Point à Binot, a distance of nine leagues. And the transports not being able to go to the former would go to fort presqu'île, which is the entrepôt for the stores sent to the different posts on Belle River.

The voyageurs would only have to carry their merchandise up to fort Frontenac, where they would embark on vessels which traverse Lake Ontario, going and coming to Niagara—a passage of seventy leagues, and at the latter place the portage of this merchandise and other goods, might be made by horses; and a regulation might be made of how much the voyageurs should pay for goods and merchandise from fort Frontenac, which would be much lower than the expense of bark canoes and engagés as I will demonstrate.

A large canoe costs . . . . 500 fr.
Six engagés at 250 fr. . . . . 1500 f.
One hundred livres of biscuit per man at 20 fr. . . . . 120 f.
Twenty-five livres of lard per man at 60 c. . . . . 90 f.
For tools for the canoe . . . . 20 f.

Total . . . . 2260 fr.

It should be noted that a bark canoe carries about four thousand weight. Thus, all the goods that the voyageurs carry up to the Upper Country for trade cost more than ten sols per livre for transportation. It is true that a part of their return comes down with the same men and canoe. Thus the king could charge twenty francs per hundred weight to carry merchandise from fort Frontenac to detroit, and twelve francs a package from detroit to fort Frontenac. The voyageurs who would follow their packages, could go down to Montreal on their own account; the king would lend them only canoes or bateaux.

These same transports could likewise by crossing Lake Huron

communicate with Michilimakina, which is the entrepôt of the northern posts; and even go through Lake Michigan as far as La Baye [Green Bay] a hundred leagues from Michilimakina, and even as far as Saint-Joseph.

Michilmakina.—Michilmakina is distant from Montreal travelling by the grand river three hundred leagues; from Detroit a hundred leagues and more. This post is situated between lake Michigan and lake Huron; when the navigators had acquired experience on these lakes, knowing the different shelters and anchorages and retreats in case of bad weather, one could use these vessels for transporting all the goods for the posts of the north. Detroit, having become a considerable place, would be in position to furnish merchandise to all these several places. By this means voyageurs would be freed from taking up bark canoes by the grand river, which is very troublesome on account of the great number of rapids and portages which the engagés make. Eighty bark canoes ordinarily go up each year, or about six to seven hundred men for that part of the country of which I speak; and by these means it would not be necessary. This would conserve the men in Canada, and augment the number of laborers which are the basis of the state.

Following this, individuals at Detroit will make boats proper for these transports, and commerce will be much facilitated in the Upper Country, for the barks of Lake Erie will go on Lakes Huron and Michigan, and a boat of forty tons will carry twenty canoe weights, and for this vessel it will take five or six men, in place of the hundred and twenty to a hundred and forty needed for the twenty canoes.

The governor general has paid ordinarily to the voyageurs five hundred francs for each canoe-crew, as much for the gratification to the officers as for the poor families; therefore, there must be paid five hundred francs for four thousand weight that the voyageurs convey to the Upper Country, and the one returns to the other.

In following exactly that which is stipulated in a few words, one will remedy one part of the abuses which are contrary to the advantage of Canada, and in a little while will see the lands culti-vated, the habitants increasing in numbers, commerce flourishing, and the people becoming happier; it is that which I wish, not being able to do more, and having spoken the truth.

Detroit the entrepôt for the southern posts.—Detroit the entre-pôt for the southern posts, is a large town situated between Lake Erie and Lake Ste. Claire, from the entrance of Lake Erie to Detroit it is six leagues, from Detroit to Lake Ste. Claire, two; from the outlet of that lake which is seven leagues long to Lake Huron, they reckon eleven leagues.

The situation of that post is very beautiful, the climate charming, the air healthy, the land excellent and adapted to all kinds of productions; hunting is abundant. A man in fifteen days can secure three hundred head of game of different kinds, excellent to eat. The season for game lasts from February to May, and from September to Christmas.

On the north there are three leagues of land inhabited by the French, with three arpents to the habitant; to the south there are two leagues and a half thus occupied. The river as one leaves Lake Erie to go to Detroit runs northeast; it is a league and a half wide in front of the town, and has an island that serves as a common, fifty arpents long and twenty wide. It is called *Isle au Cochon* (Hog Island) [Belle Isle]. A quarter of a league above the entrance of Lake Ste. Claire is an island named *Isle du Large* (Wide Island), twenty arpents long by seven or eight wide.

The habitants raise in ordinary years two thousand five hundred minots of wheat, much hay, and Indian corn, they sometimes sow grain in the autumn, but often it produces only rye. A habitant of the place assured me that he had sown a dozen minots of very fine wheat and had harvested only very fine rye. They sow in February and March and harvest in July, the wheat production is ordinarily twentyfold.

At a day's journey from there at a large point on Lake Huron there is a stone, which is wanting at Detroit, suitable for making mill-stones. It will be necessary to encourage agriculture among the Detroit habitants by assuring them of an outlet for their products, an easy matter, by having them utilized by the garrisons of the forts. . . . These provisions will cost the king less than those sent from Mont-réal, the cost of transportation of which is immense, and the difficulty of the passage renders uncertain the subsistence of the garrisons.

It will be necessary also that the merchants of Detroit or others who might wish to establish themselves there in that capacity should have the liberty to carry back to Detroit without paying a license, the returns of packages, letters of exchange, or certificates that they carry to Mont-réal; for if this privilege is not accorded the establishment of Detroit will languish.

At this post there is a commandant, a major, and under their orders [blank] subaltern officers, the garrison of [blank] men is furnished by detached companies of marine. The post is exploited by licenses whose price is usually five hundred francs payable in cash and whose number is not fixed. The charges supported by the licenses are for the commandant, three thousand francs; for the second in command, a thousand francs; for the subalterns, five hundred francs; for the subdelegate, six hundred francs; for the interpreter, five hundred francs; for the chaplain, five hundred francs; for the surgeon, three hundred francs; each canoe is obliged to carry four hundred livres weight of merchandise for the officers and other employees of the said post, in consequence the officers engage in trade, which is thus not free, and there are abuses to correct.

The savages who come ordinarily to trade at Detroit are Hurons of the same family as those of Lorette, a perfidious, knavish tribe against whom one must be incessantly on guard. The Outawas, the Saulteux [Chippewa], and the Pouteouatamies, these latter are of all the savages the most attached to our interests, never having dipped their hands in the blood of any Frenchmen, they have even given us notice of plots formed against us by the other nations. There issues from this post between eight hundred and a thousand packages of peltry.

. . . .

Michilimakinac is a fort of standing pickets, situated on the strait of communication between Lake Michigan and Lake Huron; it is the entrepôt of the posts of the north; it is on the same footing as Detroit, entrepôt for the southern posts. It is exploited by licenses, which are six hundred francs per canoe; each canoe is obliged to carry five hundred weight for the officers, or the necessities of the garrison. This post has been reduced to a thousand francs yearly for presents to the savages, and no certificates. The commandant there has three thousand francs; the second in command, one thousand francs; and the interpreter, six hundred francs.

The savages who come to trade at this post are the Saulteux and the Outawais; there may come from there in an ordinary year, six to seven hundred packages.

. . . .

Sault de Sainte-Marie, a picket fort, is situated on the strait between Lake Superior and Lake Huron; it was established in 1750.

The trade was accorded free to the commandant in order to facilitate the establishment. The king gives five hundred francs of gratification taken from Michilimakinac, of which this post is a dependency. The savages who trade there are the Saulteux. There comes from there annually a hundred packages. The sieur Debonne and the sieur de Repentigny have the concession of this post for a hereditary seigniory.

Trade and licenses.—In almost all of the posts the house where the officer in command lodges, surrounded by pickets, is honored with the name of fort. In Canada, they call a fort a species of public shop where trade in peltries is carried on with the savages, who give them in return for these the merchandise that they need. Formerly the posts were auctioned off, and the merchants could thus obtain possession; they gave a profit to the king and paid the officer who commanded. To-day the governor general disposes of them for the benefit of his favorites, with the approbation of the court. The most important are the Sea of the West, the post of la Baye, Saint-Joseph, the Nipigons, and Michilimakinac, if they do not give at the latter place many licenses. The post of Détroit has never been given away, there they have the license system.

. . . .

Foot races.—At Détroit foot races between the savages and the Canadians are as celebrated as horse races in England. They take place in the spring. Ordinarily there are five hundred savages present, sometimes as many as fifteen hundred. The course is a half league, going and returning from Détroit to the village of the Poutéouatamis; the road is well made and wide. There are posts planted at the two extremities; the wagers are very considerable, and consist of packages of peltries laid against French merchandise such as is in use among the savages.

The most celebrated Canadian who has run and won from the savages is a certain Campo [Campeau] ; his superiority is so well recognized that he is no longer admitted to the races.

There is to be found in the customs of the savages traces of the ancient usages of the Greeks, I see especially in their warlike manners and customs those of the heroes of the *Iliad* and the *Odyssey*; some of them also have the custom like the Hebrews of separating the women in cabins apart and having no intercourse with them during their courses. The separation of the houses is perhaps too much, but not to hold intercourse is according to the principles of a healthy physique and the love of humanity, not to raise an unfortunate progeny, destined to live in infirmity.

The king gives many presents to the savages of the Upper Country, that cost in an ordinary year 150,000 francs; they supply their needs in return for peltries, and this is called carrying on trade, a custom that enriches the individuals to whom the posts are granted; in some the king reserves for himself the commerce, and as it is carried on at a disadvantage for the sole reason that it is for the king, he loses thereby each year, 100,000 crowns. These expenses are, nevertheless, much below those incurred in time of war to equip, arm, feed, reward, and give collars to so many of our domiciled savages, as well as to those of the Upper Country, when we wish them to come down to our assistance.

8: The British Come to Michigan

French control of Michigan came to an end in 1760 when, at the surrender of Montreal, the governor of New France also turned over to the British the remaining outposts of that colony, including those at Detroit, Michilimackinac, Sault Ste. Marie, and Fort St. Joseph. Although British troops did not complete the task of occupying these forts until the fall of 1761, a few British fur traders in the spring of that year hastened to these northern regions from which they had previously been excluded. A half century later, one of these traders, Alexander Henry, who was by that time enjoying a comfortable retirement in Montreal, wrote an account of his experiences in the Great Lakes area in the 1760s and 1770s. In 1761, after a brief stopover at Mackinac Island, Henry, who was then only twenty-one years old, came to the main settlement on the south side of the Straits of Mackinac. Here, among Frenchmen and Indians who throughout their lives had regarded the British as their mortal enemies, Henry and his fellow traders, in the face of this hostility, made considerable progress in establishing trading relationships with the Indians before British troops arrived in September. The Indians wanted the trading goods Henry had to offer as much as Henry wanted their furs. Henry would have some harrowing experiences with the Indians, especially at the time of the so-called massacre at Michilimackinac in 1763, but the friends he had made in 1761 helped him to survive and ultimately to prosper in the fur trade.

Henry's narrative was first published in New York in 1809. A reprint, edited by James Bain, was published in 1901, and this version in turn was reprinted in 1969 by the Charles E. Tuttle Company. Milo M. Quaife edited still another edition of Henry's account of his adventures that was published in 1921. Quaife made certain minor corrections in the original text, chiefly to eliminate obvious typographical errors. It is Quaife's edition that is used for the following selection.

A British Trader in Michigan

ALEXANDER HENRY

Leaving as speedily as possible the island of Michilimackinac I crossed the strait and landed at the fort of the same name. The distance from the island is about two leagues. I landed at four o'clock in the afternoon.

Here I put the entire charge of my effects into the hands of my assistant, Campion, between whom and myself it had been previously agreed that he should pass for the proprietor; and my men were instructed to conceal the fact that I was an Englishman.

Campion soon found a house to which I retired, and where I hoped to remain in privacy; but the men soon betrayed my secret, and I was visited by the inhabitants with great show of civility. They assured me that I could not stay at Michilimackinac without the most imminent risk; and strongly recommended that I should lose no time in making my escape to Detroit.

Though language like this could not but increase my uneasiness it did not shake my determination to remain with my property and encounter the evils with which I was threatened; and my spirits were in some measure sustained by the sentiments of Campion in this regard; for he declared his belief that the Canadian inhabitants of the fort were more hostile than the Indians as being jealous of English traders, who like myself were penetrating into the country.

Fort Michilimackinac was built by order of the governor-general of Canada, and garrisoned with a small number of militia, who, having families, soon became less soldiers than settlers. Most of those whom I found in the fort had originally served in the French army.

The fort stands on the south side of the strait which is between Lake Huron and Lake Michigan. It has an area of two acres, and is enclosed with pickets of cedar wood; and it is so near the water's edge that when the wind is in the west the waves break against the stockade. On the bastions are two small pieces of brass English cannon taken some years since by a party of Canadians who went on a plundering expedition against the posts of Hudson's Bay, which they reached by the route of the River Churchill.

Within the stockade are thirty houses, neat in their appearance, and tolerably commodious; and a church in which mass is celebrated by a Jesuit missionary. The number of families may be

From *Alexander Henry's Travels and Adventures in the Years 1760-1776*, edited with historical introduction and notes by Milo Milton Quaife (Chicago: The Lakeside Press, 1921), pp. 39-53. Footnotes in the original have been omitted.

nearly equal to that of the houses; and their subsistence is derived from the Indian traders who assemble here in their voyages to and from Montreal. Michilimackinac is the place of deposit and point of departure between the upper countries and the lower. Here the outfits are prepared for the countries of Lake Michigan and the Mississippi, Lake Superior, and the Northwest; and here the returns in furs are collected and embarked for Montreal.

I was not released from the visits and admonitions of the inhabitants of the fort before I received the equivocal intelligence that the whole band of Chipewa from the island of Michilimackinac was arrived with the intention of paying me a visit.

There was in the fort one Farley, an interpreter, lately in the employ of the French commandant. He had married a Chipewa woman and was said to possess great influence over the nation to which his wife belonged. Doubtful as to the kind of visit which I was about to receive I sent for this interpreter and requested first that he would have the kindness to be present at the interview, and secondly that he would inform me of the intentions of the band. M. Farley agreed to be present; and as to the object of the visit, replied that it was consistent with uniform custom that a stranger on his arrival should be waited upon and welcomed by the chiefs of the nation, who on their part always gave a small present, and always expected a large one; but as to the rest, declared himself unable to answer for the particular views of the Chipewa on this occasion, I being an Englishman, and the Indians having made no treaty with the English. He thought that there might be danger, the Indians having protested that they would not suffer an Englishman to remain in their part of the country. This information was far from agreeable; but there was no resource, except in fortitude and patience.

At two o'clock in the afternoon the Chipewa came to my house, about sixty in number, and headed by Minavavana, their chief. They walked in single file, each with his tomahawk in one hand and scalping knife in the other. Their bodies were naked from the waist upward, except in a few examples where blankets were thrown loosely over the shoulders. Their faces were painted with charcoal, worked up with grease; their bodies with white clay in patterns of various fancies. Some had feathers thrust through their noses, and their heads decorated with the same. It is unnecessary to dwell on the sensations with which I beheld the approach of this uncouth, if not frightful assemblage.

The chief entered first, and the rest followed without noise. On receiving a sign from the former, the latter seated themselves on the floor.

Minavavana appeared to be about fifty years of age. He was six feet in height, and had in his countenance an indescribable mixture of good and evil. Looking steadfastly at me where I sat in ceremony, with an interpreter on either hand, and several Canadians behind me, he entered at the same time into conversation with Campion, inquiring how long it was since I left Montreal, and observing that the English, as it would seem, were brave men and not afraid of death, since they dared to come as I had done fearlessly among their enemies.

The Indians now gravely smoked their pipes, while I inwardly endured the tortures of suspense. At length the pipes being finished, as well as the long pause by which they were succeeded, Minavavana, taking a few strings of wampum in his hand, began the following speech:

"Englishman, it is to you that I speak, and I demand your attention!

"Englishman, you know that the French king is our father. He promised to be such; and we in return promised to be his children. This promise we have kept.

"Englishman, it is you that have made war with this our father. You are his enemy; and how then could you have the boldness to venture among us, his children? You know that his enemies are ours.

"Englishman, we are informed that our father, the King of France, is old and infirm; and that being fatigued with making war upon your nation, he is fallen asleep. During his sleep you have taken advantage of him and possessed yourselves of Canada. But his nap is almost at an end. I think I hear him already stirring and inquiring for his children, the Indians; and when he does awake, what must become of you? He will destroy you utterly!

"Englishman, although you have conquered the French, you have not yet conquered us! We are not your slaves. These lakes, these woods and mountains were left to us by our ancestors. They are our inheritance; and we will part with them to none. Your nation supposes that we, like the white people, cannot live without bread—and pork—and beef! But you ought to know that He, the Spirit and Master of Life, has provided food for us in these spacious lakes and on these woody mountains.

"Englishman, our father, the King of France, employed our young men to make war upon your nation. In this warfare many of them have been killed, and it is our custom to retaliate until such time as the spirits of the slain are satisfied. But the spirits of the slain are to be satisfied in either of two ways; the first is by the spilling of the blood of the nation by which they fell; the other by *covering the bodies of the dead,* and thus allaying the resentment of their relations. This is done by making presents.

"Englishman, your king has never sent us any presents, nor entered into any treaty with us, wherefore he and we are still at war; and until he does these things we must consider that we have no other father, nor friend among the white men than the King of France; but for you we have taken into consideration that you have ventured your life among us in the expectation that we should not molest you. You do not come armed with an intention to make war; you come in peace to trade with us and supply us with necessaries of which we are in much want. We shall regard you, therefore, as a brother; and you may sleep tranquilly, without fear of the Chipewa. As a token of our friendship we present you with this pipe to smoke."

As Minavavana uttered these words an Indian presented me with a pipe, which, after I had drawn the smoke three times, was carried to the chief, and after him to every person in the room. This ceremony ended, the chief arose and gave me his hand in which he was followed by all the rest.

Being again seated, Minavavana requested that his young men might be allowed to taste what he called my *English milk* (meaning rum)—observing that it was long since they had tasted any, and that they were very desirous to know whether or not there were any difference between the English milk and the French.

My adventure on leaving Fort William Augustus had left an impression on my mind which made me tremble when Indians asked for rum; and I would therefore willingly have excused myself in this particular; but being informed that it was customary to comply with the request, and withal satisfied with the friendly declarations which I had received, I promised to give them a small cask at parting.

After this, by the aid of my interpreter I made a reply to the speech of Minavavana, declaring that it was the good character which I had heard of the Indians that had alone emboldened me to come among them; that their late father, the King of France, had surrendered Canada to the King of England, whom they ought now to regard as their father, and who would be as careful of them as the other had been; that I had come to furnish them with necessaries, and that their good treatment of me would be an encouragement to others. They appeared satisfied with what I said, repeating *eh!* (an expression of approbation) after hearing each particular. I had prepared a present which I now gave them with the utmost good will. At their departure I distributed a small quantity of rum.

Relieved as I now imagined myself from all occasion of anxiety as to the treatment which I was to experience from the Indians, I assorted my goods, and hired Canadian interpreters and clerks, in whose care I was to send them into Lake Michigan and the River St. Pierre, in the country of the Nadowessies, into Lake Superior among the Chipewa, and to the Grand Portage for the Northwest. Everything was ready for their departure when new dangers sprung up and threatened to overwhelm me.

At the entrance of Lake Michigan and at about twenty miles to the west of Fort Michilimackinac is the village of L'Arbre Croche, inhabited by a band of Ottawa boasting of two hundred and fifty fighting men. L'Arbre Croche is the seat of the Jesuit mission of St. Ignace de Michilimackinac, and the people are partly baptized, and partly not. The missionary resides on a farm attached to the mission and situated between the village and the fort, both of which are under his care. The Ottawa of L'Arbre Croche, who when compared with the Chipewa appear to be much advanced in civilization, grow maize for the market of Michilimackinac, where this commodity is depended upon for provisioning the canoes.

The new dangers which presented themselves came from this village of Ottawa. Everything as I have said was in readiness for the departure of my goods when accounts arrived of its approach; and shortly after, two hundred warriors entered the fort and billeted themselves in the several houses among the Canadian inhabitants. The next morning they assembled in the house which was built for the commandant, or governor, and ordered the attendance of myself and of two other merchants still later from Montreal, namely Messrs. Stanley Goddard and Ezekiel Solomons.

After entering the council room and taking our seats one of the chiefs commenced an address:

"Englishmen," he said, "we, the Ottawas were some time since informed of your arrival in this country, and of your having brought with you the goods of which we have need. At this news we were greatly pleased, believing that through your assistance our wives and children would be enabled to pass another winter; but what was our surprise, when a few days ago we were again informed that the goods which as we had expected were intended for us were on the eve of departure for distant countries, of which some are inhabited by our enemies! These accounts being spread, our wives and children came to us crying and desiring that we should go to the fort to learn with our own ears their truth or falsehood. We accordingly embarked almost naked as you see; and on our arrival here we have inquired into the accounts and found them true. We see your canoes ready to depart and find your men engaged for the Mississippi and other distant regions. "Under these circumstances we have considered the affair; and you are now sent for that you may hear our determination, which is that you shall give to each of our men, young and old, merchandise and ammunition to the amount of fifty beaver skins on credit, and for which I have no doubt of their paying you in the summer, on their return from their wintering."

A compliance with this demand would have stripped me and my fellow merchants of all our merchandise; and what rendered the affair still more serious, we even learned that these Ottawa were accustomed never to pay for what they received on credit. In reply, therefore, to the speech which we had heard, we requested that the demand contained in it might be diminished; but we were answered that the Ottawa had nothing further to say except that they would allow till the next day for reflection; after which, if compliance was not given, they would make no further application, but take into their own hands the property which they already regarded as their own, as having been brought into their country before the conclusion of any peace between themselves and the English.

We now returned to consider of our situation; and in the evening Farley, the interpreter, paid us a visit, and assured us that it was the intention of the Ottawa to put us that night to death. He advised us, as our only means of safety, to comply with the demands which had been made; but we suspected our informant of a disposition to prey upon our fears with a view to induce us to abandon the Indian trade, and resolved however this might be, rather to stand on the defensive than submit. We trusted to the house in which I lived as a fort, and armed ourselves and about thirty of our men with muskets. Whether or not the Ottawa ever intended violence we never had an opportunity of knowing; but the night passed quietly.

Early the next morning a second council was held, and the merchants were again summoned to attend. Believing that every hope of resistance would be lost, should we commit our persons into the hands of our enemies, we sent only a refusal. There was none without in whom we had any confidence, except Campion. From him we learned from time to time whatever was rumored among the Canadian inhabitants as to the designs of the Ottawa; and from him toward sunset we received the gratifying intelligence that a detachment of British soldiery, sent to garrison Michilimackinac, was distant only five miles and would enter the fort early the next morning.

Near at hand, however, as relief was reported to be, our anxiety could not but be great; for a long night was to be passed, and our fate might be decided before the morning. To increase our apprehensions, about midnight we were informed that the Ottawa were holding a council, at which no white man was permitted to be present, Farley alone excepted; and him we suspected, and afterward positively knew, to be our greatest enemy. We, on our part, remained all night upon the alert; but at daybreak to our surprise and joy we saw the Ottawa preparing to depart. By sunrise not a man of them was left in the fort; and indeed the scene was altogether changed. The inhabitants, who, while the Ottawa were present, had avoided all connection with the English traders, now came with congratulations. They related that the Ottawa had proposed to them that if joined by the Canadians they would march and attack the troops which were known to be advancing on the fort; and they added that it was their refusal which had determined the Ottawa to depart.

At noon three hundred troops of the Sixtieth Regiment, under the command of Lieutenant Lesslie, marched into the fort; and this arrival dissipated all our fears from whatever source derived. After a few days detachments were sent into the Bay des Puants [Green Bay], by which is the route to the Mississippi and at the mouth of the St. Joseph which leads to the Illinois. The Indians from all quarters came to pay their respects to the commandant; and the merchants dispatched their canoes, though it was now the middle of September, and therefore somewhat late in the season.

9: The Indian War of 1763

Unfortunately, the promising start that British fur traders had made toward developing friendly ties with the Michigan Indians was upset by the insensitive approach of some British military and civilian authorities who felt no compulsion to placate these natives now that the French and Indian War was over. This attitude helped in 1763 to bring on the greatest Indian war in American history, one that started in Michigan and is named after the leader of the Detroit River Ottawas, Pontiac. Francis Parkman, in *The Conspiracy of Pontiac*, popularized the view that this Indian chieftain had not only directed the attack on the British in Detroit but had masterminded the entire uprising that occurred among Indians from New York and Pennsylvania west to Illinois and Wisconsin. In 1947, however, a century after Parkman did his research, Howard H. Peckham, who was then head of the Indiana Historical Bureau but is generally associated with the University of Michigan's William L. Clements Library, which he has headed since 1953, published his book *Pontiac and the Indian Uprising*. Using all the material that Parkman had examined plus new sources that had come to light since Parkman's time, Peckham concluded that Pontiac can only be credited with planning and leading the attempt to drive the British out of Detroit. The Indian attacks that swept the west in the weeks after the attack on Detroit were the result, he argues, of widespread anti-British feelings that had developed since 1760 and had been aroused to a fever pitch by various French and Indian agitators.

Following Peckham's discussion of the origins of the war is an account of the beginning of the Indian siege of Detroit, from a contemporary journal kept by a Detroit resident, generally believed to have been the Frenchman, Robert Navarre.

Although Pontiac and the Indians ultimately failed in their objective of driving out the British, their efforts were not entirely in vain. Recognizing the unwise nature of their Indian policy that had brought on the war, the British changed much in that policy to which the Indians had objected, and within a few years after 1763 the Indians of Michigan and the Great Lakes area were as solidly allied with the British as they had been with the French a few years earlier.

Origins of Pontiac's War

HOWARD H. PECKHAM

During 1762 the Detroit Indians gradually discovered . . . the real nature of the Indian policy laid down by the imperceptive and overconfident General Amherst.

That revelation came slowly, but it cracked the peace which [Sir William] Johnson thought he had cemented by his grand council [in Detroit]. The Indians returned to their villages in the spring, bringing in the furs from the animals they had shot or trapped during the winter. Once more they found no rum to be had for celebration. What was more ominous to them, their ammunition was shot away and they could procure only a little more—hardly enough with which to supply their families with game during the summer.

The situation was somewhat relieved by the increased number of traders in Detroit with stocks of ammunition to sell, sometimes on credit. However, the Indians expected anything so vital to their welfare as powder to be a gift from the English, as it had been from the French, out of friendship and gratitude to an ally. It was the old Indian idea of sharing property as against the white man's concept of private property. [Captain Donald] Campbell [commander at Detroit] smoothed over this dissatisfaction as best he could by diplomatic speeches, gifts of tobacco and rum and even a little powder. The gunsmith promised by Johnson was now in Detroit ready to repair Indian arms, and the two hundred hoes were distributed to the Hurons. Campbell believed the prohibition on rum was having a good effect, but he wrote to Bouquet on July 3:

"The general says the Crown is to be no longer at the expense of maintaining the Indians, that they may very well live by their hunting, and desires to keep them scarce of powder. I should be glad to know what you do in that respect. I am certain if the Indians in this country had the least hint that we intended to prevent them from the use of ammunition, it would be impossible to keep them quiet. I dare not trust even the interpreters with the secret. The Indians are a good deal elevated on the news of a Spanish war [Spain had joined France, and Britain had thereupon declared war on her January 2, 1762] and daily reports spread amongst them that the French and Spaniards are soon to retake Quebec, etc. This goes from one nation to another, and it is impossible to prevent it. I assure you they only want a good opportunity to fall upon us if they had encouragement from an enemy."

The last sentence was prophetic. What Amherst never realized was that by his policy he was playing directly into the hands of the disaffected French. After all, France and Great Britain were still at war; the capitulation of Canada had been only one great victory. But Spain had just come into the war on the side of France, and France still held Louisiana, which province included the forts on the Mississippi and Vincennes on the Wabash. Loyal Frenchmen were still hopeful that from somewhere France might draw the strength to throw back the British and recover Canada. They were not averse to suggesting to the Indians that a new French expedition was on its way to recapture Quebec and Montreal. The Indians, knowing nothing of affairs in Europe, some of them hoping these rumors were true, often did believe them.

Moreover, the French told them that the English secretly planned to wipe out the Indians. Their first step was to deprive the Indians of ammunition so they would be unable to defend themselves. Was it not so? The Indians could not deny that they were being kept short of powder. What if the explanation whispered by the French were correct?

Affairs within the fort went along much as usual in 1762. Campbell was kept busy trying to get enough provisions forwarded to Detroit and thence distributed to the dependent posts. Sir Robert Davers, one of those British tourists still to be found in odd corners of the earth, had spent the winter in Detroit learning the Indian languages and making himself an agreeable visitor. About the first of May he left for a tour of the Lakes. Thomas Hutchins, a young native of New Jersey who had studied surveying and cartography, arrived at Detroit toward the end of April bound on a mission for George Croghan to map the Great Lakes. Campbell gave him what assistance he could and saw him safely on his way northward.

. . . .

Changes were in store for Detroit. General Amherst wanted Lake Superior explored this year and the French posts there garrisoned. The Canada he had conquered stretched clear to the upper Mississippi, and the British flag had not yet been carried beyond Green Bay. He decided to appoint Major [Henry] Gladwin to the command of Detroit and move Captain Campbell up to the fort at St. Mary's River (Sault Ste. Marie), built in 1751, where he would have charge of the Lake Superior region. However, his instructions to Gladwin allowed that officer discretion in assigning Campbell.

Gladwin arrived in Detroit on August 23, 1762, bringing with him Capt. George Etherington, Lieuts. John Jamet and Jehu Hay, and another company of the Royal Americans. Learning that the Lake Superior posts were in ruins, he decided to keep Campbell at Detroit, as well as Lieutenant Hay, who earns our gratitude for having started the next year to keep a daily diary. Gladwin sent Captain Etherington to supersede Lieutenant Leslye at Fort Michilimackinac, and Lieutenant Jamet was to occupy the fort at St. Mary's. The latter assignment proved shortlived, for on December 10 the fort burned to the ground, and Jamet took his small garrison into Fort Michilimackinac for the winter. The only other change in command was the relief of Lieutenant Meyer at Fort Sandusky, who was succeeded by his second, Ensign Christopher Pauli.

The summer and fall passed without incident among the Indians, Gladwin thought, but of one significant occurrence he never learned. On the night of September 28 a Detroit Indian reached George Croghan's house on the edge of Pittsburgh and related a strange story. He said that a secret council had been held during the summer at the Ottawa village on the Detroit River. It was attended by civil and war chiefs of the Ottawas, Chippewas, Hurons, Potawatomies, and of the tribes around Lake Superior, which latter delegates were accompanied by two Frenchmen in Indian dress. The informer did not know what was discussed in the council, but he was sure they were plotting against the English. He did know that deputies were sent to carry the council's message to the tribes on the Wabash and to the Shawnees in the Ohio Valley; otherwise the council was kept secret even from the other Indians around Detroit.

Croghan was disturbed, and two days later he related this news to three Iroquois he knew to be trustworthy and loyal. They replied that they had heard the same news from a Shawnee brave. Thereupon Croghan sent his intelligence to Johnson and Amherst. The general dimissed it with the comment that he could see nothing of consequence in it. Blindly he had just ordered a reduction in the expenses and personnel of the Indian department under Johnson, thus stopping the presents which Croghan had been giving the Indians because the fort commandants could not.

It is difficult to resist the temptation to see Pontiac's hand in this council. The Ottawas had always been most attached to the French and were least cordial to the English. Within a few short months he was to emerge as the leader of those Indians who hated the English and wanted to restore the French. He had been expressing his disgust with British rule since the previous autumn, although it does not follow that he called the conference. Much more probably the instigators of it were the two Frenchmen, who may have come from Illinois or have been acting on orders from there.

Croghan found support for his faith in the story from the report of Thomas Hutchins, who returned at the end of September from his extensive mapping tour of the Great Lakes. "They were disappointed," said Hutchins of the northern Ottawas and Chippewas, "in their expectations of my having presents for them; and as the French have always accustomed themselves, both in time of peace and during the late war, to make these people great presents three or four times a year and always allowed them a sufficient quantity of ammunition at the posts, they think it very strange that this custom should be so immediately broke off by the English, and the traders not allowed even to take so much ammunition with them as to enable those Indians to kill game sufficient for the support of their families."

In December 1762 another of Croghan's agents who had been several weeks among the Shawnees (decimated by a plague during the summer) returned and reported that they had received a war belt and hatchet from the Weas on the Wabash the previous spring, who had received it from the French in Illinois. Croghan was very pessimistic in his letter to Johnson. He warned that the western tribes believed now that the English were preparing them for annihilation and that the blow would fall as soon as all the white captives had been recovered from them.

"The Indians are a very jealous people," he reminded his superior, "and they had great expectations of being very generally supplied by us, and from their poverty and mercenary disposition they can't bear such a disappointment. Undoubtedly the general has his own reason for not allowing any present or ammunition to be given them, and I wish it may have its desired effect, but I take this opportunity to acquaint you that I dread the event as I know Indians can't long persevere. They are a rash, inconsistent people and inclined to mischief and will never consider consequences, though it may end in their ruin. Their success the beginning of this war on our frontiers is too recent in their memory to suffer them to consider their present inability to make war with us, and if the Senecas, Delawares and Shawnees should break with us, it will end in a general war with all the western nations, though they at present seem jealous of each other."

That jealousy—the inability to cooperate under a single leader— was all that saved the English from an Indian war, Croghan believed. But that leader was in the making. And the force that would modify intertribal jealousies and turn the nations against a common enemy was burgeoning in the Ohio Valley. It remained only for the coming leader to adopt this doctrine and preach it as a call to arms—then war would be inevitable.

Down in the Ohio Valley a psychopathic Delaware was having strange visions and exhorting his people to change their way of living. White men were slow to hear of him, and the few who did learn of his revolutionary doctrines did not know his name. He was called the Delaware Prophet, or the Imposter. John McCullough, who was captured on the frontier by the Delawares and taken to Mahoning on Beaver Creek, refers to him in 1762 as follows:

"My brother has gone to Tus-ca-la-ways [Tuscarawas, a Delaware town on the Tuscarawas River], about forty or fifty miles off, to see and hear a prophet that had just made his appearance amongst them. He was of the Delaware nation; I never saw nor heard him. It was said by those who went to see him, that he had certain hieroglyphics marked on a piece of parchment, denoting the probation that human beings were subjected to whilst they were living on earth, and also denoting something of a future state. They informed me that he was almost constantly crying whilst he was exhorting them. I saw a copy of his hieroglyphics, as numbers of them had got them copyed and undertook to preach or instruct others. The first (or principal doctrine) they taught them was to purify themselves from sin, which they taught they could do by the use of emetics and abstainence from carnal knowledge of the different sexes; to quit the use of fire arms, and to live entirely in their original state that they were in before the white people found out their country; nay, they taught that the fire was not pure that was made by steel and flint, but that they should make it by rubbing two sticks together. . . . It was said that their prophet taught them, or made them believe, that he had his instructions immediately from Keesh-she-la-mil-lang-up, or a being that thought us into being, and that by following his instructions they should in a few years be able to drive the white people out of their country."

The fact that the Prophet was "almost constantly crying whilst he was exhorting them" suggests his mental condition. His force as a prophet was increased by his visible sincerity and his heaven-declared authority. James Kenny, a young Quaker trader in Pittsburgh, describes him in more detail in his diary. Under date of October 15, 1762, he wrote:

"I think I have made mention before [he had not] of the Imposter which is raised amongst the Delawares, in order to show them the right way to Heaven. This plan is protrayed on a dressed leather skin and some[times] on paper; [it] fixes the earth at the bottom and heaven at the top, having a stright line from one to the other by which their forefathers used to ascend to happiness. About the middle is like a long square cutting their way to happiness at right angles and stopping them, representing the white people. The outside is a long square-like black stroke circumscribing the whole within it, and joining on the left hand, issuing from the white people's place, is cut many strokes parallel to their square of situation. All these strokes represent all the sins and vices which the Indians have learned from the white people through which now they must go, the good road being stopped. Hell being fixed not far off, there they are led irrevocably. The doctrine issued on this and the way to help it is said to be to learn to live without any trade or connections with the white people, clothing and supporting themselves as their forefathers did; it's also said that the Imposter prognosticates that there will be two or three good talks [i.e. conferences] and then war. This gains amongst them so much that mostly they have quit hunting any more than to supply nature in that way."

It seems clear from this account that the Prophet had learned a smattering of Christianity, which after meditation and self-induced visions he had adapted or misinterpreted for Indian consumption. Kenny also furnishes a clue as to where the Prophet obtained his idea of shaking off the white man's unhappy influence by going back to primitive living. In his diary for February 27, 1762, Kenny mentions that several years earlier some strange Indians from the West visited the Delaware towns. They told of their own people, who used only bows and arrows and had no dealings with the white men. The reason, of course, was that they lived beyond the reach of white traders. But the fact that there were tribes existing who could and did support themselves without firearms or other articles introduced by white men possibly impressed itself on the mind of the Prophet.

It should be noted that the Delaware Prophet was not a war chief who desired to lead a military expedition to drive out the English and restore French domination. He decried the baneful influence of all white men because it had brought the Indians to their present unhappy plight. He was an evangelist, a revivalist, preaching a new religion. He was trying to change the personal habits of the Indians in order to free them from imported vices and to make them entirely self-dependent. He gave his hearers faith and hope that they could live without the manufactures of the white man. He offered them salvation through hard work and steadfast purpose.

Reports of this doctrine spread among the Indian nations. Groups of Indians traveled far to hear the Delaware Prophet, and disciples took up his message and relayed it. From one of them, possibly from the master himself, Pontiac heard the narrative of the Prophet's vision. Whether or not he followed the interpretation to the conclusion of simple, resourceful living, he shrewdly recognized the power of the Prophet's argument. Here was an appeal that could unite the Indians in a common war effort!

The situation was indeed ripe for an explosion. The Indians' grievances against the English were solid and numerous. Foremost among them was the English refusal to supply them free ammunition for hunting. Unreasonable as such a grievance may appear today, the French had accustomed the Indians to this vital handout. When the English denied them, their refusal was akin to taking the bread from their mouths. That astute soldier of fortune, Col. Henry Bouquet, observed to General Gage as Pontiac's war was dying out: "And we have visibly brought upon us this Indian War by being too saving of a few presents to the savages which properly distributed would certainly have prevented it." Secondly, the prices of trade goods were not as low as the Indians had been led to anticipate. Thirdly, the English did not make them presents as often or as bountifully as the French had done, either as rent for the land or as gratitude for friendship. The English objected even to giving gifts when captives were returned. Fourthly, the Indians objected to the prohibition on liquor, even though the wiser chiefs regarded it as beneficial. The young braves resented it not alone because they liked to get drunk, but because as long as the French controlled the forts the English had been so generous in supplying rum. Now in control themselves, the English dropped the mask and showed their contempt for such Indian tastes.

Finally, the Indians were not slow to realize that actually the English had no liking for them. The arrogance, or reserve, toward native peoples which has usually characterized British colonial administrators was typified in Amherst. The Indians had been useful pawns during the war, and it was a stratagem of warfare to lure them away from the French. Now that Canada had surrendered and peace was in sight, the Indians had no further military value. They were not only to be dismissed, but insofar as possible ignored. Their "begging" was a nuisance and an expense, and Amherst thought he could humble them with discipline. That arrogance was further expressed in the orders forbidding the soldiers to mingle with the Indians. Neither were the savages welcomed in the forts. They were expected to state their business and get out. Gladwin himself was accused of showing contempt for Indian customs. Intermarriage was frowned upon. All this was in marked contrast to the camaraderie and friendliness of the French, many of whom had found the Indian maidens attractive enough to take as wives.

Farther east the Delawares and Iroquois had other grievances. They had been led to believe that the British were going to drive out the French and restore their invaded hunting grounds to the Indians. But after the British drove out the French, they stayed; and new settlers were moving into the Monongahela Valley, west of the mountains, and into the Susquehanna Valley, claimed by the Iroquois. Even the British military could not justify this westward expansion and did make efforts to eject the lawless squatters. The job was too big for the garrison at Fort Pitt, however, for the settlers continued to pour over the mountains. The Senecas also resented the demands of the English in criminal cases and were at the moment objecting to the surrender of the murderers of a white man for trial and punishment by Englishmen.

The Great Lakes tribes had not yet been crowded by farmer settlers, but they heard the complaints of the nations to the east of them and could see the danger ahead. The Lakes tribes had indicated their attitude toward the land to George Croghan in December 1760. They regarded it as theirs to hunt on, and the French as tenants who had been allowed a few acres here and there on which to establish trading posts and forts as much for the convenience of the Indians as for the profit of the French. The land was not theirs to transfer to the British, although they might assign them the forts agreeable to the Indian landlords. The English had to all appearances accepted this view by notifying the Indians of their intended occupation of the forts, by assuring them of generous treatment and advantageous trade (rent, in a sense), and by seeking their friendship. In other words, these savages believed that the British had succeeded the French at the western posts by permission of the Indians.

Logical as it was, this attitude was ignored by the British, who in common with other Europeans never recognized the Indian tribes as sovereign nations. They purchased land from the Indians as owners, but did so primarily as a means of avoiding expensive warfare, rather than of securing valid title. That body of usages called international law was not construed by European colonial powers as conferring any rights on savage or even un-christian nations. Such nations were not considered members of that vague entity called "the family of nations" who enjoyed the rights and were bound by the duties of international law. The United States of America was in fact the first non-European country admitted to the family of nations.

This legal concept had been expressed as recently as 1758 in a famous treatise produced by the eminent Swiss jurist, Emer de Vattel. Ignoring ethical considerations, Vattel laid down the principle that the uncertain occupancy by wandering tribes of the vast regions of the New World "cannot be held as real and lawful taking possession; and when the Nations of Europe, which are too confined at home, come upon lands which the savages have no special need of and are making no present and continuous use of, they may lawfully take possession of them and establish colonies in them." What Vattel failed to realize, of course, was that a hunting people could not settle down in one region and expect the game to remain there too. They "wandered" in search of food, and the land which the savages seemed to "have no special need of" was vital game cover which replenished itself while they hunted in a fresh region. White men not only killed off the game themselves, but by their settlements scared away the animals from formerly rich hunting areas.

Added to all these rankling thoughts in the Indian mind, plus the exhortation of the "divinely appointed" Prophet, were the intrigues of the French in Illinois urging revolt and promising aid. Possibly the Indians would have taken up the hatchet in time by themselves, although they would have been slower to act without the whispered assurances of the French. The role of the Illinois French in encouraging war was lawful prior to September 24, 1763, the date official news reached Illinois that France had signed the treaty of peace and thereby bound the Province of Louisiana to its observance. Before that date war was still in progress, and the undefeated French of Louisiana had every right to prosecute it by stirring up the Indians against the English. For the French of Canada to do so, however, was a violation of the terms of the capitulation of September 8, 1760, a point of honor in eighteenth-century warfare.

The evidence of French instigation is indirect, yet fairly conclusive. We do not know it from French sources, but both the British and Indians blamed the French, and their accusations cannot be laid entirely to prejudice in the one case or the desire to exculpate themselves in the other. There is the fact of the two Frenchmen attending the secret council in the Ottawa village, probably to bring war belts. Then the Shawnees reported that the Weas had received a war belt from the French in Illinois. Similarly, the rumor among the Detroit Indians that a French and Spanish force was on its way to retake Quebec was obviously of French origin designed to hearten the Indians to strike a blow in the West.

Johnson, Croghan, and Gladwin, who were in the best position to judge of the origin of the war, all declared definitely that the French were at the bottom of it. Lieut. Jehu Hay entered in his diary for January 14, 1764, that the Huron chiefs told the interpreter that the attack had its rise in the belts promising succour from Illinois which were circulated "two years ago"—that is, in 1762. Pontiac himself reminded his allies in May 1763 of the several belts he had received from the French urging him to make war.

Coincident with the French machinations in the West, the perennially dissatisfied Senecas in the East were promoting a definite conspiracy. Whether the Senecas were proceeding independently and on their own initiative remains in doubt. Johnson believed that the French had been tampering with them, and that the wampum belt calling for war sent out by the Senecas had been given them sometime earlier by the French. That the French at the head of the St. Lawrence were active is also suggested by the statement of Wabbicomigot, a Mississaugi-Chippewa chief, who related that St. Luc de La Corne had given him a war belt at Toronto which the chief refused.

The Senecas gave a war belt to their neighbors the Delawares with the injunction to pass it on westward. When it should reach the tribes around Fort Ouiatenon, all were to rise and put the British to death in their respective localities. The date on which the Senecas started this belt on its way is not certain, but it passed from the Delawares to the Shawnees and reached the Miamies at the head of the Wabash in March 1763. Ensign Holmes, the commandant of the fort there, then discovered it and persuaded the Miamies to deliver it to him. The Miamies related its provenance and destination and confessed having no desire to participate in such a war. They said further that the Seneca chief who started it was "the one that is always doing mischief." . . .

The route of this war belt implies that it was not intended for the tribes in Michigan. However, they were not being ignored. Another belt was sent to them directly from the Senecas early in 1763, according to an Ottawa named Notawas. The Huron chief at Sandusky, called Big Jaw, evidently saw one of the belts, for he later blamed the Senecas for starting the war. Despite the belligerent and treacherous efforts of this Iroquois tribe, the plan for a united uprising (which strategy may well have been suggested by the French) did not materialize. Their one belt did not complete its course before being discovered; the other may have encouraged the Detroit Indians to action later, but it produced no allied cooperation nor did the recipients pursue the shrewd Seneca plan for a general and simultaneous revolt.

Detroit thus was assailed from both east and west with promptings to action, and the Indians there finally accepted the initiative. This resolution was due to Pontiac, who listened to these incendiary proposals with growing approval and enthusiasm. Convinced that the Indians could and should drive out the British, he agitated for war among the Ottawas and their neighbors. Because he was an accomplished war chief and an effective orator and because he had a program of positive action backed by French promises of aid to lay before the disgruntled tribes, he naturally acquired more and more influence. As he persuaded others to agree with him he rose to leadership, not only in his village but also in the vicinity embracing the Chippewa, Huron, and Potawatomi settlements.

Pontiac's role in the approaching war was that of commander over the three villages surrounding Fort Detroit and a chief-to-be-consulted over the Chippewas and Potawatomies who came from a distance to join him. As for a general uprising of all the western tribes against all the British western posts, Pontiac may have thought of it, but his abilities were taxed in uniting his immediate neighbors and devising a surprise assault on one fort.

Perhaps the French agents assured him that they would engineer simultaneous attacks on the other forts once he took the initiative. They understood Indians well enough to know that once Pontiac was successful in capturing Detroit, the other tribes, not to be outdone, would fall on the forts in their vicinity in order to demonstrate equal prowess. Or, another possibility is that Pontiac may have privately considered moving on to another fort after taking Detroit, mustering additional tribes or villages there under his leadership and destroying that new objective, then on to another, and eventually entering western New York, Pennsylvania, or Virginia at the head of an enormous horde of allied savages.

It was not the nature of the Indian mind to foresee all consequences or to prepare for all eventualities. Nor were the Indians, of course, acquainted with the diplomatic niceties observed by European governments which would prevent the French court from countenancing a savage uprising undertaken to restore French dominion while a defeated France was seeking peace with Britain.

Pontiac planned his coup against Detroit carefully and with admirable ingenuity, but probably had only vague hopes as to his next move should he be successful. He did not even wait for an answer from the Chippewas at Saginaw Bay before making his first attempt on the fort. There was no grand conspiracy or preconcerted plan on his part embracing all the western tribes, such as the Senecas had proposed. Pontiac once referred to it as "the beaver war." What it developed into, of course, was a war for Indian independence as modified by French economic penetration. In the beginning there was only a local conspiracy at Detroit directed by Pontiac, who, however, improvised a more general uprising after his initial tactics failed. And his second attempts almost succeeded in loosening the British hold.

It was Napoleon who said that generalship is the art of improvisation.

A Contemporary View of the Beginning of the Indian Siege of Detroit in 1763

ROBERT NAVARRE (?)

May 7. The fatal day . . . having arrived for the English and perhaps for the French, Pontiac, who believed his designs still a secret, ordered in the morning that all his men should chant the war-song and paint themselves and put feathers in their hair,—an Indian custom when about to go on the warpath; moreover, all were to be armed with whatever was necessary for the attack.

Toward ten o'clock in the morning he came in his trappings to ask for a council, and it was granted. All of his men to the number of sixty who were to take part in the council entered the house of Mr. Campbell, second in command, where Mr. Gladwin, commander-in-chief, was with a part of his officers, who were all aware of the bold designs of Pontiac and had arms concealed in their pockets. The rest of the officers were occupied in getting their troops in readiness to appear when wanted. This was done with so much dispatch that the Indians did not have any occasion for suspicion. While the council was assembling, the other Ottawa Indians entered and took their places according to the plans agreed upon among them.

Pontiac in the council, thinking that it was about time for all of the people to have entered and taken positions in readiness for the attack, went out to see for himself if all his followers were ready and to give the signal which, as I have said, was to be a war-whoop. He perceived some commotion attracting the attention of his men toward the drill-ground and wanted to see what it might be. He noticed that the troops were under arms and drilling. This maneuver

From *Journal of Pontiac's Conspiracy, 1763*, edited by M. Agnes Burton, translated by R. Clyde Ford, published by Clarence Monroe Burton under the auspices of the Michigan Society of the Colonial Wars (Detroit: Speaker-Hines Printing Company, 1912), pp. 44-64. Footnotes in the original have been omitted.

augured ill for the success of his plot, inasmuch as he was surely discovered and his project defeated. He was disconcerted at this and obliged to re-enter the council room where all his men had remained waiting only for the cry to attack. They were greatly surprised when they saw him come back; they suspected that they were discovered and that, since they could no longer succeed, for the present they must leave and put off the attack to another day. They talked it over among themselves for some time, and then without saying good bye or anything they went out of the gate to regain their village where they might take other measures against discovery and succeed better.

Pontiac, upon his return to the village, found himself overwhelmed by various emotions,—anger, fury, and rage. As one might have thought, he looked like a lioness robbed of all her whelps. He assembled all his young men and made inquiries among them to see if they did not know the one that had betrayed them, "because," he said to them, "I see very well that the English have been warned." He gave them orders to try to find out the traitor in the nation, for they must kill him. But all their efforts were in vain; the one who had informed against them had taken too many precautions for them to discover him.

In the meantime, toward four o'clock in the afternoon there arrived in the village a false rumor that it was a Chippewa woman who had betrayed them, and that she was concealed in the Potawatomi village. At this report Pontiac ordered four Indians to find her and bring her to him, and these, taking delight naturally in lawlessness, were not so slow to do what their chief told them. They crossed the river directly in front of the village and passed by the Fort, quite naked but for breechclouts, with knives in their hands. They were yelling as they went along that their plan had failed, which caused the French along the shore, who knew nothing about the plot of the Indians, to think they had some evil designs either upon them or upon the English. They arrived at the Potawatomi village and actually found the woman, who had not even thought of them. Nevertheless, they took her and made her walk ahead of them, all the while uttering yells of joy as if they had a victim upon whom they were going to vent their cruelty. They took her into the Fort and before the Commandant as if to confront her with him, and demand if she was not the one who had disclosed to him their plans. They got no more satisfaction than if they had kept quiet; the Commandant ordered bread and beer for them and for her, and then they took her to their chief in their village.

It was now a question in the village of inventing some ruse to conceal their treachery and carry through their evil projects. Pontiac, whose genius constantly supplied him with new resources, said that he had thought out another scheme which would succeed better than the first one, and that the next day he would act upon it; he would go to speak with the Commandant to try to undeceive him concerning what had been told him, and he would play his part so well with these gentlemen in disproving the falsehood, that as soon as they heard him they would fall into his trap and he could accomplish his purpose before they knew it.

Fortunately, however, the Commandant and all the officers who had escaped the danger which threatened them and were safe only as long as they were on their guard, were not the kind of men to be caught by the flattering talk of a traitor; consequently, all that the enmity of Pontiac could devise against them was useless. But still he attempted to come to the Fort, as if sure of his plan, and actually did come as he had told his followers he would do.

May 8th, Sunday,

About one o'clock in the afternoon he came, accompanied by Mackatepelicite, Breton, and Chavinon, all chiefs of the same Ottawa nation. They brought with them a calumet, which they call among themselves the calumet of peace. They asked and were granted an audience by the Commandant, and did all they could with fine words to deceive him and lead him and all his troops into the snare which they had set for him. Warned of their wicked intrigues the Commandant acted as if he believed what they told him, but nevertheless was on his guard.

Pontiac told him, as proof of his cherishing no bad designs, that he had brought the pipe of peace for them to smoke together in token of agreement; and that he was going to leave it with him as a guarantee of the Indians' uprightness, and that as long as he had it he need not fear anything from them. The Commandant accepted the pipe, which he well knew was a feeble guarantee against the bad faith of an Indian. After the Commandant had received it Pontiac withdrew with his chiefs, well satisfied and believing that his tricks had succeeded and entangled the English in the snares which his wickedness had set for them. But without knowing it he was deceived in his expectations.

He and his chiefs returned to his village as happy as if they were sure of the success of their enterprise, and in a few words they reported to their young men the result of their negotiations. They sent messengers to the bad band of the Hurons and to the Potawatomies to notify them of what they had just accomplished at the Fort, and that the next day was the one which should settle the fate of these Englishmen, and that they should hold themselves ready for the first call.

In order to play his part better and make it appear that neither he nor his followers cherished evil designs any longer, Pontiac invited for four o'clock in the afternoon the good and bad Huron bands and the Potawatomies to come and play lacrosse with his young men. A good many French from each side of the river came to play also, and were well received by the three nations. The game lasted till about seven o'clock in the evening, and when it was over everybody thought of returning home. The French who lived on the Fort side of the river and had been beaten were obliged to recross the river in order to return home. As they embarked in their canoes they began to utter warwhoops and yells of victory, as the Indians do when they have won a game. The officers in command, ever on the alert, thought it was the Indians crossing to fall upon the Fort and massacre them; they ordered the gates to be closed quickly and the troops and traders to take up their positions on the ramparts for defense in case of attack. However, it was only a false alarm occasioned by the imprudence of the young Frenchmen who did not realize the situation.

Pontiac, who had no thought whatever of coming to the Fort, was for the moment occupied with the Hurons and the Potawatomies who had remained in the village. After the game he related to them all the details of the parley between the commanders and himself and his chiefs, telling them that according to the word of these gentlemen he was to return the following day to smoke the pipe of peace, or rather of treason, and that he hoped to succeed.

But he reckoned without his host.

May 9, Monday; The First day of Rogations.

Following the custom of the church the curate and all the clergy conducted the procession outside the Fort without incurring any harm. Likewise mass was celebrated, after which everybody in his own house wondered how the day would pass, knowing full well that Pontiac would make some other attempt.

The good people secretly lamented the evil fate which threatened the English, who did not have much of a force. Their garrison consisted of about one hundred and thirty troops, including the officers, eight in number, and some forty men, traders and their employees. In addition, they had two vessels of unequal size which were anchored in front of the Fort and defended the place from the side toward the river. They would have been too few if the Indians by any chance had been good soldiers.

Pontiac, who had concealed in his breast the murderous knife which was to cut short the life of these people, set out to go to the

Fort with fifty men of his nation in accordance with what he had arranged the night before with the Hurons. The others were to observe the same behavior as on the preceding Saturday.

About eleven o'clock he presented himself at the gates with his followers, but he was refused admission in pursuance of an order of the Commandant. He insisted upon entering, asking to speak to the Commandant, and saying that he and his chiefs had come only to smoke the pipe of peace in accordance with the promise which the Commandant had given them. He was told that he could easily enter, but only with twelve or fifteen of the leading men of his nation and no more. He replied that all his people wanted to smell the smoke of the peace-pipe, and that if they could not enter he would not enter either. He was promptly refused and was forced to return to his village in a bad humor. However, this disturbed these gentlemen very little. The Commandant had the French warned to keep in their houses.

Pontiac, enraged to see that his last stratagem had failed and all his projects were wrecked, caught up a tomahawk as soon as he entered his village and chanted the war-song, saying that inasmuch as he could not strike the English within the Fort he would attack those on the outside; he ordered all his people, men, women, and children, to cross the river to the side where the Fort was, in order to harass it the better, and pitch camp on the shore at Baptiste Meloche's, a mile and a quarter above the Fort. This was done promptly.

He divided his men into several bands to attack in different places; one band went half a mile back from the Fort, where an old English woman lived with her two sons who cultivated for themselves seven or eight acres of land and kept a good deal of cattle, such as oxen and cows. These poor people, suspecting nothing, were killed, scalped, their property plundered, and their house set on fire. It was a terrible spectacle to see how the fire took sides with the Indians; the dead bodies were burned up in the house. The Indians killed a part of the cattle and drove off the rest, some of which escaped into the woods and were later found by the French settlers along the coasts.

While this first band were engaged in their work of carnage, the other band went to Hog Island where there lived a man named Fisher, a former sergeant of the English army. This man with his family of five or six persons was working for half the profit a little farm which the English officers had appropriated for themselves. These good people, thinking of nothing but their work, became at a moment when they least expected it victims of the fury of the

Indians, who fell upon the man and scalped him; they wanted to carry his wife away prisoner because she was pretty, but she would not go, saying that since her husband was dead she wished to die with him. They killed her and her woman servant, and carried off the two little children to their village to be slaves.

A Frenchman by the name of Goslin who was working on the island squaring building timbers had not been informed of what was about to happen to Fisher. Upon hearing the cries of the Indians as they landed on the island, he thought to save himself from the danger which seemed to threaten him as much as the English: he was caught upon the beach by the Indians who put him in a canoe and told him to stay there, saying that he had nothing to fear for himself as they did not intend to do him any harm. He did not believe it nor want to stay where they had put him. His unbelief cost him dear, for, upon trying to escape into the depths of the island, the Indians took him for some fleeing Englishman; they ran after him and killed him, and when they were upon the point of scalping him they recognized that it was a Frenchman. They placed him in their canoe and gave him to the French who buried him in the cemetery.

About four o'clock in the afternoon an inhabitant of the East Coast, Mr. Desnoyers, who had gone to the pine woods sixty miles above the fort to fell building timber, returned with the Chippewas of Saginaw who escorted him. Through him one learned of the death of two officers, one of whom was Mr. Robertson, ship captain, the other a Sir Knight and colonel of militia. These two gentlemen, acting under orders of the Commandant, had gone with ten soldiers and a Pawnee servant to sound the channels to see if there was enough water for a vessel to pass in case of need. When they left the Fort they had heard nothing about the wicked designs of the Indians and they travelled peacefully along, thinking themselves quite safe. As they were passing to the right of the pine woods the Frenchmen who were working there and had been warned of the evil intentions of the Indians toward the English called to them to put them on their guard. They turned in but would not believe what the French told them, saying that when they left the Fort everything was quiet. The Frenchmen warned them again and again and advised them not to go farther, as the Indians would prevent them, and they would better return to the Fort, but they would not listen to the warnings and went on their way. They encountered some Indians encamped upon a point at the edge of the river, and these seeing them pass called to them and showed them some meat and other supplies to entice them. Still they would not halt there and this offended the Indians who pursued and killed them, with the exception of a young man fifteen or sixteen years old and the Pawnee, whom they took to make slaves of.

The two Ottawa bands who had made the attack in the two places I have described, acting under the orders of Pontiac, their chief, came back to camp after their exploit and related with gusto all the circumstances of their cruel expedition, among other things the death of Goslin whom they had killed by mistake,—a thing that saddened them for some time.

After hearing this story from his young men, Pontiac called all of his followers together before him in order to take new measures to approach the Fort and attack it without risk to them. This was not very difficult to do, seeing that there were several barns and stables sixty-five yards to the rear of the Fort; they belonged to several private individuals who lived in the Fort.

To the northeast, at the right of the gate, about a hundred feet away, was a big garden with the gardener's house,—the whole property belonging to Mr. La Butte, the interpreter. All these buildings were so many entrenchments in the shelter of which the Indians could approach the Fort without any danger; they had discovered this and had made use of the buildings for some time to annoy the Fort. After these new measures were taken the Indians rested, waiting for the next day in order to begin their attack in a new way.

While the Indians were making their arrangements to harass the Fort, the Commandant ordered the two gates at each end to be closed, not to be opened again till the end of this war, but the one which faced the southwest was opened twice more to permit the cows which belonged to the inhabitants of the Fort to enter, and then it was also closed. The only one left was the one facing the river which was opened from time to time for the public needs, because it was guarded by the sloops, which the Indians feared greatly.

Toward six o'clock in the evening Mr. La Butte went out several times by order of the Commandant to placate the Indians and try to pump their secrets out of them. But the Indians, and Pontiac in particular, grew tired of his visits and told him to go back to the Fort and stay there or they would all fall upon him. Seeing that nothing could be gained he went back to the Fort, letting the English hope that the Indians would be more easy to deal with the next day.

In the evening at general orders the Commandant announced that all the English in the Fort, traders and soldiers, should relieve one another at guard duty every six hours on the ramparts all night so as not to be surprised in case of attack at daybreak, which is the hour the Indians usually attack when they are carrying on war. The Commandant himself set the example and spent the night standing sentinel with his officers upon the battery.

10: The French in Detroit

Although Michigan was controlled by the British after 1760, the French continued to comprise by far the largest number of residents in the several settlements that had been established. In fact, the majority of Michigan's white population was French-speaking long after the Americans took over in 1796. The French element has been dealt with rather shabbily by many writers who, since the days of Henry Hamilton, British lieutenant governor at Detroit in the 1770s, have frequently depicted these people as fun-loving, lazy, and ignorant, and, in the case of later writers such as Francis Parkman, have contrasted them unfavorably with the Yankee pioneers of the nineteenth century. A somewhat more sympathetic view of the French was presented by Henry Utley as part of the pioneering multi-volume history of Michigan that he and Byron M. Cutcheon, in collaboration with Clarence M. Burton, wrote in 1906. Utley, who was a Detroit journalist for some twenty years before becoming head of the Detroit Public Library in 1885, a post he held until 1912, found much that was admirable in the French character, and felt that the French influence was still a powerful force in Detroit at the beginning of the twentieth century. However, the conservative French influence in business matters that Utley felt had been the strength of Detroit's economic development was rapidly being dissipated in 1906 by the wild speculative tendencies generated by the new automobile industry.

A Reflection on the French Character

HENRY M. UTLEY

Lieutenant-Governor Hamilton, . . . describes the French peasant settled at Detroit as a lazy, happy-go-lucky sort of fellow, contented to satisfy his stomach in a moderate way and let the world take care of itself. He had no ambitions beyond his modest sphere

From *Michigan as a Province, Territory and State, the Twenty-Sixth Member of the Federal Union,* Clarence M. Burton, advisory editor (New York: The Publishing Society of Michigan, 1906), I, 311-322. Footnotes in the original have been omitted.

in life. As a farmer he was indifferent. In spite of a luxuriant virgin soil, a superb climate and abundant crops his cattle starved in winter for lack of fodder. He drove a shaggy little pony, about two-thirds the size of an average horse, possessed of a number of vicious traits, exceedingly tough and hardy and able to pick up its living the year round. His pigs were of the "razor back" variety. They had enormous appetites, and though in season they found an abundant supply of acorns and beech nuts, they never, by any possible exaggeration, could be considered fat. He knew nothing of sheep raising—evidently had little use for wool and no predilection for mutton. His implements were as crude as his system of farming—a plow and a harrow, a spade and a hoe, a sickle and a flail, made up the list. The licensed blacksmith fashioned these according to his best instincts. They might have been more service-able if they had been better made, but they served. The dwellings were patterned after those of the peasantry of the home country. They were of wood, sometimes the exterior covered with clap-boards, one and one-half stories high, the long stretch of roof sloping toward the street, pierced with dormer windows. The little garden in front of the house was protected by pickets and was given over to onions, lettuce, artichokes, cucumbers and other garden stuff. The kitchen was at the back of the house and here and under the side windows flourished bachelor buttons, pinks, hollyhocks and other more or less gaudy flowers. Everything which drew its sustenance from the earth grew vigorously. The day of the destruc-tive bug and worm had not yet arrived. The grasshopper was on hand, but the mosquito was about the only really pestiferous insect, and it distributed malaria with the greatest impartiality. The or-chards were behind the houses. They furnished a great variety of delicious fruits. Apples, pears, plums, quinces, grapes were among the best grown anywhere. Young trees or cuttings must have been brought over from France, for here are found varieties not known elsewhere in the country. Some of the apples still maintain them-selves as favorites, in spite of all competition. Of course, none of the original apple trees remain, but the varieties have been perpetu-ated. Quite a number of the pear trees, however, are still bearing fruit after a century and a half. The expansion of the city has destroyed the trees, with very few exceptions, on the American side of the river. But on the other side, especially in the vicinity of Sandwich, many of the pear trees still flourish. They have grown to enormous size and the annual crops which they shower down upon the heads of the present generation are proportionate to their size. The fruit is not large, but in flavor and quality it is not surpassed by any known variety.

The French settled at Detroit were, for the most part, of a different class from those found at Quebec and Montreal. These latter were of the educated noblesse. Some were doubtless worthless and dissolute scions of noble houses who sought in the new world to retrieve their fallen fortunes or to start amid more favorable surroundings a new course of life. Some were of refined tastes and aristocratic manners. They brought with them the French language, which they spoke in all its purity. This purity was preserved in the face of adverse circumstances until in our own day it has been said that the French one hears in Quebec is more Parisian than that heard in Paris itself. The settlers upon the St. Lawrence were well up in the social scale. The old feudal scheme of society was perpetuated in a small way. The lord of the manor established his castle in the midst of his estate and his retainers grouped their houses thereabout under his patronage. Cadillac came to Detroit with some such notions, but they did not survive his departure. With few exceptions, the settlers at Detroit were peasants. They came mainly from Normandy and Picardy. They were uneducated. Some of them could write their own names, in a way, as we have evidence in existing documents, but beyond that they attempted nothing with the pen. They were devoted to the services of the church. Their moral characters were above reproach. They married early and reared numerous children. There were no opportunities for instruction, except such as the priests afforded. Later regular schools were established which were under the care of philanthropic ladies, but the instruction was naturally of a quite primary character. Even this was not practicable in the early period. The residents found their time fully occupied in protecting their lives in the presence of the savages and in raising food for their own sustenance. Besides, there did not appear to be much necessity for education. They had nothing to read and as for writing, it was a luxury they could not afford.

The French people were quite moral and correct in their habits. The wild and reckless *coureurs de bois* had a fondness for ardent spirits in common with their Indian friends. They were also dissolute and addicted to a plurality of wives. But the peasants who lived quietly on their farms could not be charged with any such disregard of the moral code. They drank, upon occasion, as was the universal custom of the time, but rarely did one become besotted. The long summer evenings were spent in the open air. Canoeing upon the river was naturally a favorite pastime. Gallantry toward ladies has always been a French characteristic, as have social festivities generally. So, young men and maidens were likely to be found in each other's company either upon the river or upon the lawns. Barbecues were a form of recreation in which the elders indulged themselves. The open-air roast furnished a hearty feast, washed down with generous potations of homemade wine or cider. Even in modern times, the old-fashioned barbecue has been a notable feature of social festivities and not infrequently has it helped to draw out a crowd to listen to the orations on political occasions.

In winter when the little settlement was completely shut in from the outside world and compelled to rely solely upon itself, life was by no means stagnant. There was nothing to do but to seek pleasure. Balls and parties made up the whole round. It is said that every house held a fiddle and some one who could manipulate it. The word had only to be passed as to the rallying point and there the crowd was sure to be found and dancing was kept up from dark to dawn. Up near the mouth of Connor's creek was a large marsh called the Grand Marais. This froze solid late in the fall and generally so continued through the winter. Here the young men built a rude cabin of ample proportions, long and narrow, with huge chimney and fire-place at each end, and fitted out with tables and benches. This was known as the Hotel du Grand Marais. Here on winter evenings the young folks gathered, driving thither in their carioles on the smooth ice along the margin of the river. Arriving, the well filled boxes and baskets were unloaded upon the tables and all sat down to a toothsome feast. This disposed of, the tables were cleared, shoved back against the wall, and dancing was the order until morning. The crisp winter air was a tonic for the appetite as well as an incentive to the vigorous exercise which followed. The military officers of the fort, who found time hanging rather heavily upon their hands, with only the dull routine of garrison duty to attend to, constituted an important element of the social life. They found plenty of pretty, attractive young women for partners at the balls. An officer in uniform somehow appeals to the feminine heart, and so the admiration was doubtless mutual.

Pony racing on the ice was always a seasonable diversion for the men. Every Johnny Couteau had a pony of uncertain speed. He might challenge the whole town, or the whole town might challenge him, and then there were doings. Sometimes these races took place on the smooth ice along the margin of the river, but more frequently upon the Rouge, which being of sluggish current furnished ice which made an ideal track for that kind of sport, especially so on account of the curving of the channel which afforded spectators an unobstructed view. Every Sunday after mass the crowd gathered at the appointed place and the fun was on. The challenged and the challenger brought out their ponies and scored for a start, while the crowd sized up the animals and the betting was furious. There was no starter, no jockey, no book-maker, no drawing for the pole. Each driver handled the reins over his own animal. He maneuvered for position and took his chances with his adversary. And when at last the ponies were off for the mile stretch down the river, the excitement among the multitude on the bank was something tremendous. If ever violence was done to the French language, it was upon such occasions, when individual opinions were struggling for utterance from hundreds of throats. Large sums of money changed hands, considering the financial resources of the town. The descendents of these same Frenchmen up to recent years, at least, still raced their ponies on the frozen surface of the Rouge. The sport drew a bigger and rougher crowd than in the early day. The rough element which imbibes freely and proves itself a noisome nuisance was made up wholly of Americans. Johnny Couteau is naturally of a somewhat excitable nature, but he still behaves himself and relishes the sport for the excitement and uncertainty there is in it. His language now is a mixture of French and English, which adds flavor to the other ludicrous features of the affair.

The characteristic French fondness for dress is noted by several writers of the time. The farmers must have been prosperous to be able to dress their wives and daughters in silks and satins. They undoubtedly raised large crops of wheat and Indian corn, which sold to the garrison and English residents at good prices. The money they thus received they spent freely with the merchants. It is said the stores contained finery of all sorts and descriptions which sold for little more than the same articles were quoted at in New York. So the people indulged in the pomps and vanities of dress and showed their fondness for amusements to quite as great extent as did those in France or elsewhere, who might be presumed more able to do so.

Isaac Weld, an Irish gentleman of some literary prominence, visited Detroit in 1795. He describes the place and the people at some length. He says, speaking of the town, that it "consists of several streets which run parallel with the river which are intersected by others at right angles. They are all very narrow and not being paved, dirty in the extreme whenever it happens to rain. For the accommodation of passengers, however, there are footways in most of them formed of square logs laid transversely close to each other. About two-thirds of the inhabitants of Detroit are of French extraction and the greater part of the inhabitants both above and below the town are of the same description. The former are mostly engaged in trade, and they all appear to be much on an equality. The stores and shops in the town are well furnished and you may buy fine cloth, linen, etc. and every article of wearing apparel as good in their kind, and nearly on as reasonable terms as you can purchase them in New York or Philadelphia. The country round Detroit is uncommonly flat, and in none of the rivers is there fall sufficient to turn even a grist mill. The current of Detroit river itself is stronger than that of any others, and a floating mill was once invented by a Frenchman which was chained in the middle of the river where it was thought the stream would be sufficiently swift to turn the water wheel. The building of it was attended with considerable expense to the inhabitants, but after it was finished it by no means answered their expectations. They grind their corn at present by windmills, which I do not remember to have seen in any other part of America." His observations respecting water mills were at fault. There were several streams which afforded current sufficient to turn a water wheel. One of these was the Savoyord which flowed through what is now the heart of the city. Knaggs' creek, a little further to the westward, was another. There were two water mills on Bloody Run and others on Connor's creek and elsewhere. The windmills he speaks of were quite a conspicuous feature of the landscape in their day. They were inexpensively built, wooden affairs with canvas sails to catch the wind, these sails being thrown into position by means of a long timber sweep operated by hand.

What he says about the impassable condition of the unpaved streets will be recognized as truthful by every one who has seen such streets in the modern metropolis of Michigan. After heavy rain and at certain seasons they are literally a sea of mud of uncertain depth. The considerable mixture of clay in the soil prevents the water from sinking into the ground and the contour is not such as to accomplish natural drainage. The vehicle almost exclusively in use by the French was a two-wheeled cart. The pony which drew the cart was not very strong and it was not an uncommon spectacle at certain times to see the whole turnout stuck solidly fast in the mud, only to be pried out with a stout fence rail. The two-wheeled cart was used for all sorts of purposes. In it the farmer hauled his produce to market. In it, seated upon the boards of the bottom, rendered more comfortable by plenty of hay and buffalo robes, the family of the farmer from Grosse Pointe or Ecorces was driven to church on Sunday morning and to mass on saints' days. The cargo of the cart was discharged from the rear. If it was produce, the staple which held down the front of the box was unbolted and the contents were dumped. If the cargo was human, the cart was backed up to the church steps or to the horse block and the people stepped out as gracefully as circumstances would permit. Cases have been known when the mischievous small boy loosened the staple in such way that chattering girls were unexpectedly dumped in the middle of the road. The public vehicle, and possibly the family coach of the nabob, was the calache. This is a two-wheeled affair with low wheels, the body mounted on leather strap springs, and furnished with a folding top, or hood. The average habitant could not, of course, afford so expensive a vehicle. The date of the arrival in Detroit of the first one is not known, but it seems certain that they were never quite common. The tradition which has come down from a former generation is that ladies dressed in the height of fashion and in the richest silks have been seen riding in the streets seated upon the floor of the ordinary springless cart. One can imagine that it was not an easy vehicle to climb into or alight from, and that the occupant jolting over the rough roads experienced anything but the poetry of motion.

The old habitants were generously hospitable. As seems to be almost universally the case, pioneers are gratified at the opportunity for entertaining strangers. Their very isolation arouses a feeling of sympathy and they cordially welcome visitors. It was a common saying of the early settlers that the latch string of the rude cabin in the clearing was always hanging outside the door, so that whoever desired might lift the latch and enter. He was sure to find a cordial welcome. This feeling of humanity and sympathy is not characteristic of one nationality more than another; it pertains to all. The French pioneer was pleased to receive a friend, though he had never seen him before and might never see him again, and to furnish him with food and lodging, without expecting or accepting any compensation.

The old habitant was rather close in money matters. This was perhaps the result of early training, for it had always been necessary for him to practice the most rigid economy. He was conservative to the last degree. As the town expanded and his acres were in demand for building lots he would not sell; neither would he make improvements. He would lease and let his tenant make improvements. This policy has resulted in making some of his descendants rich. He did not take kindly to new fangled notions. He preferred to plod along in the old-fashioned way. It has been remarked that this old French spirit has characterized Detroit down to the opening of the present century. The city has never entertained anything in the nature of a boom. It has been considered rather slow and unenterprising. Nevertheless, it has flourished in a business sense and its growth and expansions have kept pace with that of other and better advertised cities. Its conservatism has on more than one occasion proved a strong staff of support, especially in the face of financial panics and monetary revolutions. Speculation has never run rampant. Business of all kinds has been done on a modest basis, and although it may have been considered a slow town, it was an eminently safe and reliable one. So, even in modern times, when the descendants of the old habitants form but a mere handful of its population, the spirit of the former generation seems to pervade the city. In the long run, perhaps, it is better that this is so.

11: A Party at Michilimackinac in 1769

Preponderant as the French were in the total population at Detroit and Michilimackinac during the British period, it was nevertheless a rare occasion when a Frenchman associated on an equal basis with the much smaller number of British soldiers and fur traders who were the social elite of these communities. Although this latter class of citizens enjoyed far more comforts than one would imagine in such remote posts, the style of life was sometimes rather rugged, as one would expect in such frontier wilderness surroundings, and as is evidenced in the following excerpt from a journal kept by Daniel Morison, surgeon's mate at Michilimackinac, between 1769 and 1772. A genteel party, gotten up by Dr. Morison and the prominent trader, Isaac Todd, among others, turned into a nightmare with the arrival of some rowdy party-crashers, headed by Ensign Robert Johnstone (or Johnson, as the name sometimes appears in other sources). In spite of the unintentionally hilarious nature of Morison's account of what happened, his journal does underline the degree to which the British officers were a law unto themselves at this time in Michigan. Civilian authority was nonexistent, leaving the officers free to make life miserable for anyone they did not like with little fear of having their authority challenged.

Morison's manuscript journal was discovered in London, England, in 1914, by Clarence M. Burton, who purchased it for fifty-five dollars and added it to his Burton Historical Collection, now a division of the Detroit Public Library. The complete text of the journal was not published until 1960, when it appeared as one of the series of publications put out by the Mackinac Island State Park Commission, the state agency that has, since the late 1950s, reconstructed much of the old fort at Michilimackinac (present-day Mackinaw City).

One Aspect of Social Life at Michilimackinac

DANIEL MORISON

Narrative of an Action of Burglary and felony perpetrated on the Dwelling House & person of Daniel Morison, Surgeon's mate of the

From *The Doctor's Secret Journal*, edited by George S. May (Mackinac Island: Fort Mackinac Division Press, 1960), pp. 12-18. Reprinted by permission of Mackinac Island State Park Commission.

2d. Battn. 60th Regt. at Michilamackinac the Seventh day of November (about 5 Oclock in the morning) in the Year one thousand seven hundred & sixty nine, Vizt:

That the evening before being the sixth of November, Isaac Todd, merchant, William Maxwell, commissary of provisions & I proposed to give an Entertainment at Sergt. [Thomas] MacMurrays to which we Severally invited such people as we thought (in such a remote corner) qualified to make the evening pass agreeably. Accordingly we met, and everything was carried on with the greatest Decency & innocent Mirth till John Chinn & Forrest Oaks, traders, joined us.

After drinking a glass round, John Chinn (who appeared to be the worse of liquor) before & at supper began to be troublesome, opened upon me with Volleys of ragged raillery (without the least provocation on my side) and that blended with Opprobrious Expressions, namely, that I was an officer in the Rebellion &c. in the Year 1745 [the abortive Scottish attempt to place Bonnie Prince Charlie on the British throne], which tho' I knew was an arrant untruth, did not think it prudent to make the proper answer his wrongious Assertions deserved, [but] waved it off in the smoothest manner, lest the Company should be disturbed. Notwithstanding, our merriment was in a great measure unhinged, as the said John Chinn's only pleasure consisted chiefly in being officious, by hobb or nobbing with everyone [who] would chuse to drink with him, & indeed importunely pouring perpetually in upon those who did not chuse to drink more than would do them good.

About an hour of eleven o'clock, Ens. Robert Johnstone (who for ought I know invited himself) came in, accompanied by Ens. John Strickland & Mr. [George] Main. We continued thus till about one O'clock in the morning, when Numbers of our Company thought proper to retire. I proposed retiring also, but Isaac Todd insisted upon my spending one hour or two more with them. Rather than disoblige I consented.

About half one hour after, Ens. Johnstone asked the Company how their punch pleased them. They answered, well enough. Then he, the said Ens. Johnstone, blabbed out publickly, Vauntingly & wantonly, he had mingled four ounces of Jallap [a purgative] with the water that was a boiling for proportioning the Punch & Sangary [wine spiced and diluted with water]. This giddy Declaration, instead of meeting with approbation, occasioned the interjection of one universal sneer. I said nothing tho' I perfectly knew such irregular proceedings could not be intended for good. Therefore I silently winked over it, as others did; at the same time took particular notice that Ens. Johnstone drank nothing but wine all the night over.

John Chinn and Forrest Oaks, who left the Company about one o'clock, seemingly fuddled, returned to the charge one hour & one half thereafter. The abovesaid John Chinn appeared to be as unruly as ever. In short, conversation became very insipid. Drinking was the principal amusement, varnished over with various inconsistencys. At length time dragged on very heavily. Consequently [I] excused myself to be away, pleading the part I had to act in regard to my department. Upon which John Chinn swore by a bloody Oath he would come with a Hatchet and pull down my house, if I did not stay a little longer. To palliate this foolish menace, I thought it prudent to humour, [rather] than exasperate [him] on that Occasion.

[I] continued in [his] company till about four o'clock, then sheered off quietly not imagineing he would persist in his folly. [I] went to bed without dread or fear, as I gave no other plausible offense except what my absence suggested to them. But the Sequel will evidently discover the Maliciousness of their perverse intentions, for about five o'clock in the morning the seventh of November abovesaid, the door of my house was forcibly broke open, one plank of the Doorleaf, bars, bolt &c. pulled down to the floor. Upon entering my Room they also broke down my stove which was strongly made of bricks, clay & lime. This unwarrantable deed was principally perpetrated by Ens. Robert Johnstone of the 2d Battn. & Oaks the trader.

So fast was I asleep [that I] knew nothing of these violent proceedings until Oaks Surprized me out of a profound sleep, tumbling in roughly in my bed [and] bawling loudly, "Doctor, Doctor, damn your blood, get up & give us a bowl of Toddy, other wise You'll repent it."

I wakened as out of a dream. He, the said Oaks' next question was if I had my durk by my bed-side. I answered, "Never in time of peace." Upon this I called to my servant John Forbes to light a candle, which was no sooner done, & set upon the table at my bed side after my servant retired to the kitchen, then the said Ens. Johnstone kicked down & overturned the table, candle, candlestick, &c. topsy turvy in great wrath.

"Is this You, Ens. Johnstone," says I, "who behaves so rudely."

"You ly," he says, "I am a gentleman."

I made answer that his rude behavior betrayed the contrary in the eyes of good men.

Then he swore bloodily in the height of Rage, he would shew me that he was a gentleman & immediately fell upon, attacked & pelted me violently in my naked bed, he & his abbettor Oaks. The room being dark all my attempts of defence were rendered ineffectual by Oaks's exerting his outmost strength to entangle me in my sheets & bed-Cloathes out of which I struggled to extricate myself like à fish entangled in a net. They pelted me pell-mell with incessant blows repeatedly, on the face, left breast, &c., to the Effusion of my blood. Before I could recover myself out of the jeopardy into which I was involved, my shirt, sheets & pillowcase [were] all bespattered with gore & blood in my naked bed until Sergt. McMurray & Arthur Ross, soldier, with the assistance of my servant, John Forbes, turned them out of the Room. Otherwise it is [hard] to know where the consequences would end. William Maxwell, the Commissary, & Christian Burgy, trader, came in who saw my face bruised all over, besmeared [with] Blood.

In the meantime Forrest Oaks had the impudence to come back again, & upon a rehearsal of my bad useage, very unmannerly gave me the ly twice or thrice, in my own house. To this Sergt. Mac-Murray, Mr. Maxwell & the abovesaid Christian Burgy was present, who can testify in this, as well as other Circumstances. I imagined he intended this insult as a provocation to stirr me up to do something rash, of which he might make a handle to invalidate my pretensions to Justice on account of his being accessory to the violent attack upon my person as abovesaid.

Whether there were more accomplices [who] acted in conjunction with Ens. Johnstone & Forrest Oaks at the breakeing of my house &c., I cannot positively determine (the room being dark) except what may be inferred from a chain of Circumstances. For John Chinn (whose mind it seems was so replete with the dregs of his former menaces abovesaid, as if he intended to make his menace good) he, the said John Chinn, was met by Isaac Todd on his way to my house, with a great Hatchet in his hand. Mr. Todd asked where he was going. The said John Chinn answered, to break down the Doctor's house. Upon which Mr. Todd, partly by persuasion, & partly by dint of strength, brought him home to his lodgeing.

Whether it was before this, or after, I cannot say, my servant John Forbes catched the said John Chinn at the porch before my broken door, with a large Hatchet, while the assailants abovesaid, to wit, Ens. Johnstone & Oaks, were perpetrating their malicious designs against me. He, the said John Forbes, asked the said John Chinn what was he going to do with that Hatchet. John Chinn replyed, to break down the Doctor's house. After a little altercation my servant persuaded him to deliver up the Hatchet.

No sooner the assailants abovesaid was expelled the house, as above mentioned, then the said John Chinn entered my house abruptly, as straight as a rush, & with an air of authority, impudently (tho' he saw my face &c. all over with blood besmeared) minding his belly more than my hard treatment asked if I should give him a bowl of Toddy, in presence of Mr. Maxwell & Mr. Burgy.

When these irregular proceedings perspired [sic!] the most considerable gentlemen in the Garrison came to see me, to wit, Capt. [Beamsley] Glazier [commandant, 1768-70], Lieut. Nordberg, Lieut. [John] Christie, Ens. Strickland, Mr. Todd, Mr. Main, Mr. [Charles?] Morison, Mr. Maxwell & Christian Burgy, who can all & one of them attest they plainly saw that the door of my house &c. were forcibly broke open as abovesaid, & that my face &c. was all over besmeared with blood & gore, & my shirt, sheets, pillowcase, were plentifully bespattered with blood also.

John Chinn, upon Recollecting what he had done, [realized he had] forgot his Hatchet, which he was very impatient to have in his possession once more, as it was then in custody of my servant John Forbes for about half one hour. The said John Chinn employed Christian Burgy, abovesaid, to bring it back to him. I did not chuse to give it, but upon the said Christian Burgy's earnest Expostulations I complied, & ordered my servant to deliver it. At the same time [I] told Christian Burgy it was to the same purpose, as he & my servant could testify with Isaac Todd, [to] the maliciousness of his [Chinn's] unwarrantable intentions as abovesaid.

Soon after Ens. Johnstone & his abbettor Forrest Oaks had been expelled my house, he, the said Ens. Johnstone, went to Ens. Strickland's. The abovesaid Isaac Todd happened to be there, who upon Johnston's appearing, observed blood upon his hands &c. [Isaac Todd] asked him, where he had been. The said Ensign Johnstone replyed Vauntingly, he was giveing some knocks to the Doctor.

About half one hour after seven the evening before, Ens. Johnstone with some other accomplices were discovered scaling up a ladder opposite to which there was a half door, up the loft, at the lower end of my house. My servant John Forbes & another soldier observing a noise, as if the half door was thrown down upon the loft, [started out] but before my servant & the other soldier could get out to make a real discovery, the attempters were scattered about different ways. What their intentions were in regard to this little Enterprise depends upon them to explain but the judicious may readily conclude it a prelude to their malicious perpetrations before daylight next morning.

Before, at, or about six weeks preceeding the 7th November abovesaid, there was a strong report prevailed in [the] Garrison (which I am now persuaded was not without foundation) that the said Ens. Johnstone, being in company with some gentlemen in the fort, had breathed out menaceing and malevolent expressions against me, threatening he would use me ill.

Ens. Johnstone's reason for this extravagant Declaration I am yet a stranger to, as it is conscious to myself I never did in word or deed give him any just grounds of provocation. Notwithstanding this surmise, I took no further notice of [it] than studying to evade his Company, excepting behaveing with common civility on general terms, as I knew his Character among the public to be of a turbulent & troublesome, meddling [and] loquacious Disposition.

Upon the whole, I believe, it will not be attended with much Difficulty to investigate sufficient evidences, who will attest to the Veracity of the above, when they are legally called upon to declare their Sentiments, Solemnly without the least partiality or mental reservation in presence of any competent Tribunal, by which it will evidently appear (to the Judicious) with other concurring Circumstances that the forcibly breaking up of my house &c., together with the violent assault upon my person as above specifyed, may be justly attributed to premeditated & malicious intentions. Authentick witnesses to prove the last assertion are Isaac Todd, Benjiman Roberts, late Lieut. in the 46th Regt., Benjiman Frobbisher, merchant, & William Maxwell, Commissary of Provisions in this Fort.

12: A Poet Looks at Michigan

Michigan's first poet is a title one could bestow upon Arent Schuyler de Peyster, who commanded the British garrison at Michilimackinac from 1774 to 1779, at which time he and his men were transferred to Detroit, where de Peyster was in command until 1784. From time to time Major de Peyster wrote verses that, like the prose of Dr. Morison, give us additional insights into the life of the British soldier in these years—riding on the ice of the River Rouge (or River Red, as de Peyster prefers to call it) in horse-drawn vehicles known as carioles to enjoy an outdoor feast of barbecued venison (*croupe en grillade*); gathering maple sugar with their Indian friends at Michilimackinac; drilling; and being shipped out for a new assignment, leaving behind their Indian mistresses and children, with all the weeping and wailing that has always accompanied such departures.

De Peyster eventually retired from military service and settled in Scotland, where he became a friend of Robert Burns. The last poem that Burns wrote, it is said, is one that he addressed to his friend when the latter sent around a messenger to inquire into the health of the poet, who had but a few days left before he died. The two men are buried in the same cemetery in Dumfries.

The selections from de Peyster's versifying efforts that follow are taken from an edition of his work that was published in New York in 1888, an edition that included some additional material written by a descendant, J. Watts de Peyster, a New Yorker whose historical interests led to a truly prodigious output of articles, pamphlets and books on a wide range of subjects.

Selected Michigan Poems

ARENT SCHUYLER DE PEYSTER

RED RIVER

A song descriptive of the diversion of carioling, or staying upon the Ice at the Post of Detroit, in North America.

Tune—The Banks of the Dee.

In winter, when rivers and lakes do cease flowing,
    The Limnades (Lake Nymphs) to warm shelter all fled;
When ships are unrigged, and their boats do cease rowing,
    'Tis then we drive up and down sweet River Red.

Freeze River Red, sweet serpentine river,
    Where swift carioling is dear to me ever;
While frost-bound, the *Dunmore,* the *Gage,* and *Endeavour,*
    Your ice bears me on to a *croupe en grillade.*

Our bodies wrapped up in a robe lined with sable,
    A mask o'er the face, and fur cap on the head,
We drive out to dinner—where there is no table,
    No chairs we can sit on, or stools in their stead.

Freeze River Red, sweet serpentine river,
    Where sweet carioling is dear to me ever;
To woods, where on bear skins, we sit down so clever,
    While served by the *Marquis* with *croupe en grillade.*

"Une Verre de Madeir," with his aspect so pleasing,
He serves to each lady (who takes it in turn)
And says, *Chere Madame, dis will keep you* from freezing,
    Was warm you within where the fire it would burn.

Freeze River Red, sweet serpentine river,
    For your carioling is dear to me ever;
Where served by the *Marquis* so polite and clever,
    With smiles, and Madeir, and a *croupe en grillade.*

The goblet goes round, while sweet echo's repeating
    The words which have passed through each fair lady's lips;
Wild deer (with projected long ears) leave off eating,
    And bears sit attentive, erect on their hips.

Freeze River Red, sweet serpentine river,
    Your fine wooded banks shall be dear to me ever,

From *Miscellanies, by an Officer, 1774-1813* . . . (New York: A. E. Chasmar & Company, 1888), pp. 35-40, 42-43. Footnotes in the original have been omitted.

Where echo repeats Madame's *Chançon* so clever,
    Distinctly you hear it say *croupe-en-grillade*.

The fort gun proclaims when 'tis time for returning,
    Our pacers all eager at home to be fed;
We leave all the fragments, and wood clove for burning,
    For those who may next drive up sweet River Red.

Freeze River Red, sweet serpentine river,
    On you, carioling, be dear to me ever,
Where wit and good humor were ne'er known to sever,
    While drinking a glass to a *croupe en grillade*.

THE DRILL SERGEANT
AT MITCHILIMACKINAC, 1775

To the Tune of—"The Happy Beggars."

Come, stand well to your order,
Make not the least false motion,
    Eyes to the right,
    Thumb, muzzle tight,
Lads, you have the true notion.
    Here and there,
    Everywhere,
That the *King's* boys may be found,
    Fight and die,
    Be the cry
Ere in battle to give ground.

Come briskly to the shoulder,
And mind when you make ready,
    No *quid* must slide
    From side to side,
To make your heads unsteady,
    Here and there,
    Everywhere,
That the King's boys may be found,
    Fight and die,
    Be the cry,
Ere in battle to give ground.

(The 3d, 4th, 5th, 6th and 7th stanzas were lost.)

We beat them at the Cedars,
With those we call our light men;

Who that same day,
Heard *Yankeys* say,
They never saw such tight men;
Here and there,
Everywhere,
That the King's boys may be found;
Fight and die,
Be the cry,
Ere in battle to give ground.

A SONG

Composed on board of the sloop Welcome, while she was getting under weigh to sail with the troops from Mitchilimackinack to Detroit, on the 20th of September, 1779;

Tune—"To all you ladies now at land."

Now to Mitchilimackinack,
  We soldiers bid adieu,
And leave each squa a child on back,
  Nay some are left with two.
When you return, my lads, take care
  Their boys don't take you by the hair,
With a war-whoop that shall rend the air,
  And use their scalping knives.

To see squas weeping on the strand,
  Indeed it is no joke;
Who does not wish a countermand,
  Must have a heart of oak.
There's buxom Moll, and Farlys three,
  And many other girls I see,
With a fal la la la la la la,
  Who thought themselves good wives.

With *Panies'* scalps hung at their ears,
  Young war-chiefs pay their court;
Aware that sighs and floods of tears,
  Must waft us from this port,
The Zephyrs and the Limnades too,
  Incline young chiefs to favor you,
With fal la la la la la la.

If I had time now I could name,
  Of belles, at least a score;

Some that from lake Superior came,
    And some bred on this shore.
But see!—the anchor is a-peak,
    And I've no time more rhyme to seek,
Sing fal lal la la la la
    Fal la la la la la la.

THE MAPLE SUGAR MAKERS

Tune—Jolly Beggars.

I'll sling my papoo's cradle, said Kitchenegoe's Meg,
With kettle, bowl, and ladle, and scoutawaba keg.
    A sug'ring I will go, will go, will go,
        A sug'ring I will go.

Nasib and Charlotte *Farlie,* of whom the lads are fond,
Shall drag their father early out to the twelve mile pond.
    A sug'ring I will go, &c.

Come, Nebenaquoidoquoi, and join the jovial crew,
Sheeshib and Matchinoqui shall tap a tree with you,
    A sug'ring I will go, &c.

Bright Kesis, deign to aid us, and make the sap to run,
Eninga, who arrayed us, at least should have a turn,
    A sug'ring I will go, &c.

In kettles we will boil it, on fires between the rocks,
And lest the snow should spoil it, there tramp it in mococks,
    A sug'ring I will go, &c.

Of all our occupations, sweet sug'ring is the best,
Then girls and their relations can give their lovers rest,
    A sug'ring I will go, &c.

But when the season's over, it will not be amiss,
That I should give my lover a sissobaquet [sugar or sweet] kiss,
    A sug'ring we will go, &c.

13: The Fort St. Joseph Affair of 1781

The outbreak of the American Revolution in 1775 would have a decisive effect upon Michigan's development, for in 1783 Michigan would be made part of the new United States of America, although the British would not turn the area over to the Americans until 1796. During the war Michigan was a British stronghold from which King George's forces sought to maintain control of the west. Numerous raiding parties were organized at Detroit and Michilimackinac to attack the Americans in Kentucky and elsewhere. No fighting occurred on Michigan soil, but in the winter of 1781 a curious military action took place at old Fort St. Joseph (modern-day Niles), which had not been occupied by British troops since Pontiac's war. This action involved not American or British soldiers but Spanish militia and their allies. What they were doing there has long been a subject of surprisingly great interest and dispute among many historians. The most thorough discussion of the incident is the one that follows, written by Lawrence Kinnaird, and published in 1932 in the *Mississippi Valley Historical Review*, the historical quarterly now known as the *Journal of American History*. The casual reader will probably be astonished to learn of the number of writers who have looked into this affair. Three different interpretations of what was behind the Spanish expedition had been advanced before Kinnaird in 1932 came up with still a fourth viewpoint. Some may wonder why so much time and effort has been expended in examining what would appear to have been an event of very slight significance. But aside from the actual subject matter with which he is concerned, Kinnaird's article is instructive because it illustrates the dangers of a narrow approach to the study of Michigan's history. Much of what has happened in Michigan cannot be really understood without taking into account the larger picture of which these events are only a part. The events at Fort St. Joseph have little meaning if some effort is not made to tie them in with related actions at St. Louis, Madrid, Paris, and other distant points. To accomplish this, the Michigan historian, as Kinnaird amply demonstrates, may find himself engaging in research in sources and at locations that at first glance would seem to have no possible connection with Michigan. Too often the local historian is too provincial in his approach to his subject.

The Spanish Expedition Against Fort St. Joseph in 1781, A New Interpretation

LAWRENCE KINNAIRD

In the days of the Revolutionary War a British post named St. Joseph was located upon the river of the same name within the district of Michilimackinac at the present site of Niles, Michigan. This post was captured and plundered, on February 12, 1781, by a band of white men and Indians. Many historians have written of the episode, but there has been marked disagreement among them. Accounts vary in respect both to the participants in the attack and the motives which prompted it, but in general they may be divided into three groups according to the following interpretations. First, the St. Joseph expedition was sent out from St. Louis as a diplomatic move on the part of the Spanish government to establish a claim to territory east of the Mississippi. Second, the affair was merely a frontier foray undertaken against the British by Frenchmen of Cahokia and St. Louis for motives of plunder and revenge. Third, the undertaking was a defensive measure on the part of the Spaniards to prevent a threatened British attack upon St. Louis. The purpose of this article is to examine critically former studies of the St. Joseph episode in an endeavor to arrive at a more complete and more authentic interpretation.

St. Joseph was an insignificant post which, in June, 1780, had only fifteen houses and a population of forty-eight French half-breeds. The attack upon the place might have been forgotten had it not, at the close of the Revolutionary War, become associated with the claims of Spain to territory east of the Mississippi River. The *Gaceta de Madrid*, on March 12, 1782, published an account of the capture of St. Joseph by a Spanish force sent from St. Louis and supported by a party of Indians. According to the *Gaceta*, Don Eugenio Pouré, the commander of the expedition, "took possession in the name of the King of that place and its dependencies, and of the river of the Illinois, in consequence whereof the standard of his Majesty was displayed there during the whole time." Captain Pouré took the English flag "and delivered it on his arrival at St. Louis to Don Francisco Cruzat, the commandant of that post."

The Spanish diplomats, during the negotiations preceding the peace at the end of the Revolutionary War, made use of the St.

From *Mississippi Valley Historical Review*, XIX (September, 1932), 173-191, by permission of the Organization of American Historians. Footnotes in the original have been omitted.

Joseph incident to support their claims to territory east of the Mississippi. At that time the American negotiators believed the expedition had been undertaken in accordance with directions from Madrid. They were justified in the belief because the Spanish government had made known to Congress, in 1780, through the French minister, Chevalier de la Luzerne, that it considered the territory lying west of the proclamation line of 1763 as a field for "making a permanent conquest for the Spanish crown." During the peace negotiations of 1782 Spain opposed the efforts of the United States to secure the Mississippi as her western boundary and was supported by France.

The American diplomats finally overcame this opposition by making a separate treaty with Great Britain; but Spain refused to acknowledge officially the western claims of the United States until the signing of Pinckney's treaty in 1795. Under the circumstances both Franklin and Jay naturally regarded the St. Joseph expedition as a deliberate attempt by the Spanish government to establish a title to lands east of the Mississippi in the region north of the Ohio. Franklin did not hesitate to say that he believed the affair was a part of Spain's policy to "shut us up within the Appalachian Mountains." Jay supported this opinion by calling attention to the care with which the Spanish commander of the expedition had taken possession of the territory for Spain.

In fact it was chiefly through Jay that the St. Joseph affair became known to historians in the United States, for he sent both a copy and a translation of the article in the *Gaceta de Madrid* to Secretary of Foreign Affairs Robert R. Livingston. The Spanish narrative in this manner came to be published in the *Secret Journals of Congress*, and in the *Correspondence of the American Revolution*, edited by Jared Sparks. The information contained in these works in turn formed the basis for the accounts of the St. Joseph expedition written by John B. Dillon in the *History of Indiana* (Indianapolis, 1843), James H. Perkins in the *Annals of the West* (Cincinnati, 1846), John Reynolds in the *Pioneer History of Illinois* (Belleville, 1852), Rufus Blanchard in the *Discovery and Conquests of the North-West* (Wheaton, 1879), and others. It was not strange, therefore, that most of the earlier historians who wrote upon various aspects of the Revolutionary War in the West should come to the conclusion that the St. Joseph expedition was prompted by Spain's territorial ambitions.

The diplomatic interpretation of the episode was presented in greatest detail by Edward G. Mason in an article entitled "March of the Spaniards across Illinois." This study, published in 1886 in the *Magazine of American History*, was devoted entirely to the expedition against Fort St. Joseph. Although Mason's chief source of information was the brief account of the affair printed in the *Gaceta de Madrid* of March 12, 1782, his narrative was interesting and colorful. He explained that, as the war in the West progressed, Spain became more and more unfriendly to the United States "until it was apparent that nothing less than the entire valley of the Mississippi would satisfy the ambition of the Spaniards. Their conquests of Baton Rouge and Natchez were made to serve as a basis for title to the whole eastern side of the Lower Mississippi, as far as the Ohio. They needed something more, in order that they might include in their demands what was afterward known as the North-west Territory." Mason was more emphatic than any other historian in his insistence that the St. Joseph expedition could be explained only as a result of diplomatic and political motives. "As an illustration of that crafty diplomacy which sought to control both the Old World and the New, it may repay study," he wrote. "How little did those light-hearted soldiers and their red allies know that they were but the pawns in the great game whereof the players were at Paris and Madrid!"

The diplomatic explanation of the St. Joseph affair was accepted by many historians after Mason. It has been restated with only minor variations by William F. Poole in a chapter of Winsor's *Narrative and Critical History of America* entitled "The West from the Treaty of Peace with France, 1763, to the Treaty of Peace with England, 1783," by Justin Winsor in his *Westward Movement*, by Claude H. Van Tyne in *The American Revolution*, by Reuben G. Thwaites in *France in America*, by Daniel McCoy in an article entitled "Old Fort St. Joseph," by Louis Houck in *History of Missouri*, and by others.

A gradual change in the interpretation of the St. Joseph episode was brought about by the publication of documentary material dealing with the subject. The first volume of the *Calendar of Virginia State Papers* made its appearance in 1875. Douglas Brymner began the publication of the calendar of the Haldimand collection in the 1884 *Report on Canadian Archives*. The Pioneer Society of the State of Michigan in 1886 published the first installment of the Haldimand Papers in volume IX of the *Collections*. Other material found its way into print, chiefly in the *Collections* of the Michigan Pioneer and Historical Society, the State Historical Society of Wisconsin, and the Illinois State Historical Library.

[Theodore] Roosevelt in *The Winning of the West* did not attribute much importance to the capture of Fort St. Joseph. He dismissed the incident with the statement that "in reality it was a mere plundering foray." He explained that after the departure of the enemy "the British at once retook possession of the place, and, indeed, were for some time ignorant whether the raiders had been Americans or Spaniards."

Arthur C. Boggess, writing in 1906, introduced certain new elements into the St. Joseph narrative by a careful study of documentary material already published upon the subject. "According to a Spanish account," he wrote, "the party consisted of sixty-five militia men and sixty Indians, while an American account declares it to have contained thirty Spaniards, twenty men from Cahokia, and two hundred Indians." Boggess indicated that there was a connection between the attack upon St. Joseph in 1781 and the ill-fated expeditions organized among the Illinois French in 1780 by Augustin Mottin de la Balme. Thus a new motive for the undertaking was suggested. "The purpose of the expedition," he stated, "was to retaliate upon the British for the attack on St. Louis and for the defeat of La Balme."

Clarence W. Alvord, late professor of history at the University of Illinois, borrowed the manuscript of Boggess' work, *The Settlement of Illinois, 1778-1830,* before it was published "to use in the preparation of his article on the County of Illinois." Alvord described the St. Joseph expedition briefly in his introduction to the *Cahokia Records* published in 1907, and in December of the same year he read a paper before the State Historical Society of Missouri entitled "The Conquest of St. Joseph, Michigan, by the Spaniards in 1781" in which he elaborated upon the ideas contained in the Boggess study. Although Alvord used in his paper most of the references cited by Boggess upon the subject, he made no mention of the latter's work. His discussion of the St. Joseph expedition, however, was more detailed than that of Boggess and was critical in character. Alvord directed his criticism chiefly against Mason and the historians who had accepted his version. He asserted that Mason had told "the story of this 'March of the Spaniards across Illinois' in eighteen pages with no more information on the subject than is afforded by the brief description in the Madrid Gazette; but his description gives evidence of such detailed knowledge that it has carried conviction with it." Alvord thought that "the demands of diplomacy" were responsible for the article in the *Gaceta de Madrid* and gave it small consideration as a piece of historical evidence.

All accounts of the St. Joseph affair based upon the Spanish narrative emphasized the following points. The expedition was sent out by Cruzat, the Spanish commandant at St. Louis, and was composed of Spanish soldiers and Indians. The post St. Joseph was taken, prisoners were captured, and English goods were seized or destroyed. The commanding officer, a Spanish subject, actually took possession of the territory for the King of Spain. Lastly, the enterprise was all a part of a scheme to strengthen Spain's claim to territory east of the Mississippi. Alvord made the statement that there was "sufficient warrant to suspect the truth of almost every one of these points."

His account of the affair was in substance as follows: In the summer of 1780, there came to the Illinois country a French officer by the name of Augustin de la Balme, who proposed to raise, from among the French population, a force for the purpose of attacking Detroit and invading Canada. He succeeded in collecting a small number of men, and, with one detachment, he reached and occupied Miami about the last of October, 1780. Shortly afterward, the Indians attacked the party, killing De la Balme and thirty of his men. In the meantime his other detachment, composed of men from Cahokia, under the command of Jean Baptiste Hamelin, advanced against St. Joseph. This party succeeded in surprising the post while the Potawatomies, who lived near it, were absent on their hunt. The place was plundered and twenty-two prisoners were taken. The Cahokians then turned toward home, but were overtaken by the British and Indians, who killed four, wounded two, and took seven prisoners.

According to Alvord, the survivors of the expedition returned to Cahokia where they incited the French people to avenge the death of their fellow citizens. The hope of recapturing the lost plunder was an additional incentive for another expedition. Appeals were made to the people of St. Louis, who were also French. Cahokia raised a force of twenty men; St. Louis, thirty; and two hundred friendly Indians joined the expedition. The band set out just twenty-eight days after the first party had met its defeat. The services of Louis Chevalier, who was on very friendly terms with the Potawatomies, were secured, and he succeeded in inducing these Indians to remain neutral. This accomplished, St. Joseph was easily surprised and plundered. The British officers were unable to induce the Potawatomies to pursue the invaders as they had done before.

The foregoing account, Alvord asserted, was the true story of the capture of St. Joseph. This version of the affair was based largely upon a letter written to Colonel Slaughter by Captain McCarty, whom Alvord believed to have been living in Cahokia during the winter of 1780 and 1781. The letter by McCarty, dated January 27, 1781, had been one of the important pieces of evidence previously used by Boggess. Alvord also utilized a story which Governor John Reynolds had heard in Cahokia from one of the survivors of the first expedition against St. Joseph. Alvord stated that the "leader of the expedition was Jean Baptiste Mailhet of Peoria," rather than

Eugene Pouré. He believed that the Spaniards had little or nothing to do with the affair and asserted that "there is no evidence that the taking of St. Joseph was in accordance with the instructions from the home government or even from the governor of Louisiana."

Almost simultaneously with the appearance of Alvord's article a Spanish document was published by Reuben G. Thwaites, in his "British Régime in Wisconsin," which contained an expression of satisfaction by the King of Spain himself at the capture of St. Joseph and instructions that the officers in charge be rewarded. The following year Louis Houck, in the *Spanish Régime in Missouri*, published a brief statement of the affair written by Carondelet, governor of Louisiana. At about the same time Robert L. Schuyler, in the *Transition in Illinois from British to American Government*, attempted an interesting combination of certain elements of the accounts of Boggess and Alvord with those of the Spanish version. He explained that, after the defeat of De la Balme, "the Cahokians, eager for revenge, then raised a party of about twenty men. Francisco Cruzat, who had succeeded Leyba as commandant of St. Louis, was at the same time organizing an expedition to attack British posts east of the Mississippi. The two enterprises appear to have been united, and a mixed party of Spaniards, French creoles and Indians, under a Spaniard, Eugenio Pourée, marched to St. Joseph in January, 1781."

Frederick J. Teggart of the University of California wrote for the *Missouri Historical Review* in 1911, an article entitled "The Capture of St. Joseph, Michigan, by the Spaniards in 1781," in which he challenged the accuracy of Alvord's conclusions. Teggart proved by the use of Spanish manuscripts in the Pinart-Bancroft Collection of Louisiana Papers, Bancroft Library, that the account of the expedition as originally related in the *Gaceta de Madrid* was substantially correct. The most important of the documents used by Teggart were the letters of Malliet to Cruzat, January 9, 1781, and Cruzat to Miró, August 6, 1781, together with the "act of possession" drawn up at St. Joseph by the officers of the expedition on February 12 of the same year. The letter to Miró was especially important because it contained Cruzat's official report of the expedition. Using these Spanish manuscripts, Teggart gave an account of the St. Joseph affair which may be summarized as follows:

A detachment of sixty-five Spanish soldiers and sixty Indians set out from the town of St. Louis on January 2, 1781, to attack the British post of St. Joseph. This force was under the command of Captain Eugene Pouré of the second militia company of St. Louis. Charles Tayon was ensign, and Louis Chevalier was chosen by Cruzat as interpreter. The Indians were led by the chiefs El Heturno and Naquiguen. The expedition set out by boat and ascended the Mississippi and Illinois rivers to a point where the latter was frozen over. A party of twelve Spanish militia men under the command of Jean Baptiste Malliet, who had been stationed on the Illinois River as an outpost against the British, joined Pouré's party en route. Leaving the boats and all unnecessary articles, the band made a twenty day march to St. Joseph, experiencing "all that can be imagined of cold, peril and hunger."

The Potawatomies were persuaded to remain neutral by a promise of half the booty to be taken at the post. At seven o'clock in the morning of February 12, 1781, Pouré led his detachment across the ice of the river, took the post of St. Joseph completely by surprise, and made prisoners all who were found in it. Referring to the manuscripts used by Teggart we learn that Pouré, with his detachment standing at arms, "planted the royal colors in the center of the place" and read a proclamation in which he said: "I annex and incorporate with the domains of his Very Catholic Majesty, the King of Spain, my master, from now on and forever, this post of St. Joseph and its dependencies, with the river of the same name, and that of Islinois, which flows into the Missicipy River." After occupying St. Joseph for one day Pouré led his men back to St. Louis where they arrived on March 6.

This is the version of the capture of Fort St. Joseph given by the Spanish manuscripts and followed by Teggart. There seems to be no good reason to doubt its accuracy. The recent investigations of Abraham P. Nasatir, who is probably the best authority upon the history of Spanish Illinois, have brought to light some new information upon the subject, but, in general, have substantiated Teggart's narrative. Although Nasatir has treated the St. Joseph affair merely as an incident in the study of the *Anglo-Spanish Frontier in the Illinois Country during the American Revolution,* he has written one of the best accounts of it.

The description of the St. Joseph expedition itself now seems to be fairly complete, but the origin of the plan and the motives for it have not been so well determined. Milo M. Quaife in his work, *Chicago and the Old Northwest,* commented upon this fact: "Three detailed studies of this expedition have been made. The conclusions of the first, by Edward G. Mason, were generally accepted by scholars as valid until Professor Clarence W. Alvord's study appeared. His conclusions differ materially from those reached by Mason. More recently Frederick J. Teggart has challenged Alvord's conclusions." Most of the earlier writers who followed the account given in the *Gaceta de Madrid* believed the purpose of the expedition was to establish a Spanish claim to territory east of the

Mississippi, although this object was not stated in the Spanish article itself. Developing ideas expressed upon the subject by Roosevelt and Boggess, Alvord succeeded in casting much doubt upon, if not entirely discrediting, the diplomatic interpretation. "It is quite evident," he asserted, "that the expedition was conceived by the Cahokians to revenge the defeat of their friends who had been sent out by De la Balme, and that a second motive was the hope of plundering the property which was known to be unprotected at St. Joseph."

Teggart asserted that Alvord's "explanation of the origin of the expedition must be noticed, not because of its having either merit or probability, but because the author speaks with the prestige of a professor in the University of Illinois." He then proceeded to discredit the evidence used by Alvord in much the same way that Alvord had discredited Mason's article. Teggart believed that Cruzat had devised the scheme to capture St. Joseph in an attempt to prevent an impending expedition of the British against St. Louis. This town had been attacked the year before by the English and Indians. The assault had failed, but it was reported that the British had sent supplies to St. Joseph with which they intended to outfit another expedition in the following year. "The expedition," concluded Teggart, "was the direct result of information Cruzat had received of preparations by the English for a second attack on St. Louis in the spring of 1781." To strengthen his point he called attention to the recapture of Vincennes by the Americans, and stated that "if anything is wanting to complete the evidence it is supplied by the fact that Cruzat had before him the example of George Rogers Clark who, in 1779, had undertaken a similar march for a similar purpose."

A number of questions may be asked which raise doubts as to whether the reason just stated would have been sufficient justification for sending any force upon such a hazardous venture. In the first place, were there sufficient supplies at the little post of St. Joseph to recruit the neighboring Indians and to outfit a second expedition against St. Louis? The stores at the post in all probability had already been damaged considerably, since the Cahokians had captured the place scarcely a month before. If there were sufficient supplies at St. Joseph to equip an expedition against Spanish Illinois, would it be probable that the British would have left them unprotected after having already suffered one raid?

Furthermore, would the destruction of a small post like St. Joseph have given sufficient assurance of the prevention of an attack upon St. Louis to warrant Cruzat in sending a much needed force upon a two months' journey through hostile country in the middle of winter? In regard to this point, Alvord correctly asserted that "the description of the village is sufficient to show that British resources were in no ways impaired, nor could this slight success prevent the British making other military operations in the region." Alvord also made the statement that as late as December 22, only eleven days before the start of the St. Joseph expedition, "Cruzat at St. Louis knew nothing about it." This assertion was given upon the evidently reliable authority of a letter from Bernardo de Gálvez to Cruzat, dated February 15, 1781. If Cruzat planned the expedition as a measure primarily to prevent an attack upon St. Louis the following spring, is it not likely that he would have had it under consideration for more than eleven days, and that he would, at this time, have given Governor Gálvez some definite information about it?

Finally, was there sufficient danger of a British attack upon Spanish Illinois in the spring of 1781 to justify Cruzat's sending any men away upon an apparently reckless venture rather than keeping them at St. Louis and employing them in preparations for defense? Cruzat wrote to Governor Gálvez on November 14, 1780, only seven weeks before Pouré and his men set out from St. Louis: "I have learned that a great number of Indians of different nations, and even of the same nations who came to attack us last spring, are now getting ready to come next spring with the idea of soliciting our clemency and alliance." Apparently other motives than those already stated were involved in the Spanish expedition against St. Joseph. But to determine them obviously would be a difficult task, for, in all probability, Cruzat himself was the only man able to give all the reasons for the undertaking. The only possibility of a solution of the problem seemed to be through the discovery of new evidence.

A careful check of all the documentary material used by previous writers was first made in order to determine whether any fact had been overlooked or misinterpreted. This investigation led to the conclusion that the work had been very well done. The search, however, did result in the finding of one clue. Cruzat began his letter of August 6 to Miró with the following sentence: "On January 2nd of the present year, as I have written to the governor on the 10th of the same month and year, Don Eugenio Pourre, the captain of the second militia company . . . left this city of San Luis with a detachment of sixty-five militia men and about sixty Indians." The foregoing statement indicated that there had been a letter written by Cruzat to the governor of Louisiana on January 10, 1781.

An examination of other accounts of the St. Joseph affair revealed the fact that the letter of January 10, 1781, had not been used. Written while the expedition was in progress, it would be almost certain to contain valuable information. Was this letter still in existence and if so, where was it likely to be found? The first supposition would be that the manuscript, if still preserved, would be among the Papeles de Cuba in the Archivo General de Indias, Seville, Spain; but this was only one of many possibilities. The letter might be in one of the other Spanish archives or in another section of the Archivo General de Indias. It might even be in the Archivo Nacional at Havana, Cuba, for certain of the Louisiana manuscripts apparently were overlooked at the time the Spanish government removed 2336 *legajos* of papers from Cuba to the Archivo General de Indias in 1888 and 1889. The search for the document constituted a problem in heuristic that is of no importance here. It is sufficient to say that it was eventually found in the collection of Louisiana Papers now deposited in the Bancroft Library at the University of California. This group of manuscripts was originally a part of the Papeles de Cuba and is of great importance for the study of the history of the Spanish régime in the Mississippi Valley.

The letter justified the search for it. Writing just eight days after Pouré's force had left St. Louis, Cruzat not only explained the origin of the expedition to Governor Gálvez, but carefully stated the reasons why he had been compelled to send it and listed them in the order of importance. The letter is as follows;

> MY DEAR SIR: On the 26th of last month the chief, El Heturnò, arrived, bringing me news of the destruction (by a party of Canadians of the Strait [Detroit] under the leadership of a certain Dequente [De Quindre]) of a detachment of seventeen Frenchmen who had set out nearly three months ago from the pueblo of Kaò for the purpose of going to take possession of the Fort of San Joseph, situated in the English dependency fifty-five leagues from the bank of the river. In it there are four persons commissioned by the English, with seventeen men and a considerable quantity of all sorts of merchandise, which they use only to purchase maize and different kinds of provisions from the neighboring Indians, in order to collect in the fort a store of supplies for the expeditions which they are planning against us. In addition to this, they excite and urge the above-mentioned Indian nations to commit in their hostilities their customary cruelties, of which we have had bitter experiences.
>
> The urging of the Indian Heturnò, both on his own account and in behalf of Naquiguen, both chiefs being already known to your Lordship, that I should make an expedition against the English of the Fort of San Joseph, together with the reasons which I shall state to your Lordship, and which I believe to be well founded, compelled me to arrange for

the departure from this town, as quickly as possible, on the first of this current month, a detachment of sixty volunteers under the orders of the Captain of Militia Don Eugenio Purè, a person skilled in war and accustomed to waging it in these countries. He, together with the two chiefs mentioned, El Heturnò and Naquiguen, and several others from the bank of the Ylinueses who take their nations with them, form a force sufficient to send to San Joseph endeavoring to destroy everything that the enemy has in it. For if these stores remained in the hands of the English, they would be of assistance in furthering their hostile plans. I believe that the measures I have taken will be effective in realizing our hopes. Indeed, it has been indispensable for me to take this step, as I am going to tell your Lordship.

FIRST. For me not to have consented to the petition of El Heturnò and Naquiguen would have been to demonstrate to them our weakness and to make evident to them our inadequate forces; and perhaps, if they had learned of these facts, it might be sufficient reason for them to change sides, notwithstanding the evident signs of friendship which they have given us. For the Indians are in the habit of following the strongest one, and the English would not have failed to take advantage of this event, nor would we have escaped experiencing the fatal results of the unfriendliness and inconstancy of the two chiefs referred to.

SECOND. To go to San Joseph and seize the fort, the English commissioners, the merchandise, and the provisions would have the effect of terrorizing the surrounding nations. It would take from them the men who are inciting them to evil acts, and would deprive them of powder and merchandise given to them by the English for hunting and making war upon us. By this means would be accomplished both the destruction of the fort and the supply of provisions in it; and, even though the English might not be prevented entirely from carrying out their intentions, it would cut off their resources in part and lessen their hopes of having in that place a store of provisions with which to supply those who may attempt to come by that way to attack us this spring.

By permitting El Heturnò and Naquiguen to go to make war and giving them forces against our enemies we shall succeed in turning our allied nations against those who are opposed to us; and since both sides are bent on sacrificing themselves mutually, it will compel our Indian allies to be loyal during the war because they will have need of our help to defend themselves. The enemy will not then be able to attack us so easily on account of the opposition and resistance which they will meet from the Indians friendly to us.

With the savages it is always necessary, in order to preserve oneself from their destructive inclinations, to keep them occupied by bringing about disagreements among them, and causing them to war among themselves. This has always been experienced in these countries and every day it is proved more and more. These reasons, and many others which your Lordship may think of, compelled me to take the unavoidable step of sending the detachment referred to with the Indians who asked for and were enthusiastic for this expedition. I gave them everything necessary for the success I desire. I am sure that everything that I have done in connection with this affair will meet with your Lordship's approval.

God keep your Lordship many years. San Luis de Ylinueses, January 10, 1781.

I kiss your Lordship's hand. Your most faithful servant,

FRANCO. CRUZAT [rubric].

The foregoing document amplifies the historical work already done upon the St. Joseph affair. It shows the possibility of reconciling, in a measure, two heretofore conflicting opinions concerning the motives of the enterprise. The incentive of the Indian chiefs, who proposed the expedition, and of their followers, was the desire to plunder the store at St. Joseph. Probably any Cahokians who volunteered went with Pouré for the same reason. On the other hand, one of several motives which induced Cruzat to yield to the urging of the Indians was the hope that a destruction of the supplies at St. Joseph would render more difficult the outfitting of an expedition against St. Louis in the following spring, although this in itself was not sufficient to warrant the undertaking.

The most important points brought out in the letter of January 10, 1781, have not been discussed in former studies. Cruzat's explanation of the St. Joseph episode differs from the three previous interpretations as much as these differ from each other. The expedition was not planned by Spanish diplomats at Madrid, nor by irate Frenchmen at Cahokia; neither was Cruzat himself the originator of the project. The scheme was proposed to the lieutenant-governor by the Milwaukee chiefs, El Heturno and Naquiguen. Cruzat did not decide to send the expedition because he hoped to establish Spanish claims to territory east of the Mississippi, nor because he desired to avenge the defeat of De la Balme; neither did he dispatch it primarily to prevent an expected attack upon St. Louis in the spring of 1782 by the British.

The whole affair was a manifestation of Spain's Indian policy. The very existence of the settlements in Spanish Illinois depended upon maintaining friendly relations with neighboring Indian tribes. Indian alliances for frontier defense had already been used by the Spaniards in Texas and lower Louisiana against both the Apaches and the English. A similar system was later followed in the Old Southwest where Spain attempted to control the Indian nations by means of treaties, subsidies, and agents, and use them as a buffer against the expansion of the United States. Cruzat hoped that the attack upon Fort St. Joseph would bring about hostilities between the Milwaukees and the Indians who adhered to the British, thereby forcing the former in the future to remain loyal to Spain. Above all, the safety of the entire district demanded that the requests of the Indians be complied with lest they learn the weakness of the Spaniards and go over to the British. Cruzat, therefore, yielded to their urging because he dared not refuse.

Part III

1800-1865

Introduction

During the first half of the nineteenth century Michigan's history was unique, but it also reflected national issues and policies. Prior to its official acceptance into the Union in 1837, the territorial leaders were appointed in Washington and quite naturally both Whigs and Democrats selected officials demonstrating loyalty to their own parties. Yet, despite the spoils system, several worthy and able leaders did come to serve in Michigan, and some of these gained public office and trust after the region became a state with democratically elected officials.

Men like Lewis Cass and Stevens T. Mason were among those who helped bridge the gap from territory to state. Their efforts to encourage an influx of settlers and the internal development of the territory complemented the national urge to open and explore the entire North American continent. The acquisition of Indian lands and the discovery of natural resources were for Lewis Cass major concerns. He was notably successful in negotiating Indian treaties, and thus expanded those regions available to prospective residents.

In the welter of Michigan settlement, a single driving force is not readily discernible. Yet it is certain that Michigan's natural advantages required careful examination and honest publicity before large numbers of newcomers would be attracted into the territory. Official requirements for admission to the federal union demanded a resident populace of sixty thousand, and statehood was a necessary prerequisite to local control of cultural pursuits. Hence, Lewis Cass and others attempted to secure information concerning the opportunities that Michigan offered, and his Schoolcraft Expedition in 1820 was designed to provide evidence of Michigan's economic potential.

Statehood was not an end in itself, but served mainly to facilitate continued settlement and exploitation. Boom towns with banks, realtors, and eager investors began to spring up in Southern Michigan. Farmers occupied the rich soils, and immigrant groups from Germany and the Netherlands acquired sufficient territory to erect islands of ethnic culture. In 1840 the Douglas Houghton Survey provided additional substance to claims that opportunities of all sorts were available in Michigan. Thereafter Lake Superior carried copper, iron and fish to urban centers around the Great Lakes.

A western region, deeply influenced by settlers from New England and areas surrounding the Erie Canal, Michigan's institutional and social concerns reflected a northern perspective. Public education on all levels received popular support and governmental attention. Anti-slavery sentiment flourished, and Michigan's regiments were among the most enthusiastic combatants in President Lincoln's army.

Returning from Virginia to Michigan, a perceptive Civil War veteran would have been impressed by the variety of opportunities in his home state. Farms continued to flourish. Merchants could choose their port, while mining, lumbering and shipping offered additional employment. If he were inclined to none of those, there was a growing University in Ann Arbor able to train our veteran for medicine or the law.

1: Political Affairs

Father Gabriel Richard, an exile from France during the French Revolution, came to serve Detroit's numerous French-Catholic populace in 1798. Not content with the ordinary duties of the priesthood, Richard launched an ambitious educational program that included the preparation of day-school teachers as well as the training of nearby Indians. He hoped to prepare them for a more settled life in white society, and thus his Spring Hill school emphasized the acquisition of domestic skills for girls and mechanical trades for boys.

Demonstrating a wide variety of interest, Richard served as the first Vice President of the Catholepistemiad in 1817 (known since 1837 as the University of Michigan). He set up the first book printing press in Detroit and was a territorial delegate to the United States Congress in 1823.

Gabriel Richard: Frontier Ambassador (Detroit, 1958), by Frank B. Woodford and Albert Hyma, is the standard biography of the French priest, but Sister Dolorita Mast has also written an excellent biographical account entitled *Always the Priest: The Life of Gabriel Richard* (Baltimore, 1966).

The Educator

ALBERT HYMA and FRANK B. WOODFORD

One had only to scratch Gabriel Richard, priest, very lightly to find Gabriel Richard, schoolmaster.

His background, training, and expressed interest, all indicate that he regarded education and the development of schools as an integral part of his ministry. From the time he left the seminary, Richard considered himself destined for a career within the church as a scholar and educator, instead of as a priest primarily devoted to pastoral work or the missionary life. The vocation of seminary

From *Gabriel Richard: Frontier Ambassador,* pp. 80-90. Copyright © 1958 by Wayne State University Press. Reprinted by permission. Footnotes in the original have been omitted.

professor had strong appeal for him; his early plans envisioned a continuance of that role, even after he was forced to leave France and go to the United States. He never abandoned hope of finding that niche in life. No matter where he set his feet, no matter how raw the wilderness or crude his surroundings, he always saw, just ahead, a school or a seminary. The realization of one, or the other, or both, was part of the task to which he was dedicated. The history of education in the early stages of territorial development is virtually his personal history.

He was admirably equipped for the role of educator, possessing all the attributes of a scholar, plus a quick, eager and penetrating mind. One of his colleagues said that he spoke and wrote seven languages; in all probability at least one of them was an Indian tongue. The breadth of his interests is revealed, as much as any-where, in his library, a collection which at one time must have been fairly extensive. It is easy to believe that in his day it was without equal in Michigan. He apparently was not a particularly creative scholar; what he wrote himself consisted mainly of philosophical analysis and comment on the works of others. Yet, these were often acute and, as related to his time, occasionally profound. He careful-ly preserved much of this material, some of it dating back to his own seminary days. When Theophilus Mettez learned the book-binder's art, Richard kept him well occupied binding his treatises and commentaries, some printed, some in manuscript form. He wanted to save these against the day when they would be used again as the basis of discourses and lectures in his own seminary. The greater part of this material, naturally, was theological. Some of it was related to such fields as philosophy, rhetoric and physics. There were treatises on divine attributes, human behavior and canonical law.

. . . .

There were occasions when Richard's educational projects ap-peared grandiose and impracticable. There was, for example, his plan for a seminary in the Illinois country. Obviously, it could not be a success both from the standpoint of the small population from which students would be drawn and from the generally low level of educational background which existed on the frontier. At the time, Richard was new in the country; he may have been disappointed that he was not able to stay in Baltimore or Georgetown as a mathematics instructor. He was trained for the task; and when he reached the Illinois country, and later in Michigan, he did not want that training to be wasted. Accordingly, he may have felt the urge to utilize it without first weighing how effective it could be.

In Detroit, his opportunities were somewhat better. There existed among the general population a small element of sufficient wealth and culture to give education real meaning. Some of the people, principally the English and Americans, sent their children to eastern schools and academies. Others used facilities closer at hand. There had been itinerant schoolmasters and private schools in Detroit long before Richard's arrival; there would be others during most of his residence there. But such instruction was for the fortunate few, and at best, it was somewhat haphazard and uncertain. There was no general system of schools for the sons and daughters of the poor, or even for those in moderate circumstances. The French, exhibiting little interest in learning, probably would not have taken advantage of them in any case.

· ·

The fire of 1805 seems to have ignited in Richard a new determination to get his school plans under way. If conditions following that disaster were not exactly propitious for such an undertaking, the challenge was that much greater. Schools were opened shortly thereafter, both for boys and girls. Unfortunately, not much is known about them; the information which has come down is incomplete and often confusing. The first accomplishments are described by Paré who says there was most likely a boys' school in existence in 1806; four schools are mentioned for 1808, although there is no proof that all of them were sponsored by Richard. An account of 1808, which Paré accepts with some reservations, takes note of an academy for young men under the direction of Richard, with assistance of a M. Salliere, "a young professor of literature, chemistry, and astronomy, whom Father Richard had brought from France. . . ."

It was to obtain support for these efforts, the last mentioned in particular, that on October 3, 1806 Richard petitioned the Governor and Judges in the following terms:

"Gabriel Richard prays that for the purpose of erecting a College in which will be taught the languages ancient and modern, and several sciences and enabling him to render the education partly Gratuitous, the Corner lot on the military square of the section number 3 and the whole same section or a part thereof according to the will and benevolence of the Legislature be given." This request was supplemented by another submitted by two instructresses in a girls' school sponsored by the priest, in which the authorities were asked to donate still another lot "for the purpose of erecting a young ladies school."

· ·

Providing funds for educating Indians was part of a broad policy, very dear to the heart of President Jefferson. It would be, he hoped, the means whereby the tribes would be put through the civilizing process and transformed from nomadic hunters into sedentary farmers. This policy was based in part upon what Jefferson considered to be lofty humanitarian principles; in part it was a means of rationalizing the grab of Indian lands at a tiny fraction of their real worth. Whether acquisition of Indian lands was good or bad from the national standpoint, it was definitely not good for the Indians; and it contributed to the frightful incidents which marked the War of 1812 in the west. Richard, as a representative of a highly civilized European society, subscribed to Jefferson's plan and became an instrument by which it was implemented. His concern was not with obtaining vast tracts of hunting domain. On the contrary, as has been seen, he objected vigorously when he felt the Indians were being victimized by the government. His chief interest was in winning infidel souls. To his way of thinking, the most logical manner in which this could be accomplished was through the civilizing process. In his mind, the two things went hand in hand.

This was the germ of the idea behind his Spring Hill farm. This enterprise was to be both church and school, and the latter was to provide him opportunity to conduct some very interesting educational experiments. First, and most important, the Spring Hill community would enable him to educate Indian and white children together, a process which, he felt, would create understanding and break down the barriers between the two races.

He described this plan to the President when he first sought to obtain Spring Hill; it was his justification for asking that the property be given to him. After reading Richard's letter, written sometime early in 1808, Jefferson passed it on to his Secretary of War with the comment that "the writer appears to have that sincere enthusiasm for his undertaking which will ensure success. The education of the common people around Detroit is a most desirable object, and the proposition of extending their views to the teaching the Indian boys & girls to read & write, agriculture & mechanic trades to the former, spinning & weaving to the latter, may perhaps be acceded to by us advantageously. . . ."

Encouraged by Jefferson's favorable reaction, Richard petitioned Congress for an outright grant of Spring Hill during his visit to Washington early in 1809. He went further, and in the name of the Wyandots who, he claimed, had given him authority to represent them, he requested that a farm allotment be given to the head of each family of the tribe, and to each youth "who shall be placed and will have remained Eight years and been Educated in the above mentioned Seminary." These farms were to be cut out of a tract between the Huron and Ecorse rivers, then occupied by the Wyandots. The parts not subdivided, he suggested, might be kept as a reserve for the endowment of the school. Parts of the reserve "could be used and cultivated, as praemiums, by Such Indian children who shall have made more progress in the said Seminary." The management of the entire enterprise, he urged, should be under the local Catholic priest.

Undoubtedly, the subject matter of this petition had been discussed with the President before it was presented to Congress; in fact, the whole idea strongly suggests that the course Richard followed was laid out for him by the President. The petition was received and referred to the House committee on public lands, and there, due to other more pressing considerations, it languished.

With this appeal to Congress, Richard also undertook to submit, with the prior approval of the President, and at the request of Governor Hull, a comprehensive prospectus for a system of education especially adapted for use in Michigan Territory. The tone of much of this outline has a surprisingly modern sound.

He first proposed establishing several free primary schools at distances of from five to six miles from each other. He conceded the difficulty of staffing such schools because of the shortage of trained teachers. "In fact," he declared, "the worst trade in the territory of Michigan is to be a school-master." For this reason, government subsidy would be necessary because qualified instructors could not exist on the contributions which parents of the pupils would be able to make. This incapacity, he continued, was the result of a lack of industrial enterprise among Michigan's inhabitants. To remedy this, he recommended "that the theory and practice of Agriculture and of the most useful arts and Trades, as carpenter, black-smith, shoemaker, weaver &c. may become a part of the System of Education of the youth. . . . "

Richard then proceeded to lay out a curriculum for boys and girls which included reading, writing, "ortography," arithmetic, geography, "use of the Globes," grammar, history, natural philosophy, and composition, while advanced students would be taught languages and higher mathematics.

"The young ladies," he explained, "shall be instructed in the different branches of needlework, sewing, knitting, spinning, &c. the husbandry shall not be omitted, nor such of the fine arts as music drawing & which may contribute to the youth an innocent amusement."

Recreation would have an important place in Richard's program. "Children," he declared, "must be led to science and virtue by a flowery road. The hope of pleasure shall be the best allurement to study. It is a great & very useful art to surround the most important truths with a circle of agreable Ideas. The Thorns of the most severe virtue, are charming when they are conveniently twisted with the flowers of pleasure. The wise Nature leads man to the food of his body by attraction of pleasure. As the truth and knowledge are the food of our mind, a wise instructor must surround it with the honey of amusement and pleasure."

He then went on in his comprehensive prospectus, to discuss what should be done for the children of Indians who, he contemplated, would be admitted to his school on an equal footing with the whites. This, of course, was the crux of his civilizing process. Indian pupils would be exposed to the basic academic subjects, but the major emphasis would be on vocational studies, including "hoeing, gardening, plowhing &c."

"Let them," he suggested, "make their own bred, raise hemp & flax, let them make their own cloths, let them learn to build their own houses, let them take care of the sheep which will supply the wool to cloth them. Let the Girls spin that wool, and moove the shuttle, let them meelk the cows, raise large quantity of chicken &c. &c."

Those who proved to be proficient scholars should be rewarded with tools and household implements to be given them "at appointed times in the middle of many spectators under the shade of trees planted by themselves, at the sound of the greeting and martial music executed by their companions of the school &c. Such public exhibitions should certainly excite the ambition of the children and draw the attention of their parents.—Let it be a rule that at the end of their education, one cow, a pair of oxen or a horse, and a farm of so many acres of land more or less in proportion of the progress made by each, be given as rewards."

The net result, he concluded, would be that the Indians would realize "they are all Brothers, and believe to be one and same people and one family."

Unfortunately for Richard, Thomas Jefferson was no longer President after March 4, 1809. He was succeeded by James Madison who, at the moment, was more concerned with allaying the dangers of a British-Indian war and matters of foreign policy than he was with Indian education. A new Congress was in Washington and Richard's school prospectus ended up in some departmental pigeon-hole. His reliance upon Jefferson's promises of financial aid for Spring Hill brought him only disappointment. The government's failure to carry out this program weighed on Jefferson's conscience, and from his retirement at Monticello, he called Madison's attention to the assurance that had been given Richard.

Nevertheless, Spring Hill was not entirely neglected by the government. In a progress report to Madison, made just before he lost the property, Richard said he had five or six persons employed at the farm as instructors and several pupils whose exact number he did not specify. Under the arrangement worked out with Jefferson, the Indian children were being taught useful trades by a weaver, a printer and bookbinder, a mason and a carpenter. He needed more buildings, he said, and he recommended that the government add a blacksmith and a shoemaker to his staff. The carpenter, weaver and other artisans, whose continued services he hoped for, were regular government employes of the Indian Department, assigned in accordance with treaties. They were attached to the school as a matter of convenience, as the place where they could work most effectively.

Of course, Richard needed money, too. He asked that the Richard Press be given the contract for government printing; he also requested an additional allowance to buy clothing for the Indian children who came to him—most of them, he observed, "almost naked, dirt & worms Excepted."

The loss of Spring Hill seriously dampened Richard's educational plans. The Loranger farm to which he was forced to move lacked facilities; the government also, about that time, seems to have withdrawn much of its support. Then the War of 1812 gave him another setback. It was at least five years after the loss of Spring Hill before he was again able to give serious attention to his schools. Even then, he had nothing as elaborate as he had earlier contemplated. After the war, with new territorial leaders and with many new Yankee settlers moving into the Territory, more attention began to be given to a publicly supported system of schools. The attainment of that goal required many more years of planning, debate and legislation; Richard did not live to see it completely realized. But during that period he struggled along in his humble way, doing what he could. The records are meager; however, he always managed to have a few pupils under his supervision, and to that extent he helped to bridge the gap to a public system of schools.

Even in the face of his deepest disappointment, he did not lose hope. In 1811, when his Spring Hill program was at low ebb, he was still able to write to a sympathetic Jefferson with words of resolution.

"I have not given up & will not give up the design of Instructing Indian children. I am certain that with constancy we shall succeed."

Richard won the complete confidence of the Indians by his compassionate and humane attitude. An example of his influence, and the respect in which the Indians held him, is related in an account of an appeal made to him by the Indian Pokagon, who asked Richard to send a missionary to the band of Pottawatomies of which Pokagon was chief. To prove to Richard that he was a good Christian, Pokagon fell to his knees and recited the Lord's Prayer, an Ave Maria, the Apostles' Creed and the Ten Commandments. Richard, it was said, was deeply touched by this demonstration of piety.

Only once was Richard in danger from the Indians. That, if the account can be believed, occurred when sickness swept through a band camped near Spring Hill farm. A council was held, and it was decided the "black robe" was the cause. It was decreed that Richard be tomahawked. Before the sentence could be carried out, wiser members of the tribe prevailed and the Indians sought elsewhere to place the blame.

Gabriel Richard was an idealist, but practical things are frequently instituted upon the designs of dreamers. That was true in his case, particularly in the field of instruction of the Indians. Out of his early efforts came a government policy which was followed well into the twentieth century.

"When the War Department sought to formulate a plan of education that would measure up to the needs of the Indian, it took over a system presented by Father Richard to the United States Congress a decade before." So says one authority on the subject. "The Government had at last caught up with the man who failed because he was ahead of his time. The circular of 1819 states explicitly that those who expected government aid must include in the course of study, in addition to reading, writing and arithmetic, practical knowledge in agriculture and the mechanical arts for the boys, while spinning, weaving, and sewing must be taught to the girls. This plan adopted by the government became the basis of all later training in the Indian schools throughout the United States. Deservedly then might Father Richard bear the title, 'Father of Modern Indian Education.' "

During the War of 1812 Lewis Cass came to Michigan as a colonel in General William Hull's service. An impetuous young officer, who chafed under the slow, cautious leadership of General Hull, Cass criticized him frequently, and finally, when Hull surrendered Detroit to the British without resistance, Cass initiated proceedings that led to the General's court-martial. Although convicted on two counts, Hull's death penalty was remanded by President James Monroe, probably because the old soldier had served courageously in the Revolutionary War.

Cass was born in New Hampshire, studied law in Ohio, and became Michigan's territorial governor in 1814. He traveled with Schoolcraft during the 1820 Expedition and established his reputation as an astute negotiator among the Indians. Cass remains one of the most distinguished leaders in Michigan's history, and his career passed beyond the borders of the state and into the arena of national affairs.

In Washington, D.C., he served as President Andrew Jackson's Secretary of War (1831), Minister to France (1836), and in the United States Senate (1845-1851). An unsuccessful candidate for the United States Presidency in 1848, Cass took up the Secretary of State's office under President James Buchanan, but when the President offered no serious opposition to Southern secession, Cass resigned his post.

Lewis Cass has received much biographical attention, including Andrew C. McLaughlin's scholarly efforts in *Lewis Cass* (Boston, 1891). More recent accounts are Frank B. Woodford's *Lewis Cass, The Last Jeffersonian* (New Brunswick, 1950), and Willis Dunbar's *Lewis Cass* (Grand Rapids, 1970).

Henry R. Schoolcraft's famous work, instigated in part by Lewis Cass, has been published by Philip P. Mason in his *Schoolcraft's Expedition to Lake Iaska* (East Lansing, 1958), and by Schoolcraft himself in *Historical and Statistical Information . . .* , six vols. (Philadelphia, 1851-1857).

Indian Affairs: Alarms and Excursions

FRANK B. WOODFORD

Had Cass's duties in the Northwest been confined exclusively to the civil administration of Michigan Territory, he would have held no sinecure. His was a dual role; a lesser man would have found it difficult to wear his toga of proconsulship. For he was also ex-officio superintendent of Indian affairs, not only for Michigan, but for most of the original Northwest Territory, with jurisdiction over sub-agencies in Ohio, Indiana and Illinois. Almost half of his time was devoted to his work with the Indians. He was away from his seat of government, at times, for weeks and months on end, experiencing hardships of wilderness travel which taxed his physical capacities to the utmost.

He had been led by official duties, he said, "to travel almost all the western region north of the Ohio and east of the Mississippi." Hardly a forest stream large enough to float a birch canoe was unknown to him. Nearly every tribe south of Canada and east of central Minnesota was visited by him, and he was known personally to literally thousands of Indians.

What Cass accomplished for Michigan Territory as its governor was, in a sense, a local effort benefitting directly only the relatively small community which he served. But in his administration of Indian affairs he was performing a national function. Through selfless diligence, patience and courage, Lewis Cass laid the foundation for an enlightened Federal policy toward the aborigine. It was conceived of an understanding of the Indian, his problems, his relation to the whites, and an appreciation of the government's obligation to him. One noted historian claims that Cass's influence over the Indians was so great that the actual possession of the Northwest was due to his exertions.

From the standpoint of the government in Washington, Cass was charged with keeping the Indians off the warpath and obtaining land cessions from them. As a practical matter, these two things usually went hand in hand. But as the frontiers advanced and land-hungry migrants reached out eagerly for what belonged to the Indian, conflict became inevitable. To obtain these lands peaceably was Cass's first charge, and how effectively he performed it is attested by the fact that between the close of the War of 1812 and the time of the Black Hawk uprising, there was not a single Indian war in the territory under his jurisdiction. Yet during the same period Cass extinguished, through treaty or purchase, Indian title to literally millions of acres of land including most of Michigan, Wisconsin and northern Minnesota.

His success was the result of a strong sense of justice and a sympathetic understanding of the Indian's position. He never permitted pity to swerve him from his duty, but at the same time he never stooped to trickery. He felt always that he shared his obligation to the government with one equally great to the Indians. That made him the perfect, trusted mediator.

"I have frequently conversed with them upon their situation and prospects," he told Secretary of War Crawford, "and have found them deeply sensible of their forlorn condition, and anxiously desirous of meliorating it. I doubt whether the eye of humanity in a survey of the world could discover a race of men more helpless and wretched." The compassion aroused by his personal observations prompted him to write to Crawford's successor, John C. Calhoun: "The time has arrived when we should be known to the Indians by every humane and benevolent exertion." And again: "They should be protected in all their just rights, and secured from their own improvidences, as well as from the avarice of the whites." Territory should be acquired of them, he declared, only when necessary for the use of the whites and when it could be spared without injury to the Indians.

This, in sum, was the credo guiding Cass's relations with the savages. It was not lost upon them. For a generation they recognized him as their friend and champion. William Johnston, a half-breed Chippewa, spoke, perhaps for all of his brethren when he stated:

"He [Cass] has done much to raise the standard of Indian character in the United States. . . . Lewis Cass, in carrying out the orders of the War Department respecting the Indians, has always performed them with feelings of regard and friendship." Os-Kotchee—Big Belly—the northern Indians affectionately called him.

During his superintendency Cass negotiated eighteen major treaties with the tribes of the Northwest. In 1819, in order to increase the public domain, Cass made a treaty with the Chippewas for the benefit of his own territory. This agreement added six million acres, some of it the world's finest timberland, in an area which included the Saginaw River valley and the central and northeastern portions of Michigan's lower peninsula. These Chippewas were noted for their truculence; they had caused most of the trouble at Detroit after the war. As a precaution, a detachment of soldiers was sent by schooner to the head of Saginaw Bay. With an interpreter, Cass set out on horseback to make the hundred-mile journey through uncharted forests. He opened the council on September 24 where the city of Saginaw now stands.

In authorizing this treaty, Calhoun suggested the desirability of persuading the Saginaw tribes not only to give up their lands but to migrate farther west. On the scene, Cass decided not to follow these instructions. While he advocated voluntary removal as a happy solution to the Indian problem, he quickly perceived that the Chippewas were in no mood to entertain such a proposal. Acting on his own initiative, he reached an agreement for the transfer of the tribal lands in return for cash payments and a system of annuities. The latter arrangement was an elastic one—one thousand dollars and "the payment of whatever additional sum the Government of the United States might think they ought to receive, in such a manner, as would be most useful to them." To cover this loose agreement, a stipulation was inserted in the treaty binding the government to furnish the Indians with the services of a blacksmith, and to supply them with livestock, farming implements, and teachers to instruct them in agriculture.

"In taking this course," Cass told Calhoun by way of explanation, "I was influenced by the consideration, that the negotiator of an Indian treaty is not always the best judge of the value of the purchase or of the amount which should be paid for it. Sometimes too much has been allowed, and at other times too little. . . . He is not sent upon such a negotiation to ascertain the lowest possible sum for which the miserable remnant of those, who once occupied our country, are willing to treat, and to seize with avidity the occasion to purchase. . . . Certain I am, that both you and the President would censure me, and justly too, were I governed in my intercourse with the Indians by such principles."

Such fair treatment was not wasted upon the Indians. With the treaty signed, sealed, and safely in his pocket, Cass turned homeward. He had not gone far when he was overtaken by Washmenon-deguet, a chief who had been deputed by his tribe to follow the white ambassador "and express to him their entire satisfaction with the arrangement and their thankfulness for the kindness and attention shown to them." Everybody was happy, and within three years there were thirty-two townships platted in the ceded area, ready for settlement.

From the fur traders and the Indians Cass heard strange stories about the mysterious and fabulous north country. In Lake Huron, near Mackinac, it was said that there were islands of "Plaster of Paris." In the Lake Superior country, the Indians told of a river containing boulders of pure copper. Even the indefiniteness of the boundaries of his territory, as vaguely shown on maps, fascinated him. The western limits of Michigan were roughly described as the upper Mississippi River. But where, Cass asked, were the headwaters of this stream? The Indians and the voyageurs only shrugged when asked. Until the river's source was found, his knowledge of the domain he ruled was imperfect.

There was only one sure way to get the answer he sought. That was to go and find out for himself. This exciting proposition was submitted to Calhoun in 1819, and Cass found no lack of arguments to win the government's approval. There was, for instance, the matter, discussed for some time, of obtaining a site for a military post at Sault Ste. Marie. Besides the reports of iron, copper and silver ores, private interests had been clamoring to exploit the gypsum deposits. Cass recommended to the War Department that no licenses be granted until permission had been obtained from the Indian owners of the Huron islands.

There were remote tribes in the far northwest with whom the American authorities had no contact. "We are very little acquainted with these Indians," Cass remarked, "and I indulge the expectation that such a visit would be productive of beneficial effects." He wanted to know more about their numbers, customs and languages, and to what extent they were under British influence. There had been alarming reports that trouble was brewing between the Chippewas on the upper Mississippi and the Sioux beyond the river. If such a conflict got out of hand it might endanger settlements and army posts in the Wisconsin and Minnesota districts.

Official concern over that possibility was heightened by grapevine rumors to the effect that the northern Indians were restless as a result of the Creek and Seminole wars, of which they had heard. "A war belt from the South, probably from the Indians engaged in hostility in that quarter, but said to be from the Spaniards, has passed through this Country," Cass reported to Calhoun. It was something to be looked into.

It might be a good idea, too, he suggested, to examine the flora and fauna, and "I think it very important to carry the flag of the United States to these remote regions where it has never been borne by any person in a public station."

As a clincher, Cass assured Calhoun that the cost of such an expedition would be negligible. "All that will be required is an ordinary birch canoe, and permission to employ a competent number of Canadian boatmen. The whole expense will be confined within narrow limits, and no appropriation will be necessary to defray it." Calhoun gave his enthusiastic approval.

The winter and spring of 1820 were spent in preparation. Birch canoes were ordered from the Saginaw Bay Chippewas, considered master craftsmen. They had to be well built. Canoe travel, Cass confessed, sometimes made him seasick. Supplies, presents for the Indians, and scientific equipment had to be obtained, and the personnel selected. It already had been agreed that a detail of soldiers should go along to give "greater effect to any representations which might be made to the Indians." Cass was authorized also to take with him ten Ottawa, Chippewa and Shawnee braves as guides and hunters, under the supervision of two experienced interpreters.

An Albany glass blower turned geologist, Henry Rowe Schoolcraft was selected by the War Department to go along as the government's natural historian. The assignment of chief topographer went to Captain D. B. Douglass, professor of engineering at

West Point. Lieutenant Eneas Mackay, an artillery officer, was put in command of ten soldiers. Cass picked Dr. Alexander Wolcott, Indian agent at Chicago, as physician; and three young Detroiters, James Duane Doty as expedition secretary, Charles C. Trowbridge as assistant topographer, and Major Robert A. Forsyth as Cass's personal secretary, made up the group. Besides general leadership of the enterprise, Cass reserved for himself the duty of observing the Indians.

It would have been impossible to assemble another group with as wide a range of intellectual interests, with such universal inquisitiveness, and of such complete congeniality. What started as a party of strangers ended with friendships which were to endure through the lifetimes of them all. Through a compatibility of interests, a routine journey of exploration became a scientific expedition of first importance.

Schoolcraft and Captain Douglass arrived in Detroit on May 7, 1820, but the time for departure was still more than two weeks away. A thousand last-minute details demanded attention. The canoes were delivered—three of them, thirty to thirty-six feet long and of seven-foot beam, equipped with mast and sail and flying the national emblem at the stern.

"It was necessary," Schoolcraft reported, "to have mosquito bars, knapsacks, and various contrivances. . . . The public armorer had orders to furnish me suitable hammers and other minerological apparatus for preparing and packing specimens."

. . . .

So they proceeded. Into Lake Huron, across treacherous Saginaw Bay, they skirted the east shore of the Michigan peninsula until, on June 6, the flotilla touched the beach at Mackinac Island. The guns in the fort atop the bluff boomed a welcome salute, and the party was greeted by the commandant Captain Benjamin K. Pierce, a brother of Franklin Pierce. The first leg of the journey had been completed.

The party spent a week at Mackinac. While Cass attended to the gypsum deposits and won the Indians' sanction of their commercial development, his companions marvelled at the scenery—"sublime views of a most illimitable and magnificent water prospect"—or observed the Indians who came to trade at John Jacob Astor's American Fur Company store.

The mail caught up with them, and Cass received an urgent commission from the new secretary of state John Quincy Adams.

He was requested to make inquiry concerning the fate of a boy, Peter Hoffman, who in 1813, at the age of five, had been stolen by the Indians from his home in Indiana. The lad's frantic father had never given up searching for his son, and finally appealed for assistance to the State Department. Cass made an investigation which brought only partial success. He ascertained that Peter had been carried to Mackinac and had been purchased from his captors by one John Adair, a member of the British garrison during the war.

"This Adair and his wife were much attached to the boy," Cass learned, "and avowed their determination of adopting him as their son." But he could report nothing more with certainty. Adair's corps, he said, was disbanded, some of the men going home to England, others settling near Quebec and Kingston.

Peter Hoffman was never found, although the father, acting on Cass's lead, scoured the country around Quebec and Kingston. His, at least, was the small solace of knowing that the lad was alive and well cared for—a comfort denied the relatives of most captives of the Indians.

The expedition's first big task lay ahead of it at Sault Ste. Marie, and the reports filtering through from there were none too assuring. The Chippewas knew what the United States wanted of them—the cession of a tract of land on which to build a fort. The Indians wanted none of it. For many years in their remote country they had been having things pretty much their own way, without government interference or restraint. Regular visitors to the British post at Drummond's Island, they felt much closer to the English than to the Americans. They were said to be awaiting Cass's party in a dangerous mood.

Actually the government was asking nothing to which it was not legally entitled. Both the French and British had maintained military establishments at the Sault on land given them by the Indians. The Treaty of Greenville recognized the American rights of succession to all British and French titles in the Northwest Territory.

Under the circumstances, it was decided to take along reinforcements. When they left Mackinac they were accompanied by Captain Pierce's brother and second in command, Lieutenant John S. Pierce, and twenty-two regulars. The expedition, now numbering sixty-four persons, reached the Sault after a couple of days' paddling. The Indians were out in force to meet them, firing their guns into the air and shouting "bosho," the Chippewa equivalent of "bon jour."

But this welcome was not convincing, and in making camp, precautions were taken against a surprise attack which, they later learned, the natives were planning.

"Our line may have looked offensively demonstrative to the Chippewas, who regarded it . . . with unfriendly feelings," Schoolcraft commented.

Early next morning a council convened in the American camp. The scene was an impressive one. Painted and feathered, decked in their ceremonial ornaments and medals, the Indians seated themselves solemnly in front of the governor's marquee, with a tempting array of presents spread out before them. But there was tension in the air. The Indians, one of the interpreters intuitively felt, "did not look right."

After the traditional pipe was smoked, James Riley, a halfbreed interpreter, got to his feet and described the purpose of the conclave and what the American government expected to receive from the Indians. No attempt was made to hide the fact that a fort was to be erected and garrisoned by the United States. One chief then turned to Cass and explained that the Indians were willing to grant land concessions provided no military post was involved. It would be a bad thing to bring soldiers to the Sault, he said. The young men might steal the garrison's cattle.

Cass assured him that any uneasiness on that score was unnecessary. American soldiers could take care of themselves and their property. Moreover, he added—and he became quite emphatic—they needed to give themselves no concern whatever about the Americans' intentions.

"So sure as the sun which was then arising, would set in the west," he declared, "so sure would an American garrison be sent to that place, whether they renewed the grant or not."

At these words, Sassaba, a leader of the extremist party, who had fought with Tecumseh at the Thames, rose from his place in the half circle. Quivering with rage, he confronted Cass. His appearance, spectacular under the most ordinary circumstances, now was almost terrifying.

"Beginning at the top," said Trowbridge, describing the chief, "an eagle's feather, bear's grease, vermillion and indigo; a red British military coat, with two enormous epaulets, a large British silver medal, breech clout, leggins and moccasins."

Sassaba did not beat around the bush. "He did not like Americans," he stated bluntly. "He did not like the great White Father at Washington, and they (the Indians) would not sell him any of their lands, and if he (General Cass) and his soldiers did not leave, they would all be killed."

With that grim ultimatum, Sassaba drove his war lance into the ground at Cass's feet. Kicking the presents out of his path, he marched stiffly off to his own camp. One by one the other chiefs and their followers silently rose and went after him. Over in the Chippewa village the braves could be seen arming. The women and children scuttled into the woods. To the Americans it looked like a showdown, and they made ready for the attack they felt certain was coming. Suddenly, as they waited, a British Union Jack was unfurled on a pole in front of Sassaba's lodge. Here was defiance with a vengeance.

If he was to save face, Cass could not ignore this challenge. Not for a moment did he hesitate. Instructing the military to hold their ground, he started, unarmed and accompanied only by Riley, across the no-man's land separating the two camps. Schoolcraft and some of the others tried to follow him but were waved back. Straight into the center of the Indian camp he strode, ignoring the threatening looks of the braves. Stamping determinedly up to Sassaba's lodge, he pulled down the flag, tossed it contemptuously on the ground and trod on it.

"Then I was afraid," said Riley. But Cass was unperturbed. Boldly entering Sassaba's lodge, he read the riot act to that worthy in unmistakable terms. The hoisting of that flag, he declared firmly, was an affront which would not be tolerated. The soil on which they stood was American soil, and two flags could not fly there in friendship or in enmity. The United States was the supreme power, and the Indians, he warned, had better recognize the fact. Otherwise a strong foot would be placed upon their necks and they would be crushed. With this declaration he turned on his heel, picked up the trampled flag, and returned to his own camp, leaving the Indians speechless at his audacity. It was a display of personal courage of a type which appealed to the Indians, and which aroused their admiration. Schoolcraft, no less impressed than the Chippewas, observed that the governor's action "betoken[s] a knowledge of Indian character of which we never dreamed."

It was effective. The chiefs finally sent word that they would resume the council, which reconvened in the early evening. Sassaba and one or two other hot-heads had packed their gear and departed, leaving behind those who could be persuaded to reason. The atmosphere was entirely changed. Hostility had given way to a conciliatory feeling, and in this spirit an understanding was quickly reached. The following day Cass sent a copy of the agreement to Calhoun. It contained a cession of a piece of land on the St. Mary's River, ten miles square.

"I did not require the Indians to cede us a larger tract," he explained, "because more would be useless for the objects, which the Government have in view, and because it is important to our character and influence among them, that our first demand should be distinctly marked with moderation. . . . You will find that the right of fishing is secured them. Common humanity, as well as their urgent entreaties, required such a stipulation in their favor."

Leaving the Sault on June 18, the expedition followed the Michigan coast of Lake Superior, marvelling in passing at the beauty of the Pictured Rocks and the other wild scenes, which Cass thought surpassed the Niagara or the Potomac in grandeur. Schoolcraft found abundant traces of iron and copper, and the Indian guides helpfully ranged the shores seeking unusual pebbles which they brought to him. They named him "Paguabekiega," or "He-who-strikes-the-rock."

Lake Superior weather is uncertain, and the party, at the mercy of sudden squalls, was wet and miserable half the time. Poor Doty had to sit up all alone one night when a storm blew down the tents, to see that the waves did not wash away the supplies. But life had its little compensations. Two days later he recorded happily in his journal that he had feasted on sturgeon and wild strawberries. On fine days, as they paddled along, the various members of the group took turns reading aloud from the books which were invariably a part of Cass's baggage on any trip he took. Evening campfires were enlivened by discussions, generally led by Cass, on some literary or scientific subject.

On June 27 they were at the mouth of the Ontonagon, or Copper River, where the copper boulder was said to be. The next day Schoolcraft, Dr. Wolcott and Captain Douglass ascended the river to hunt for it, Cass and some of the others following, with local Indians as guides. The weather was extremely hot, and when he overtook Schoolcraft, Cass was nearly exhausted and decided to turn back. While the others continued their search upstream, Cass's guide succeeded in getting lost in his own woods, and the governor wandered aimlessly around for the rest of the day.

Thirty miles from the mouth of the Ontonagon they came upon the object of their search, a lump of copper partly immersed in the river.

"The rock consists of a mass of native copper in a tabular boulder of serpentine," Schoolcraft noted. "Its face is almost purely metallic, and more splendent than appears to consist with its being purely metallic copper. There is no appearance of oxidation. Its size, roughly measured, is three feet four inches, by three feet eight inches, and about twelve or fourteen inches thick in the thickest part." He estimated its copper content at a ton or a ton and a half. Although he broke his hammer trying to chip off a sample, he had seen enough to know that he possessed the key to a veritable mineral treasure house.

. . . .

Cass's interest in the American Indian had several facets. As a public problem it required his attention as an administrator. To that he added a useful scientific and historical curiosity. Better than most people of his day, Cass understood the unhappy situation in which the Indian was placed, as white migration inexorably pressed back the limits of the frontier. It was perfectly clear to him that the two races could not live side by side unless the Indian accepted the white man's standard of civilization. And with little possibility of that, the Indian was the one who had to give ground.

The Indian seemed to be doomed through natural circumstances. Clearing the forests and fencing the fields drove off the game—and with it went his way of life. Introduction of firearms among the Indians hastened the wildlife depopulation, for he hunted, as did everything else, without moderation. Then, too, the Indian was not conditioned to the habits and customs of the whites. What a decline in his food supply did not accomplish, smallpox and whisky did.

"Their contact with the whites has subjected them to moral and physical evils, which threaten at no distant day to extirpate the small number that remains," said Cass. "The chase affords them a scanty and precarious supply, and the purchases of land, which we are continually making and settling, will circumscribe the Territory, within which their game abounds, to such a degree, as to render it impracticable for them to subsist by hunting."

The public responsibility to the savages was clear to Cass. It called for an official paternalism "that the propensity of the Indian for war should be checked, and themselves restrained within reasonable limits; that they should be protected in all their just rights, & secured from their own improvidence, as well as from the avarice of the whites, & that the Territory should be occupied for permanent improvement, whenever it was necessary for the one party, & could be spared without injury by the other. . . . They have a right to expect much. In fact we must think for them. We must frequently promote their interest against their inclination, and no plan for the improvement of their condition will ever be practicable or efficacious, to the promotion of which their consent must in the first instance be obtained."

Efforts, he believed, should be made to teach them to live as the whites did, and for their education he advocated that in each treaty provision should be made to provide them at government expense with the services of "a saddler, a carpenter, a Cooper, a wheel-wright, a Tailor and an Armourer." But Cass was astute enough to realize that the Indian could not be brought into the fold of white civilization over night. "Any change to be permanent," he said, "must be gradual and general. We must teach the Indians, by their own observation, the value of our institutions."

Whisky was the curse of the Indian and the *bête noir* of the humane and conscientious agent who dealt with him. Cass had ample opportunity to witness its ravaging effects. At nearly every Indian conclave which he attended, he warned the braves of what they were letting themselves in for if they persisted in drinking. Despite his abhorrence of the custom of observing the successful conclusion of a treaty by knocking in the head of a whisky keg, Cass was himself sometimes an unwilling party to such practices. The Indians insisted that liquor must be furnished before agreeing to attend a council. Cass had to comply, but he never did so from choice, nor did he use whisky to take advantage of the Indians in his negotiations with them.

"I am," he once declared, "utterly opposed to the introduction of spirituous liquors into the Indian Country. Their effects are too obvious to admit of doubt, and too deleterious to the morals and manners of the Indians to allow their use to them."

On one occasion, at Prairie du Chien, when the Indians demanded liquor, Cass delivered a stern temperance lecture, and then caused several kegs to be emptied on the ground before the anguished eyes of the warriors, to prove that it was not from parsimony that it was denied them.

Federal law prohibited the sale of whisky within Indian lands, but there was nothing to prevent the Indians from coming into white settlements and buying as much as they could hold. Moreover, there was a constant, illegal traffic on the part of traders smuggling spirits to the savages. Cass attempted to plug the loopholes through which liquor flowed by having the territorial legislature outlaw the sale or gift of whisky to the Indians. He also authorized his subagents to examine the packs of traders entering Indian territory, and confiscate their contraband and impound their trade goods if they were bootlegging.

Nevertheless, Cass felt on occasion that he was fighting a losing battle. Both Federal and territorial statutes contained provisions which permitted designated officials to authorize distribution of liquor under certain conditions. Widespread abuse of this privilege resulted.

"So long as the law remains in the statute book I have no power to check its operation," he complained. "It is an authority, which I have never exercised and which I would be unwilling to exercise unless in some extreme case. . . . I am perfectly aware, that the law is daily violated here and elsewhere. . . ."

During Cass's administration the first steps were taken to move the Indians from their original homes to new lands in the wilderness. A colony of Oneidas from central New York was transplanted, partly through his efforts, to Wisconsin. It was the original experiment in "removal." Cass favored it in principle. But, he insisted, removal should be voluntary, and those not desiring to move should be "protected in their rights of occupation. To which may be added that land may be laid off in fee to such families as remain & as we presume, may wish to receive it."

It was not uncommon for local administration of Indian affairs to be placed in the hands of missionaries, generally well-intentioned and often capable people, who did their best within the limitations placed upon them. A number of missions operated successfully within Cass's jurisdiction, and he was instrumental in establishing at least one. The Carey Mission, in particular, backed by the Board of Managers of the Baptist Missionary Convention, was run by the Reverend Isaac McCoy among the Pottawatomies near present-day Niles, Michigan. Cass had great respect for Mr. McCoy and to some extent became the patron of his establishment. He employed McCoy as subagent in a number of government dealings with the tribe, and he named the missionary as head of a commission to go to Kansas to seek new homes for the Pottawatomies.

However, he was realistic about the missions and those in charge of them. "I fear," he wrote, "that missionaries are sometimes afraid to tell the worst part of the story lest the benevolent societies and individuals who patronize the missions should become discouraged and decline the prosecution of the undertaking."

Cass's own warm and intelligent interest in the Indian lent facility to his pen. For several years he endeavored to present the Indian as he really was—a human creature of many virtues and many faults, rather than the bloodthirsty villain or the noble child of nature which popular writers persisted in parading. To know his problems, Cass contended, it was first necessary to know the Indian. His expedition of 1820 set him on the right path. It resulted in his writing a learned pamphlet on Indian languages and dialects, an undertaking preceding the one which Schoolcraft later was to do on a larger scale.

He concluded that a "conventional and uniform orthography" was necessary for proper investigation of aboriginal tongues. The Sioux language he regarded "as one of the most barren which is spoken by any of our aboriginal tribes." The Wyandotte dialect he called the worst "spoken by man since the confusion of tongues at the Tower of Babel. . . . It is harsh, gutteral & indistinguishable, Filled with intonations that seem to start from the Speaker with great pain and effort." That he was familiar with the speech of most of the Northwestern tribes is evident from his writing.

Indian lore he found a fascinating subject. Soon after his arrival at Detroit in 1813, he began a systematic interrogation of the old French inhabitants for their recollections of Pontiac's war of 1763 with the idea of writing a biography of the Ottawa chief. He persuaded Tarhe, a Wyandotte chief, to give him an eye-witness account of the torture and death of Colonel William Crawford during the Revolution. Trowbridge and others who accompanied him on his expeditions were encouraged to gather their legends and tribal histories from the Indians.

The information he accumulated over the years brought him into demand as a reviewer and critic. In 1823 a James Dunn Hunter, who claimed to have been kidnapped as a child and raised by the trans-Mississippi Indians, wrote a book of his adventures which achieved wide popularity in the East and in England. Asked to discuss the book in the columns of the *North American Review,* Cass proved that Hunter was an imposter and his story a fraud. This annoyed the British critics who had hailed Hunter's narrative as a literary "find." They frostily rejected Cass's documented exposure as unworthy of consideration, because no investigation of the facts had been made by British scholars.

"Where an educated Englishman does not go," Cass replied tartly, "nothing can be known."

Anything about the Indians was, in fact, grist to Cass's mill. No book on the subject was considered authentic unless it carried his endorsement. His notes were added to Schoolcraft's *Narrative,* and to Henry Whiting's *Ontwa* and *Sannillac,* precursors of *Hiawatha.* Their success was partly due to his efforts. "A poem of great merit and by a native American is now printing in New York," Cass informed a Washington editor concerning *Ontwa.* "To show that the author adhered with fidelity to Indian usages, at his request, I furnished him with a body of notes which are appended to the poem." He requested the editor to give *Ontwa* good notices.

The notes and material Cass gathered about Pontiac were later given to Francis Parkman and used as the basis for the *Conspiracy of Pontiac.* Parkman also drew on Cass's material in writing *LaSalle.* On more than one occasion Parkman recognized his obligations to Cass.

"I have already been so much indebted to you for assistance in my investigation with Indian history," Parkman wrote in 1846, just before setting out on a western trip. He asked Cass for letters of introduction to persons on the frontier. Cass obliged and *The Oregon Trail* was the result of that journey.

Thus American literature is richer because of Lewis Cass.

Clearly written and meticulously researched, F. Clever Bald's *Michigan in Four Centuries* (New York, 1954) is one of two recently published general Michigan histories. Bald's treatment of Stevens T. Mason provides an excellent summary of the state's constitutional beginnings and the achievements of the "boy governor." Mason's programs, particularly free banking and state-financed internal improvements, have been criticized frequently, but his flamboyant leadership continues to attract admirers. Two of his most able appointees, John D. Pierce as the first superintendent of public instruction, and Douglas Houghton as state geologist, continue to reflect favorably on the first elected Governor of Michigan.

Specific studies of Stevens T. Mason include Lawton T. Heman's *Life and Times of Stevens T. Mason* (Lansing, 1930), and a biography by Kent Sagendorph, *Stevens T. Mason, Misunderstood Patriot* (New York, 1947). John D. Pierce and Douglas Houghton are discussed in Clyde R. Ford's "The Life and Work of John D. Pierce," *Michigan Pioneer and Historical Collections,* XXXV (1907) and *Douglas Houghton, Michigan's Pioneer Geologist* (Detroit, 1954), by Edsel Rintala.

The Boy Governor Does a Man's Job

F. CLEVER BALD

The years from 1831 to 1837 were notable for many changes and exciting events in Michigan Territory. Leadership was in the hands of Stevens Thomson Mason, the Boy Governor. Under his guidance a constitution was adopted, Michigan became a state not recognized

From *Michigan in Four Centuries* (New York: Harper and Row, 1954), pp. 188-202. Partially reprinted by permission of the History Division, Michigan Department of State. Footnotes in the original have been omitted.

by Congress, and finally, admittance to the Union was secured. During this period occurred the Black Hawk War, the Toledo War, two cholera epidemics, the operation of the first railroad, a great boom in real estate, and a tremendous growth in population.

General John T. Mason was appointed secretary of Michigan Territory in 1830. A member of the Mason family of Virginia, he had been living for some years in Kentucky. Stevens T. Mason, eighteen-year-old son of the new secretary, helped his father in the performance of his official duties, became well acquainted with the work, and made a favorable impression on Governor Cass.

In the summer of 1831 John T. Mason decided to go to Texas to look after some land claims there. He and Stevens T. went to Washington and visited President Jackson. John T. Mason resigned his office and asked the President to appoint his son to the position. Pleased with the boy's evident ability, Jackson granted the request and named him secretary of Michigan Territory.

News of the appointment reached Detroit before Mason returned. Because he was an outsider and not yet of age, some of the leading citizens of Detroit called a meeting to protest against the appointment of "the stripling." After his arrival, a committee was sent to interview him and report. He received the members courteously and answered their questions, readily admitting that he was only nineteen years old.

After hearing the report of the committee, the leaders of the opposition drew up a memorial to the President, asking him to remove the boy from office. The Whig newspapers took up the issue and attacked the new secretary vigorously.

Mason acted wisely. First he wrote a long letter to President Jackson, explaining that the opposition to him was purely political and asking for the President's support. Then he published an address in which he promised to seek advice from older men and to serve the people faithfully. His frank appeal did much to disarm hostility, but the newspapers which were antagonistic to Jackson continued to attack him.   On July 24, 1831, Lewis Cass administered the oath of office to Stevens T. Mason, attended a farewell banquet arranged by citizens in his honor, and departed for Washington to serve as Secretary of War. Jackson appointed George B. Porter of Pennsylvania as governor. He did not reach Detroit until September 17, and he was frequently absent from the Territory thereafter. During these periods Mason was acting governor, and after Porter died in July, 1834, he continued to serve in that capacity, for Michigan never had another territorial governor. Because he was intelligent, industrious, and modest, he soon won the enthusiastic support of the people.

An Indian uprising in northern Illinois and in Michigan Territory west of Lake Michigan occurred in the spring and summer of 1832. For a time it checked migration into the southwestern counties, and greatly exaggerated reports of widespread Indian hostility frightened settlers as far east as Detroit. The occasion of the disturbance was the crossing of the Mississippi River by Black Hawk and his "British band" into northern Illinois. This leader of the Sauk and Foxes was greatly feared. He was known to be resentful because he had been forced to move beyond the Mississippi, leaving the villages and the cornfields of his people to the white settlers.

When he crossed over into Illinois near the mouth of the Rock River, Black Hawk was accompanied by about five hundred mounted warriors and an equal number of women and children. He declared that his purpose was to plant corn in his old fields, and the fact that he brought women and children with him makes it appear that he had no immediate intention of making war. Nevertheless, crossing the Mississippi eastward had been prohibited by treaty, and the settlers demanded protection.

The governor of Illinois called out the militia, and regulars were sent up the Mississippi River from St. Louis. Gathering a force of about four thousand men, General Henry Atkinson sent them up the Rock River in pursuit of Black Hawk. As he retreated, Black Hawk's band killed settlers who had not had time to escape. He called upon the other Indian tribes for assistance, but none rallied to his cause.

News of Black Hawk's depredations crossed Lake Michigan and spread through the settlements along the Chicago Road. Rumors ran riot from village to village and from farm to farm: Black Hawk himself was in Michigan; the Chippewa and Ottawa had joined him; the Potawatomi who inhabited the region were sharpening their hatchets to fall upon the settlers. Without waiting for orders, able-bodied men in some communities shouldered their guns and gathered to protect their families.

A request for assistance from the Indian agent at Chicago and increasing uneasiness among the people caused Acting Governor Mason to order Major General John R. Williams to call the militia near Detroit into service. About three hundred men, answering the call, assembled at Conrad Ten Eyck's tavern on the Chicago Road, now in Dearborn. Brigadier General Joseph W. Brown at Tecumseh mustered five companies from Clinton, Adrian, Tecumseh, Blissfield, and Palmyra and marched them to Niles. General Williams and his men started west on May 25.

Meanwhile a message from Chicago informed Mason that the dangers had been greatly exaggerated, and the Michigan troops would not be needed. The acting governor sent off a courier with orders for the militia to return. At Saline he overtook the army. General Williams ordered the men to return to Detroit, but, with his staff and a detachment of mounted men, rode on to Chicago. There was no need for going farther because sufficient settlers in Illinois had rallied to expel the invaders. General Brown released his men to return to their farms.

An overwhelming army of regulars and militia under General Atkinson drove the Sauk and Foxes across the Illinois line into the part of Michigan Territory that is now Wisconsin. Near the present city of Madison, Black Hawk made a brief stand. Forced to retire, he reached the Mississippi. There near the mouth of the Bad Axe River, while he was attempting to send women and children across to the western bank, the pursuing force overtook him. His offer to surrender was rejected.

An army transport, the *Warrior*, blocked escape by water. Caught between the guns of the steamer and the troops on shore, on August 2 the Indians were almost annihilated. Seeing that further resistance was useless, Black Hawk retired to the dells of the Wisconsin River. He was captured by two Winnebago and taken a prisoner to Prairie du Chien.

Black Hawk made peace with the government, and in 1833 he was taken on a tour of the East in order to impress him with the foolishness of defying the power of the United States. On his return journey he was brought to Detroit on July 4, 1833. There the whole town had gathered at the wharf to see him. Wearing a long blue coat, a white high hat, and spectacles, and carrying a cane, he conducted himself with dignity. The growth of the town since the War of 1812, when he had last seen it, amazed him. The next day Black Hawk paid a courtesy call on Acting Governor Mason.

Although Black Hawk's warriors never extended their attacks into the area of the present state, the war brought suffering and death into the territory. General Winfield Scott was ordered by President Jackson to lead United States troops from the East to take part in the Black Hawk War. Traveling from Fortress Monroe, Virginia, they embarked at Buffalo for Chicago.

On July 4, 1832, one of the transports tied up at Detroit. Suddenly, a number of the soldiers were stricken with cholera. Taken ashore for treatment, eleven died during the night. City authorities ordered the transport to leave the wharf, but the damage had already been done. The dread disease began to attack civilians, and on July 6 two died. Panic ensued. Many left the city to escape the mysterious sickness which struck without warning and killed its victims quickly.

So many became ill that the second floor of the Capitol was made into a hospital, and physicians in the city courageously attended the sick, although there was little they could do. Many died; some recovered. Father Richard also labored manfully, helping to care for the victims. A cart went through the city streets day and night, with attendants who cried as they went, "Bring out your dead."

Frightened Detroiters fled from what seemed to them a doomed city. To prevent introduction of the disease, other towns stationed armed guards on the roads to stop stagecoaches and individual travelers. At Ypsilanti, a coach from Detroit carrying passengers and the mail was halted by shooting one of the horses, and Secretary Mason, traveling west by the Chicago Road on official business, was arrested.

These precautions were not entirely successful. Near Fort Gratiot one of General Scott's transports stopped to put the sick ashore because there were too many to be cared for on the ship. Fearful of taking the disease, many of the soldiers who were not yet ill deserted and scattered throughout the countryside, spreading it among civilians. Of the outlying towns in which cholera appeared, Marshall suffered most. There, of the seventy inhabitants, eighteen were stricken, and eight died, among them the wife of the Reverend John D. Pierce.

The disease abated early in September. On the thirteenth of the month Father Gabriel Richard died, the last victim of the plague from which he had saved many sufferers by his unceasing toil. So ended the thirty-four years of service to Detroit and Michigan of this man who had been a mighty influence for good as priest, educator, and civic leader.

Another cholera epidemic appeared in Detroit in the summer of 1834. Though of shorter duration, it was more deadly than the former one. Seven per cent of the city's population died during the month of August.

The restlessness of the western Indians in general and the Black Hawk War in particular called attention to the need for a depot of arms, ammunition, and supplies for the western garrison posts closer to them than the existing ones. For that purpose, the United States Government selected a site on the Chicago Road near the River Rouge about ten miles west of Detroit.

Work was begun in 1833. Bricks were made of clay taken from a nearby pit and eleven buildings were erected around a square eight hundred feet on a side. The buildings were connected by a high brick wall which made a solid enclosure. Named the Detroit Arsenal, it was used by the government until 1873. The town of

Dearborn grew up around it. For many years the commandant's residence on the corner of Michigan and Monroe was used as the city police station. In 1948 the building was given to the Dearborn Historical Commission to be maintained as a museum of local history.

In 1832, the year of the Black Hawk War and of the first cholera epidemic, the Legislative Council asked the inhabitants of the Territory to vote on the question of becoming a state. The number of ballots cast was small, but a majority favored statehood. The Legislative Council petitioned Congress to pass an enabling act giving the people the privilege of making a constitution for a state which would have for its southern boundary the line mentioned in the Ordinance of 1787 and in the act establishing Michigan Territory, that is, a line from the southernmost point of Lake Michigan due east to Lake Erie.

The claiming of the Ordinance line aroused the opposition of Ohio because, if it were granted, Toledo would be in Michigan. Ohio was building a canal to connect Lake Erie with the Ohio River, and Toledo was intended to be the northern terminus.

Strange as it may seem, the northern boundary of Ohio had never been established. When the constitution of the state was being written in 1802, the latitude of the southern extremity of Lake Michigan was unknown. Fearing that the Ordinance line might strike Lake Erie farther south than they wished, the delegates described the northern boundary as either the one provided by the Ordinance or, if that should strike Lake Erie below Maumee Bay, a line from the southern extremity of Lake Michigan to the northern cape of the bay. Congress admitted Ohio with this uncertain boundary, but in 1805 it established Michigan Territory with the Ordinance line as the southern boundary.

In order to settle the matter, Congress in 1812 directed that the Ordinance line be run. Action was deferred until after the war, when Edward Tiffin, surveyor general of the United States and formerly governor of Ohio, was ordered to have the work done. Following Tiffin's instructions, his deputy, William Harris, in 1817, marked the boundary desired by Ohio. The Harris line put Toledo in Ohio.

Governor Cass protested vigorously to the United States Government, and President James Monroe ordered a new survey in accord with the act which established Michigan Territory. In 1818 John A. Fulton ran the line, which fell below Toledo, putting it in Michigan. The land between the Harris and the Fulton lines, a tapering piece five to eight miles wide, was called the Toledo Strip. Michigan, of course, was satisfied, if Ohio was not; but Fulton's survey was inaccurate and Congress ordered a resurvey. The Talcott Line, named for the surveyor who ran it in 1834, was nearly identical with the Fulton Line.

Michigan seemed to have a clear title to the Toledo Strip. The official Talcott Line supported her contention, territorial officers had governed the disputed area, public land there had been sold from the Monroe land office, county courts of Michigan had sat there, and the inhabitants had voted in territorial elections. Political considerations, however, outweighed Michigan's rights. Michigan had only a nonvoting delegate in Congress; Ohio had senators and representatives. Indiana and Illinois, each of which had pushed its northern boundary above the Ordinance line, supported Ohio. President Jackson, at first, seemed to favor Michigan's cause; but an election year was approaching, and he could not afford to offend three states, with the possibility of losing their electoral votes. Until Michigan entered the Union, she would have no vote for President. Politically, her position was very weak.

To Stevens T. Mason it seemed that Michigan would never become a state if she had to depend on an enabling act by Congress. After Governor Porter died in July, 1834, Mason was acting governor again, and he began a campaign to make the territory a state. When the Legislative Council met in September, he asked that a census be taken as a first step. The returns showed that there were 85,856 people in the territory east of Lake Michigan.

Mason urged further action, calling attention to the clause in the Ordinance of 1787 which promised a territory having sixty thousand free inhabitants entrance into the Union after making a constitution and organizing a state government. Following the acting governor's instructions, the Council called a constitutional convention to meet in May, 1835. Mason declared that such measures were legal, and the people accepted him as their leader.

When word reached Michigan that Ohio authorities intended to extend their jurisdiction over the disputed strip on April 1, 1835, the Council passed an act providing penalties of fine or imprisonment against anyone, except territorial officers or officers of the United States, who might attempt to perform governmental duties there. In spite of this threat, Governor Robert Lucas of Ohio was determined to re-mark the Harris Line and to enforce Ohio Law in the Toledo Strip. To protect the surveyors he ordered militia to Perrysburg on the Maumee River.

Acting Governor Mason was equally determined to prevent what he considered invasion of Michigan's rights. Ordering General Joseph W. Brown to Monroe to assemble the militia, he joined him there on April 1, 1835, to direct operations. The Toledo War was about to begin. The first move was to send General Brown as deputy sheriff with an armed posse into Toledo to arrest Ohio officials. Mason had decided not to use uniformed militia unless the sheriff's men were unable to enforce the law. After making some arrests and causing some damage to property, the posse returned to Monroe. One of the prisoners, Benjamin F. Stickney, refusing either to walk or ride, was tied on a horse and so delivered to the jail in Monroe.

Other raids were made on Toledo, and on April 26 another posse pounced upon Ohio's commissioners and surveyors rerunning the Harris Line in Lenawee County, fourteen miles south of Adrian. The commissioners escaped, but deputies from Tecumseh and Adrian captured nine of the party. All were released on bail except one who refused to furnish it. He was held in the county prison.

While these attempts to maintain the jurisdiction of Michigan Territory were taking place, two commissioners sent by President Jackson to negotiate with Lucas and Mason arrived on the scene. They reminded both governors that the President had warned them not to use force in trying to settle the dispute, and urged them to accept Jackson's recommendation that the matter be left to the decision of Congress in December. Although Lucas insisted on rerunning the Harris Line, he agreed to a suggestion by the commissioners that Michigan and Ohio govern the region jointly for the present. He had nothing to lose by waiting for action by Congress.

The commissioners tried to persuade Mason to have the charges against the Ohio officials dropped. He rejected the suggestion, and he refused to agree to joint government. He did agree to call a special session of the Council to lay the matter before it. Mason believed that the Council would support his stand, and he had no faith in Congress.

The constitutional convention met in the Capitol in Detroit on May 11, 1835, and it adjourned on June 24 after having completed its task. The constitution of 1835 was the best one Michigan has had. Like the Constitution of the United States, it provided a framework of government and left legislation to the legislature. Like the President, the governor was given the power to appoint judges and the principal officers of administration—secretary of state, auditor general, attorney general, and even county prosecutors—with the consent of the senate. The governor had great responsibilities, and he had sufficient power to meet them.

Although Michigan Territory had had a unicameral council, the constitution provided for a bicameral legislature. The house of representatives was to consist of from forty-eight to one hundred members; the senate was to have one third as many members as the house. Elections were to be held annually. Representatives were given terms of one year; senators, two years. The two houses elected the state treasurer. The people were given the privilege of electing the governor, lieutenant governor, members of the legislature, and local officials.

Article Ten dealt with education. One clause provided for a superintendent of public instruction to be named by the governor with the consent of both houses of the legislature. This provision is an indication of the importance which the delegates attached to the office. No other state constitution at the time contained such a clause. Elsewhere, the superintendent was a statutory officer whose position could be abolished by the legislature. The Michigan delegates made him a constitutional officer so that his position would be secure.

The same article also required the legislature to provide for a system of common schools to be open at least three months a year. The state was to give financial assistance. Actually, this clause did not guarantee free public schools. Rate bills were still issued, and the level of education varied greatly from district to district.

Article Ten also prescribed that the proceeds from the sale of land given by the United States for the support of schools should be put into a perpetual fund and the interest used to maintain schools. Income from lands granted for the University was required by the same article to be used only for the University.

The constitution contained a bill of rights meant to protect the liberties of the citizens, and qualifications for voting were liberal. Besides giving the franchise to all white male citizens above the age of twenty-one after a six months' residence, the constitution permitted all white male inhabitants to vote if they were twenty-one years old or over and were living in the Territory at the time the constitution was signed.

Amendments to the constitution might be made by a two thirds vote of each house of the legislature, ratified by a majority of the people voting on the proposal. A method was provided also for revising the constitution or making a new one.

A miscellaneous provision required the state government to encourage internal improvements, that is, transportation by roads, canals, and navigable waters. Although extravagant application of this clause almost bankrupted the state, the constitution, as a whole, was an excellent instrument of government.

Among the delegates who made the constitution were many able men. Some were already well known throughout the Territory; others reached high political positions later. Among those who had been in public life for a number of years were William Woodbridge and John Biddle, both Whigs of Detroit. Although the Democrats had a majority in the convention, Biddle was elected president. Another prominent Whig, but a newcomer in Michigan, was Townsend E. Gidley of Jackson County. Among the Democrats John Norvell of Detroit was leader of the liberals and Lucius Lyon, from Kalamazoo County, of the conservatives. Other delegates who had active parts in the convention were Edward Mundy of Washtenaw County, Ross Wilkins and John R. Williams of Detroit, Edward D. Ellis and Robert McCelland of Monroe, John S. Barry of St. Joseph County, John J. Adam of Lenawee, Hezekiah G. Wells of Kalamazoo, and Isaac Crary of Calhoun. Crary is especially notable for his report on education, which was written into the constitution and was the foundation upon which Michigan's school system was eventually established.

During June and July the Toledo War went on. Posses from Monroe County made several raids to arrest Ohio officials, and on one occasion Two Stickney, resisting arrest, stabbed Joseph Wood, a deputy sheriff of Monroe County, and escaped. In July, Secretary of War Lewis Cass went to Detroit and tried to cool the belligerent ardor of his young friend, the acting governor. Mason, however, rejected his advice to have the cases against Ohio officials dismissed and was willing only to await the decision of the Legislative Council.

When the Council met in August, it supported the acting governor's stand and appropriated funds to carry on the contest. This action followed that of the Ohio Legislature, which had voted money to Governor Lucas. It had also organized Lucas County in the disputed area and named September 7 as the date for a session of court to be held in Toledo. The official record of such a session, the legislature believed, would prove that Toledo was within the jurisdiction of Ohio.

President Jackson, entirely out of patience with Mason, removed him from office on August 29, 1835. Before a successor arrived to take his place, a session of the court of common pleas of the second Ohio judicial circuit had been held in Toledo. General Joseph W. Brown, with about one thousand men, marched into Toledo on September 7, the day set for the meeting, but the Ohio judges had outwitted him. With an armed bodyguard they had quietly gone into town shortly after midnight, held a brief session of court, signed the record, and left. Their departure was hastened by the false report that General Brown was searching for them.

Later in the day, when the general arrived, he learned that he was too late. He retired with his soldiers to Monroe, where he dismissed them. The Toledo War was over, but the boundary remained undrawn.

The new secretary of Michigan Territory, John S. Horner of Virginia, handed Mason his credentials and entered upon his official duties on September 21, 1835. Relations between him and Mason were polite, but some residents of the Territory resented his supplanting of their fearless leader and expressed their feelings vigorously. Horner tried to carry out the President's instructions to have the suits against the Ohio officials dismissed, but the Monroe County prosecutor paid no attention to him. In March, 1836, Horner went to Wisconsin and was appointed secretary of that territory.

The constitution signed on June 24, 1835, provided that it should be laid before the people for ratification on October 5, and that an election of state officers and of a representative to Congress be held on the same day. The voters ratified the constitution and elected Mason governor, Edward Mundy lieutenant governor, and Isaac E. Crary United States representative. When the legislature met, the two houses chose Lucius Lyon and John Norvell as Michigan's first senators. Representatives and senators went to Washington and presented their credentials, but Congress refused to admit them. Although Mason called himself governor of the State of Michigan, the state could not enter the Union without the consent of Congress.

At the time, because both the North and the South wanted to keep an equal balance in the Senate, two states were always admitted together, one slave and the other free. Arkansas was asking for admission, and she was paired with Michigan.

When the question of Michigan's admission was raised, Ohio insisted that the boundary must be drawn according to her specification. Lyon, Norvell, and Crary could only sit as spectators and listen to the oral attacks on their state delivered by Ohio men. Lyon believed that Michigan should have compensation in the North, and he urged this solution informally upon senators and representatives.

A bill establishing the Harris Line as the southern boundary and a line along the Menominee and Montreal rivers as the western boundary was passed by the Senate in March, 1836, and sent to the House. The western portion of the Upper Peninsula was attached to Michigan as indemnity for the loss of the Toledo Strip.

An act to establish Wisconsin Territory with the Menominee-Montreal River line as its northeastern boundary was approved on April 20, 1836, but the debate on the Michigan bill continued. Ohio was determined that Michigan should specifically accept the Harris Line, and so the bill contained the provision that Michigan would be admitted only after a majority of delegates elected by the people to a convention for that sole purpose should give their consent. This bill was passed and signed by the President on June 15, 1836, when he signed also an act to admit Arkansas, which became Michigan's twin state.

When news that the law had been approved reached Michigan, bitter attacks were made on the terms it contained. The Upper Peninsula was characterized as "the sterile region on the shores of Lake Superior, destined by soil and climate to remain forever a wilderness." The editor of the *Free Press* called it "the region of perpetual snows—the ultima Thule of our national domain on the North," and Lucius Lyon suggested, "there we can raise our own Indians in all time to come and supply ourselves now and then with a little bear meat for a delicacy."

Complaints, of course, were of no avail, and the Legislature, obeying the demand of Congress, directed that the people elect delegates, who should meet in Ann Arbor on September 26. Governor Mason, who had so vigorously fought for the Toledo Strip, now advised the people to accept the terms required by Congress. Senator Lyon changed his mind and predicted that the Upper Peninsula in twenty years would be worth $40,000,000, and someone else expressed the opinion that "the whitefish of Lake Superior might be a fair offset for the lost bull-frog pastures of the Maumee." Whigs and conservative Democrats, however, bitterly opposed submission to Congress and urged the people to elect delegates who would vote "No" at the convention.

The Upper Peninsula, unwanted by Michigan, was greatly desired by the people west of Lake Michigan. Since 1829 they had petitioned Congress to establish the Territory of Huron, which would include the area south of Lake Superior. Many of the people in Michilimackinac and Chippewa counties preferred to be in the proposed Huron Territory. Petitions to Congress from Sault Sainte Marie complained that it was cut off from Detroit for six months of the year and that the government of Michigan had treated the northern region as a remote and neglected colony. Congress paid no attention to these pleas.

When the Convention of Assent, as it was called, met in Ann Arbor on September 26, it was soon discovered that a majority of the delegates were dissenters. After several days of angry debate, the delegates voted twenty-eight to twenty-one to reject the demand of Congress. They adjourned on September 30.

This decision expressed the resentment of Michigan people against Congress and Ohio, but it brought the state no nearer admission to the Union. Everyone realized that eventually assent would have to be given. Besides, there were practical reasons for entering the Union as quickly as possible. A surplus in the United States Treasury was to be divided among the states; territories would receive nothing. Then, too, Congress had promised to give Michigan 5 per cent of the net proceeds from the sale of public lands within her boundaries after she became a state.

These were strong inducements, and politicians who expected to be appointed to fill national offices in the state used their influence for assent. Governor Mason suggested another convention. The Democratic party organization urged the people in each county to elect favorably disposed delegates to a convention. This was done, the dissenters refusing to take part in what they called an illegal election. Monroe County, which was especially bitter over the loss of the Toledo Strip, elected no delegates.

On December 14, 1836, the second Convention of Assent met in Ann Arbor. After declaring that Congress had no constitutional right to require assent, the delegates decided, in the interest of Michigan and as proof of her desire for harmony among the states, to assent to the boundaries prescribed. They drafted a letter to the President reporting the decision of the people of Michigan.

Although the dissenters throughout the state jeered at the action of the delegates and, because of the bitter cold weather, nicknamed the meeting the Frostbitten Convention, the action was generally accepted as inevitable. President Jackson sent the report of the Convention to Congress with a recommendation that it be accepted. After several days of heated debate, a bill to admit Michigan was passed by both houses. It was signed by President Jackson on January 26, 1837. At last Michigan was a state within the Union, and a new star appeared in the flag.

Wildcats, Railroads, and Patriots

F. CLEVER BALD

When Michigan became a state in 1837, the population was about 175,000. There were still many descendants of the French Canadians, but the majority of the inhabitants had come from New England and New York. Immigrants directly from Europe had not yet become numerous, but some Germans and Irish had already settled in the state. Twenty-two counties had been organized, all, except Mackinac and Chippewa, in the Lower Peninsula. Only the two southernmost tiers of counties were complete in 1837, but by 1840 two more were filled out, and Saginaw County was the first in the fifth tier.

Plenty of land was available for settlement, for, by treaties with the Indians, all except the western half of the Upper Peninsula had been acquired by the United States Government. The remainder was purchased in 1842. The land was surveyed and offered for sale at United States land offices within the state. Some settlers, without funds to purchase or unwilling to wait until attractive sites were placed on sale, occupied what they wanted as squatters.

Although most of the land belonged to the United States, the state also owned a considerable area. Section Sixteen of each township, by act of Congress, was conveyed to the State for the support of schools, and seventy-two sections were given to aid in establishing a university. In addition, Congress gave Michigan five sections to help defray the cost of erecting public buildings and seventy-two sections where there were salt springs. Congress also promised that 5 per cent of the net proceeds from the sale of public lands within its boundaries would be given to the state.

Besides all this, Michigan expected to receive an immediate gift of hard cash. In 1835 the national debt had been paid in full, and a surplus had begun to accumulate in the United States Treasury. Embarrassed by this unusual circumstance, Congress directed that all money over $5,000,000 in the Treasury on January 1, 1837, should be apportioned among the states according to their representation in the Electoral College and distributed as an indefinite loan in quarterly installments. Michigan received $95,000 as the first installment, and two more were paid before the law was repealed in the fall of 1837 at the request of President Martin Van Buren.

From *Michigan in Four Centuries* (New York: Harper and Row, 1954), pp. 205-210. Partially reprinted by permission of the History Division, Michigan Department of State. Footnotes in the original have been omitted.

An important natural advantage was Michigan's location in the heart of the Great Lakes region. The greater part of the outer boundary of the state was easily accessible by sailing vessels and steamships, and some of the rivers were navigable for a considerable distance inland. A steamer built at Grand Rapids in 1837 plied the Grand River between Lake Michigan and her home port, and other steamers were launched later.

By 1837 roads radiating from Detroit had been built to Chicago, to Toledo, to Flint, to Port Huron, and to Howell. There was also a highway from Monroe to Tecumseh, and the Territorial Road extended from Dearborn through Ann Arbor, Jackson, and Kalamazoo to St. Joseph on Lake Michigan.

The wealth of Michigan when it became a state was principally in agriculture. Lumbering had scarcely begun, and the fabulously rich deposits of copper and iron had not yet been discovered. There was, however, great prosperity. Money was plentiful, especially paper money, and during 1836 the sales of land by the United States at its offices in Detroit, Monroe, Kalamazoo, Flint, and Ionia had been greater than those in any other state. More than four million acres, one fourth of all the land sold in that year by all United States land offices, were sold in Michigan. Much was bought in large tracts to be held for future sale, for prices were rising.

Stevens T. Mason, the first governor of Michigan, was inaugurated on November 3, 1835. Young, enthusiastic, and affable, he was very popular. A patrician by inheritance, in politics he was a Democrat, and he was democratic in his concern for the general welfare. His message to the Legislature in January, 1837, contained recommendations for the enactment of laws on a number of important matters which he believed were necessary for the prosperity of Michigan. The newspapers supported the governor's program, and the Legislature enacted his recommendations into laws.

One important act created the office of state geologist and provided for a geological survey. The governor appointed Dr. Douglass Houghton, a brilliant young physician of Detroit, to this post. Dr. Houghton had come to Detroit in 1830 at the invitation of Governor Cass and others to deliver lectures on chemistry and geology. Although not yet twenty-one, he was a graduate of Rensselaer Polytechnic Institute and a member of its faculty. He also had been admitted to practice as a physician in New York.

His sponsors, who knew him only by reputation, were at first doubtful when they saw his youthful face and short stature. Their doubts soon vanished when they came to know him. A brilliant lecturer, a skilled physician, and a friendly person, Douglass

Houghton quickly charmed everyone he met. He decided to stay in Detroit.

That he was hardy enough to endure rough living he soon proved by accompanying Henry R. Schoolcraft in 1831 on an expedition to Lake Superior and in 1832 to discover the source of the Mississippi River. Serving as physician and botanist, he had opportunities to examine the Upper Peninsula.

As state geologist, Houghton's first exploration resulted in the discovery of salt beds in the Saginaw River valley. His most important work, however, was accomplished in the Upper Peninsula, where, in 1840, he located some of the principal copper deposits, which he reported in February, 1841.

Dr. Houghton was appointed professor of chemistry, zoology, and mineralogy in the University of Michigan in 1839. Although his duties as geologist prevented him from teaching classes, he provided many specimens for the mineral collection of the University.

In 1842 Dr. Houghton was elected mayor of Detroit. In spite of his manifold duties he had taken an active interest in improving the school system, and while he was mayor he was also president of the board of education. He had supported Dr. Zina Pitcher in his fight for tax-supported schools, and it was during his year of office that the first free public schools in Detroit and in Michigan were set in operation.

At Dr. Houghton's suggestion the state geological survey and the United States land survey were carried on co-operatively, beginning in 1844. On September 19 of that year, William A. Burt, a deputy surveyor, looking for the cause of the remarkable deviation of the compass needle, discovered a rich deposit of iron ore on the site of the present city of Negaunee.

Governor Mason on March 20, 1837, signed an act of the Legislature providing for the organization of common schools. This act was based on the report of the first superintendent of public instruction. In July, 1836, Governor Mason had appointed the Reverend John D. Pierce to this office on the recommendation of Representative Isaac E. Crary. While living in Marshall the two men had studied a report on the Prussian school system, which they believed was the best, and Crary knew that Pierce had sound ideas.

Immediately after his appointment Pierce journeyed East and conferred with leaders in education about a school plan for Michigan. On his return he wrote a comprehensive report which laid down in detail a system which included primary schools, a university, and branches of the university as intermediate institutions.

According to his plan, the schools and the university were to be free and supported by taxes. The law passed by the Legislature provided for schools in each district. No compulsion was attempted, but some financial assistance from the state was promised. Needless to say, free schools did not come at once, nor for many years; but Pierce's plan was an ideal which was finally reached and surpassed.

Through the efforts of Representative Crary in Washington, Congress gave the sixteenth section in each township to the state, instead of to each township, for the benefit of all the schools. These sections were placed in the hands of the superintendent of public instruction, and proceeds from their sale were put into the permanent primary school fund. Interest on the money in this fund was distributed to school districts.

The Legislature selected Ann Arbor as the seat of the state University, chiefly because a local land company offered forty acres free of charge. The law establishing the University followed closely the plan drawn by the Reverend John D. Pierce, a part of his report on a system of education for the state. The University was to have three departments—literature, science, and the arts, law, and medicine—and the governing body was a Board of Regents composed of twelve men appointed by the governor, who was ex-officio president of the Board, the lieutenant governor, the three judges of the supreme court, and the chancellor of the state. The seventy-two sections of land which previously had been granted by Congress were placed in the hands of a commissioner. Eventually they were sold for $547,000.

Four faculty residences and a combination dormitory, chapel, museum, library, and classroom building were erected, and the University opened in the fall of 1841 with two professors and six students. As the University was to be supported by the state, each student paid only an entrance fee of $10. Besides, he was charged $7.50 a year rent for his room. He made his own arrangements for board with a family in the town at a cost of $1.50 or $2 a week.

Student life in the University was very different then than now. The students lived in the building which later was called Mason Hall. Two shared a study, and each had his own bedroom opening into it. The boys chopped their own firewood and carried it up two or three flights of stairs. They swept the dirt from the floor out into the hall where it was gathered up by the janitor, Patrick Kelly, nicknamed "Professor of Dust and Ashes."

Every morning there was a compulsory chapel, at 5:30 in spring and fall, and at 6:30 in the winter. Afterward the students attended a recitation before going to breakfast at a boardinghouse in the town. On Sunday they were required to attend one of the Ann Arbor churches. The number of students increased from the original six to eighty-nine in 1857.

The first two professors were the Reverend George P. Williams and the Reverend Joseph Whiting. Others were added as more students enrolled. Although the University was a state institution, for many years a large proportion of the faculty members were Protestant ministers.

The same law which provided for the University authorized the Regents to establish branches to serve as preparatory schools for the University and train teachers for the common schools of the state. Nine branches—in Pontiac, Monroe, Kalamazoo, Detroit, Niles, White Pigeon, Tecumseh, Romeo, and Ann Arbor—came under the control of the Regents, who gave them some financial support. Most of these schools had been organized earlier as local academies. Because the sale of University lands did not provide as much money as had been expected, support was gradually withdrawn from the branches, and no funds were granted after 1846. Some of the branches, nevertheless, continued as academies.

A member of Douglas Houghton's geological survey party, statewide traveler and observer, Bela Hubbard published his frequently consulted *Memorials of a Half-Century* in 1887. Quite reliably Hubbard describes the people, events, and geography of early Michigan in rich detail. His comments, reproduced below, on land speculation, boom towns, and "wildcat" banks have been corroborated by other first-hand observers such as Alpheus Felch in "Early Banks and Banking in Michigan," *Michigan Pioneer and Historical Collections*, II (1880), and later in the same series by Henry M. Utley, "The Wildcat Banking System in Michigan," V (1884).

A Time of Universal Prosperity, and What Came of It

BELA HUBBARD

From *Memorials of a Half-Century* (New York: G. P. Putnam's Sons, 1887), pp. 93-105.

The years 1835, 1836 and 1837 were to Michigan one of those "periods of unexampled prosperity" with which our country has been periodically favored. In its character and results no better example has occurred in our history. This prosperous condition had begun to manifest itself in the extraordinary demand for wild lands, and in the sudden appreciation of the immense advantages possessed by a great number of places in the "West," and particularly in newly opened Michigan, for the building up of large cities. That the Peninsula possessed unequalled "water privileges" could not be doubted by any one who recognized its position on the map of the United States, almost surrounded by the waters of the Great Lakes. Interior lakes, too, were numerous, and large and rapid streams everywhere intersected the land. At least this was the case so far as the country was known, for the Government surveys had extended over not more than one-third of its surface. These surveys had opened to sale, at the low price of one dollar and twenty-five cents per acre, a most beautiful and varied country of "oak-openings" and timbered lands, with occasional small rolling prairies, all interspersed with lakes and streams. What a mine of wealth lay in a few thousand, or even a few hundred acres of such lands at the low price of a dollar and a quarter per acre!

From the very beginning of the period we are considering, and even before, a steady stream of immigration had begun to pour into the territory. It consisted mostly of people of means and respectability from the older States, led by the prospect of cheaper lands. Wagons loaded with household goods and surmounted by a live freight of women and children—the men trudging on foot—were constantly entering by the almost only door, Detroit, in great numbers, bound for some paradise in the new Eldorado. A curious spectacle at one time presented itself—literally a *drove* of men— Frenchmen from lower Canada—taken on by an adventurer to be settled upon the River St. Joseph, at the mouth of which, in the olden time, their countrymen had built a "fort" among the savages. Each had his pack, bound up in a blanket, upon his shoulders, and the baggage followed in a wagon; for the United States Government had opened a road in that direction, leading from Detroit to Chicago.

Men who never before saw a wilderness were tempted to set forth, on horseback and on foot, in the spirit which prompted so many gentlemen adventurers, in the early settlement of the New World, to swell the ranks of the colonists—the prospect of speedy and golden fortunes. The numbers that crowded to the search soon converted the ordinary slow process into a race.

Three land-offices had been opened by the Government in Michigan—one at Detroit, one at Monroe, another near the western extremity of the known portion of the territory at Kalamazoo, then called Bronson. The strife and eagerness which prevailed at these offices passed all sober bounds. They were besieged long before the hour arrived for opening; crowds of anxious faces gathered about the doors and blocked up the windows, each eager to make "entry" of some splendid tract of farming land, or better still, some magnificent site for a town, before an equally greedy speculator should discover and pounce upon the treasure.

One of these land-lookers, who had been for days traversing the woods and "taking notes," if he chanced to fall in with some one who was suspected of having seen the coveted tract, secretly hurried off, in the dead of night, determined to steal a march upon the others and secure the prize. Often, after an exhausting ride and a still more tedious waiting for his turn, he obtained his chance at the window, only to learn that a more wary applicant had been beforehand with him. What exultation if he found himself in time! What execration upon his ill fate if too late!

At the hotels were gathered animated crowds, from all quarters of the country, of speculators in lands. Every one who had secured some fortunate entry was busily proclaiming his good luck, and calculating his gains. The less fortunate, and those who were unable to convert themselves into woodsmen, were satisfied to take the accounts of others on trust, and buy at second hand, of course at a very large advance, expecting in their turn to realize a handsome increase.

Beautifully engraved maps of new city plots were executed in all haste, on which the contemplated improvements were laid down. Hotels, warehouses and banks were here erected, like palaces in fairy land; piers projected into the harbors, and steam-boats were seen entering. Wherever a crowd could be collected auctioneers were knocking down lots to eager buyers, and happy was he who secured one with a "fine water privilege," at a price a thousand fold beyond its first cost of a few days before. Nor were these improvements all upon paper. In an incredibly short time small clearings had been effected, a town plat surveyed—often half a hundred miles from the nearest actual settler—and shingle palaces arose in the wilderness, or amid the burned stumps that were left for time to remove. Prominent among these, and often the only buildings erected preliminary to the sale of lots, were a hotel and a bank.

At the admission of Michigan into the Union, in 1836, the territory contained fifteen chartered banks, with a population estimated at nearly one hundred and fifty thousand. These banks were all authorized to issue "currency." Why should these few enjoy a monopoly of so good a thing as money, which benefited all alike, and of which there could not be too much? Consequently one of the first acts of the new State government, March, 1837, was to pass a general banking law. Thus by a bold stroke monopoly was abolished, while bill-holders were made exceptionally secure by a pledge of real estate. Of this everybody held large quantities, and nothing had proved so convertible. Confidence in it was unbounded. Of course every proprietor of a "city" started a bank.

These became so numerous that money was one of the most plentiful of commodities. The new currency was made redeemable in gold and silver, and every bank was required to keep in its vaults thirty per cent of its circulation in the precious metals. When to these precautions was added the real estate, pledged for the redemption of the bills, and the whole placed under the supervision of commissioners specially appointed, and who were to visit and examine the banks every few months, could reasonable man ask for more ample security?

The banks of Eastern States, also, had a large circulation in the West, and they expanded to the full extent of their powers. The effect of such rapid increase of the circulating medium was to enhance prices of all commodities, and to stimulate speculation. Money became flush in every pocket, and all who had "the fever"— and few had not—were anxious to invest and own one or more of these farms and city lots that were held at such high value, and were making every holder rich. Poor women, who had accumulated a little spare cash, widows and sewing girls, were only too thankful when some kind friend volunteered to put them in the way of realizing some such fortunate investment. The southern counties of Michigan were speedily bought up, and the Government surveys were not rapid enough to satisfy the greed.

Stimulated by the abounding sunshine, the State, too, had entered the arena, in its official capacity, and undertaken a vast system of internal improvements, for which its bonds were outstanding to the amount of five million dollars. But already storm-clouds were gathering, which were soon to darken the whole heavens. As a ship, which for many days has sailed gallantly on its course under favoring winds, with all of its canvas spread, is forced to take in sail when a shift of the wind threatens a gale, so the banks, which had so greatly "expanded" in the breezes of universal prosperity, found it necessary to "contract" at the first suspicion of a change. Suddenly the storm fell. At the first demand to realize for their bills in specie, the banks were compelled to call in their circulation. As the whole amount of specie in the country was far below the amount of paper in circulation, many banks broke under the large demand which fell upon them as soon as the public became suspicious of their ability to pay. All were forced to contract their loans, and money was rapidly being called in, instead of being liberally paid out as before.

Money speedily became "tight." As few banks were able to sustain the pressure, it became necessary, in the view of the public authorities, to exercise the power, where it existed, to suspend specie payments. Accordingly an act was passed to that effect by the State Legislature, which was summoned for that purpose by the governor, June, 1837, only three months after the passage of the general banking law. It was thus hoped to tide over the pressure, which was believed to be but temporary.

Prior to the passage of this act, about twenty banks had registered and gone into operation under the general law. As the act did not repeal this law, many more took advantage of the privilege afforded by it of issuing irredeemable paper; so that before the inevitable end came no less than fifty banks were scattering their worthless notes as far and as widely as means could be found to effect it. But the end was close at hand. Prices fell with as magical a facility as they had risen. The real estate security of the new banks, which was supposed to be so stable, was suddenly found to be the weakest security possible. In the matter of the percentage of specie required to be kept in the vaults, it was found that the grossest frauds had been practised. Kegs filled with nails and broken glass, and having only an upper layer of coin, had been substituted in many instances, and were passed as genuine. In other cases, one institution loaned temporarily to another that was about to receive a visit from the commissioners, and the favor was reciprocated when its turn came. One by one, in rapid succession, the banks toppled to the earth, from which, like mushrooms, they had sprung, as it were, in a night. They were known universally under the name of "wildcats." The most worthless were styled "red-dog." The bills fell to a mere nominal value, or greatly depreciated, as it became known that the real estate held would suffice to redeem only a small fraction of the circulation. Much of this was found to be of no value whatever, as it represented merely swindling operations. Many a poor man thus lost all his available means of livelihood.

. . . .

One of the Michigan banks had gained an unusual share of notoriety, under the name of "The Bank of Sandstone." It was "located" at a place of that name, situated in the central part of the State, where quarries of a fine grit-stone had recently been opened.

These constituted the entire commerce of the little burg, and the solid corner-stone of the new institution, whose promises to pay were in wide circulation. An old resident of Michigan held a large quantity of these bills, and learning that the bank was "broke," came to my informant, in great distress, for advice. He was advised to go immediately to Sandstone and demand redemption, as it was understood the bank had some means, and the usual way was "first come, first served." The advice was followed. The man, on his return, called on his adviser, who inquired after his success, and was assured that it was quite complete. "I presented my roll," said he, "and was paid as follows: For every ten-dollar bill, a millstone; for every five-dollar, a grindstone, and for every one-dollar bill a whetstone!"

The year 1838 saw as "hard times" in Michigan as the two previous years had witnessed a seeming prosperity. Men of supposed large wealth, and who owned thousands of acres of wild lands, valued at hundreds of thousands of dollars, were unable to buy provision for their families, and knew not where to look for the supply of their daily wants. Farmers had neglected to cultivate their farms in the struggle to amass land. The new cities, which the magic wand of speculation had created, were left without inhabitants. Trade was paralyzed for want of money, and prices fell below the old standard. To add to the depreciation of real estate, a strong feeling arose among the actual settlers against non-resident proprietors. These were called "speculators," and many contrivances were resorted to to throw on them the burden of taxation. Thus, in opening new roads, the resident was permitted to work out his tax, at an easy rate, by an understanding with the overseers, while the law compelled the non-resident to pay a higher rate in money. Under the name of school-houses, large edifices were built and used for town-meetings and religious worship. The non-resident landowner was charged with keeping out settlers by raising the price of land, in forgetfulness of the fact that the very tide of speculation had been the means of opening up the country to future settlement. Land which had constituted the sole wealth of thousands became a drug. Large tracts were frequently abandoned to the tax-gatherer for a sum which a few years previous would not have bought a single acre. The banks did not outlive the destruction of the wealth they had fictitiously created. In two years from the act which gave them birth, it is believed, not a "wild-cat" nor "red-dog" of them all was in existence. But they left from one to two millions of dollars of their worthless bills in the hands of creditors. Four or five chartered banks only survived, and they proved fully sufficient for the wants of the population for years to come.

The year following the crash of 1838, the writer had occasion to visit the *ruins* of several of those renowned cities that had flourished so magnificently—on paper. One of these was situated on a small stream which discharged into Lake Michigan. Most of the streams on this side of the Peninsula have lakes near their outlets, originating in the setting back of the water, occasioned by the sand-bars at their mouths. These lakes are often large and deep enough for very fine harbors, but which can be made available only by the construction of piers.

The village of Port Sheldon was "located" at the outlet of one of these streams—the smallest of its kind, and without depth of water sufficient for a harbor. But one road led to it from the nearest and still distant settlement. It was in the midst of a tall forest of pines and other timber, very few of which had been cut away. The clearing disclosed a large frame building, handsomely finished outwardly, but a mere barn within, and by its side a smaller one, decorated with Grecian pillars. These were the hotel and the bank. And they were the only buildings in the place, if we except a few shanties scarcely decent for the abode of the most poverty-stricken. The bank had collapsed; the hotel was without guests; the splendid bubble had burst, and its brilliance vanished suddenly and forever. In 1865 the whole town plat, consisting of two hundred acres of very poor land, was sold for a petty sum. The long abandoned and desolate site, of which its projectors had published with prophetic foresight so many years before—"Nature seems to have done almost everything for this point, and the time is at hand when her eminent advantages will lift her to the first rank among our cities of the lakes"—was now the owlish abode of a solitary Dutchman.

Another of these town sites, which had made a great noise, was situated near the mouth of Maumee Bay of Lake Erie. It was on low, marshy land, which had been regularly laid out in streets and some twenty or more buildings erected. The high water of 1838 had converted into a marsh the whole site. All the buildings were deserted and the city was without an inhabitant. Two of the houses were pointed out—among the handsomest in the place—that had been built by poor milliner girls, who had invested in them all their earnings. They could not be approached, except by boat. This was the Port of Havre, the rival of its namesake, in the dreams of its founders and of their credulous victims, for one short year, before the waters of desolation swept away its glories.

One of the first found and most famous sites was "White-rock City." It was upon the shore of Lake Huron, at the mouth of a pretty rivulet. Maps of this "city" had been scattered far and wide, and lots sold and resold at fabulous prices. These maps represented a large and flourishing town upon a magnificent river. Piers projected into the harbor, which was filled with steam-boats, and it was evident that a thriving commerce had begun. I visited this place, during a coasting voyage, in the fall of 1837. The only approach was by the lake, for it was far removed from any road and forty miles from the nearest inhabitant, except a solitary backwoodsman. A large boulder rock in the lake marked the "harbor." The "river" was insufficient for the entrance of our log canoe. An unbroken and unsurveyed forest covered the whole site. We could not find even a solitary ruin standing alone, like that at Heliopolis, in the Egyptian desert, to mark the place of departed grandeur.

At a few of the really "eligible" sites thriving villages have since sprung up, the Government having aided to build harbors, or natural advantages existing. But most of these town sites still retain their valuable privileges unimproved, and their owners have either abandoned hope, or continue to pay taxes on some undivided one-hundredth part of a fractional "forty," purchased at city prices, that is not even marketable as farming land.

The financial reverses of 1838 were followed by another calamity, which added greatly to the distress of the settled population of the State. The season of 1839 proved very sickly. Among the permanent improvements made during flush times were numerous mills, almost every one of which formed a nucleus for a settlement. No labor or thought had been bestowed upon clearing the stumps and fallen timber from the mill ponds, and this proved a formidable source of malaria.

In the fall of that year I passed through many hamlets, and even considerable villages, where a quarter part of the population were down with fever and ague. I had often to ride miles beyond my intended resting-place, because at the tavern where I applied the family were too ill to wait upon me. At others I was enabled to find supper and a bed for myself, but had to seek accommodation for my horse where I could find it. Having myself had a touch of the ague, I carried a stock of quinine in my saddle-bags. These old-fashioned appurtenances sometimes caused me to be hailed as "doctor." On one of these occasions, finding what was the medicine required, I did not hesitate to allow the mistake to go uncorrected, made the professional visit, administered the pills, but, undoctor-like, departed without my fee.

Reaching Monroe late one evening, I anticipated no difficulty in finding comfortable quarters, for this place was, in name, at least, a city, and second only in importance to Detroit. As I entered the street, I overheard a conversation, in which occurred the not very comforting remark—"Tom, you must make the next coffin; I have worked myself almost to death at it the last week." Even in this old city it was only after much trouble that I succeeded in quartering myself in one place and my beast in another.

Most persons only laughed at those who were so unfortunate as to be seized with "fever and ager," as the popular term was for this diresome disease, as if it were a matter of course that every one must have his turn at shaking like a lamb's tail. The rival cities of Monroe and Toledo were constantly bantering each other upon the insalubrity of their neighbor's location. But this year the subject was one almost too serious for joking. Who has not noticed that we are often most inclined to make merry when we have greatest cause for sadness? So jokes carried the day. Saw-mills were spoken of as driven by fever-and-ague power. Villages were told of where the church bells were rung every half hour to mark the time for taking the inevitable quinine. On one occasion, a traveller is said to have entered a village and searched in vain for a tavern. He found the streets deserted and grass-grown. At last he followed the one which showed the most marks of travel, and it led him to—the graveyard.

2: Pioneer Life and Settlement

Although best known to Americans for his *Democracy in America* (1835), Alexis De Tocqueville wrote additional observations about the New World in *Memoirs, Letters and Remains of Alexis De Tocqueville* (Boston, 1862). In this later book, Tocqueville recorded impressions of his Michigan excursion to Pontiac and Saginaw at a time when these areas were little more than clustered shanties occupied by Indian traders, trappers, and land agents. His reports of the white settlers' ambitious efforts at land speculation and his vividly detailed portrayals of forest scenery, including its furtive native inhabitants, are among the best available.

From a literary viewpoint Tocqueville's *Memoirs* is flawed by an attempt to record the dialog of Pontiac's early residents in language more suitable to a Boston dinner party than a smoky hovel occupied by virtually illiterate frontiersmen. He romanticized where Caroline Kirkland recorded the laconic or grammatically blemished frontier dialog honestly.

Kirkland, a well-educated woman from New York, joined her husband in his speculative efforts at town development in Michigan. In lengthy letters (subsequently published in book form) to her eastern friends, she described the toils of travel, settlement, and domestic life in "Montacute," a pseudonym for Pinkney, Michigan. Her portrayals of local social behavior, in churches, homes, and the marketplace, are Kirkland's best contribution to the historian, and although her own moral judgments become obvious, she avoids the long-winded sermonic tendencies of her contemporary, James Fenimore Cooper.

Kirkland did not hesitate to record what was totally unappealing in "Montacute," but she balanced her account with sympathetic character sketches of many honest and reliable neighbors. Most remarkably, she kept humor on her sleeve, and the whole volume is, for the reader, an unlabored delight.

There is a considerable body of travel literature treating Michigan's early days, and this material includes Lansing Swan's *A Trip Through Michigan in 1841* (Rochester, 1904), as well as Charles F. Hoffman's *A Winter in the West* (Ann Arbor, 1966). In addition, a larger mass of manuscript material—diaries, day books, and letters—can be consulted in the several good manuscript libraries of Michigan.

A Fortnight in the Wilderness

ALEXIS DE TOCQUEVILLE

We did not reach Pontiac till after sunset.* Twenty very neat and pretty houses, forming so many well-provided shops, a transparent brook, a clearing of about a square half-mile surrounded by the boundless forest: this is an exact picture of Pontiac, which in twenty years hence may be a city. The sight of this place recalled to me what M. Gallatin had said to me a month before in New York: "There are no villages in America, at least, in your meaning of the word. The houses of the cultivators are scattered all over the fields.The inhabitants congregate only in order to set up a sort of market to supply the surrounding population. In these so called villages you find none but lawyers, printers, and shopkeepers."

We were taken to the best inn in Pontiac (for there are two), and as usual we were introduced into the barroom; here all, from the most opulent to the humblest shopkeeper, assemble to smoke, think, and talk politics on the footing of the most perfect equality. The owner of the house, or rather the landlord, was, I must not say a burly peasant, for there are no peasants in America, but at any rate a very stout gentleman, whose face had about as much of frankness and simplicity as that of a Norman horse-dealer. This man, for fear of intimidating you, never looked you in the face when he spoke, but waited till you were engaged in talking with some one else to consider you at his leisure; he was a deep politician, and, according to American habits, a pitiless querist. They all looked at us at first with surprise; our travelling dress and our guns proved that we were not traders, and travelling for curiosity was a thing never heard of. In order to avoid explanations, we declared at starting, that we came to buy land. The word had scarcely escaped us, when we discovered that in trying to avoid one evil, we had incurred another still more formidable.

They ceased, indeed, to treat us like extraordinary animals, but each wanted to bargain with us. To get rid of them and their farms, we told our host that before deciding on anything we wished to obtain from him useful information on the price of land, and the course of cultivation. He instantly took us into another apartment, spread out with due solemnity a map of Michigan on the oaken table in the middle of the room, and placing the candle before us, waited in silence for our inquiries. Though the reader has no

*Gustave de Beaumont traveled with Alexis de Tocqueville.
From *Memoirs, Letters and Remains of Alexis De Tocqueville* (Boston: Ticknor and Fields, 1862), pp. 156-187. Written on board the steamboat *Tuperion* in 1831.

intention of settling in an American wilderness, he may perhaps be curious to know how the thousands of Europeans and Americans who every year seek a home in this country, set about it. I shall therefore transcribe the information afforded by our host in Pontiac. We often afterwards had occasion to verify its accuracy.

"This country is not like France," said our host, after listening quietly to all our questions, and snuffing the candle. "With you labor is cheap, and land is dear. Here the price of land is nothing, but hands cannot be bought; I tell you this to show you that to settle in America as well as in Europe, one must have capital, only it must be differently employed. For my part, I should not advise any one to seek his fortune in our wilds, unless he has 150 or 200 dollars at his disposal. In Michigan, an acre never costs more than four or five shillings, when the land is waste. This is about the price of a day's work. In one day, therefore, a laborer may earn enough to purchase an acre. But the purchase made, the difficulty begins. This is the way in which we generally try to get over it.

"The settler betakes himself to his newly-acquired property with some cattle, a salted pig, two barrels of meal, and some tea. If there happens to be a hut near, he goes to it, and receives temporary hospitality. If not, he pitches his tent in the middle of the wood which is to be his field. His first care is to cut down the nearest trees; with them he quickly builds the rude log-house which you must have seen. With us, the keep of cattle costs nothing. The emigrant fastens an iron bell to their necks, and turns them into the forest. Animals thus left to themselves seldom stray far from the dwelling.

"The greatest expense is the clearing. If the pioneer brings with him a family able to help him in his first labors, the task is easy. But this is seldom the case. The emigrant is generally young, and if he has children they are small. He is therefore obliged either himself to supply all the wants of his family, or to hire the services of his neighbors. It costs from four to five dollars to clear an acre. The ground once prepared, the new owner lays out an acre in potatoes and the rest in wheat and maize. Maize is a providential gift in the wilderness; it grows in our marshes, and flourishes under the shade of the forest better than when exposed to the rays of the sun. Maize saves the emigrant's family from perishing, when poverty, sickness, or neglect has hindered his reclaiming sufficient land in the first year. The great difficulty is to get over the years which immediately succeed the first clearing. Afterwards comes competence, and later wealth."

. . . .

We resumed: "Do the ministrations of religion ever reach them?" "Very seldom. As yet we have not been able to set up public worship in our forest. Almost every summer, indeed, some Methodist ministers come to visit the new settlements. The news of their arrival spreads rapidly from dwelling to dwelling: it is the great event of the day. At the time fixed, the emigrant, with his wife and children, makes his way through the scarcely cleared paths in the forest towards the place of meeting. Settlers flock from fifty miles round. The congregation have no church to assemble in, they meet in the open air under the arches of the forest. A pulpit of rough logs, great trees cut down to serve as seats, such are the fittings of this rustic temple. The pioneers encamp with their families in the surrounding woods. Here for three days and nights, the people scarcely intermit their devotional exercises. You should see the fervent prayers and the deep attention of these men to the solemn words of the preacher. In the wilderness men are seized with a hunger for religion."

"One more question: among us it is generally thought that European emigration mainly peoples the deserts of America; how is it then that since we have been travelling in your forests we have not happened to meet a single European?" At these words, a smile of proud satisfaction spread over the countenance of our host.

"None but Americans," replied he solemnly, "are brave enough to submit to such privations, and are willing to pay such a price for competence. The European emigrant stops in the large towns of the seaboard, or in surrounding districts. There he becomes a mechanic, a laborer, or a servant. He leads an easier life than in Europe, and appears content that his children should follow his example. The American takes possession of the land, and tries to create out of it a great social position."

After pronouncing the last words, our host was silent. He let an immense column of smoke escape from his mouth, and seemed prepared to listen to what we had to tell him about our plans.

We first thanked him for his valuable information and wise counsels, assured him that some day we should profit by them, and added, "Before fixing in your country, my dear landlord, we intend to visit Saginaw, and we wish to consult you on this point." At the name of Saginaw, a remarkable change came over his features. It seemed as if he had been suddenly snatched from real life and transported to a land of wonders. His eyes dilated, his mouth fell open, and the most complete astonishment pervaded his countenance.

"You want to go to Saginaw!" exclaimed he; "to Saginaw Bay! Two foreign gentlemen, two rational men, want to go to Saginaw

Bay! It is scarcely credible." "And why not?" we replied. "But are you well aware," continued our host, "what you undertake? Do you know that Saginaw is the last inhabited spot towards the Pacific; that between this place and Saginaw lies an uncleared wilderness? Do you know that the forest is full of Indians and mosquitoes; that you must sleep at least for one night under the damp trees? Have you thought about the fever? Will you be able to get on in the wilderness, and to find your way in the labyrinth of our forests?"

After this tirade, he paused, in order to judge of the effect which he had produced. We replied: "All that may be true, but we start to-morrow for Saginaw Bay."

Our host reflected for an instant, shrugged his shoulders, and said slowly and positively, "Some paramount interest alone can induce two strangers to take such a step. No doubt you have a mistaken idea, that it is an advantage to fix as far as possible from any competition?"

We do not answer.

He continues: "Perhaps you are sent by the Canadian Fur Company to establish relations with the Indian tribes on the frontier?"

We maintain our silence.

Our host had come to an end of his conjectures, and he said no more; but he continued to muse on the strangeness of our scheme.

"Have you never been in Saginaw?" we resumed. "I," he answered, "I have been so unlucky as to go thither five or six times, but I had a motive for doing it, and you do not appear to have any." "But you forget, my worthy host, that we do not ask you if we had better go to Saginaw, but only how we can get there most easily."

Brought back thus to the matter in hand, our American recovered his presence of mind and the precision of his ideas. He explained to us in a few words and with excellent practical good sense how we should set about our journey through the wilderness, entered into the minutest details, and provided for every possible contingency. At the end of his recommendations he paused once more, to see if at length we should unfold the mystery of our journey, and perceiving that neither of us had anything more to say, he took the candle, showed us a bedroom, and after giving us a truly democratic shake of the hand, went to finish his evening in the common room.

. . . .

After we left Mr. Williams, we pursued our road through the woods. From time to time a little lake (this district is full of them) shines like a white tablecloth under the green branches. The charm of these lonely spots, as yet untenanted by man, and where peace and silence reign undisturbed, can hardly be imagined.

. . . .

Still travelling on, we reached a country of a different aspect. The ground was no longer flat, but thrown into hills and valleys. Nothing can be wilder than the appearance of some of these hills.

In one of these picturesque passes, we turned suddenly to contemplate the magnificent scene which we were leaving behind, and, to our great surprise, we saw close to us, and apparently following us step by step, a red Indian. He was a man of about thirty, tall, and admirably proportioned. His black and shining hair fell down upon his shoulders, with the exception of two tresses, which were fastened on the top of his head. His face was smeared with black and red paint. He wore a sort of very short blue blouse. His legs were covered with red *mittas,* a sort of pantaloon which reaches only to the top of the thigh, and his feet were defended by moccasins. At his side hung a knife. In his right hand he held a long rifle, and in his left two birds that he had just killed.

The first sight of this Indian made on us a far from agreeable impression. The spot was ill-suited for resisting an attack. On our right a forest of lofty pines; on our left a deep ravine, at the bottom of which a stream brawled among the rocks, hidden by the thick foliage, so that we approached it, as it were, blindfold! To seize our guns, turn round and face the Indian in the midst of the path was the affair of an instant. . . . He halted in the same manner, and for half a minute we all were silent.

His countenance presented the characteristics of the Indian race. In his deep black eyes sparkled the savage fire which still lights up those of the half-caste, and is not lost before two or three crossings of white blood. His nose was aquiline, slightly depressed at the end; his cheek-bones very high; and his wide mouth showed two rows of dazzling white teeth, proving that the savage, more cleanly than his neighbor, the American, did not pass his day in chewing tobacco-leaves.

I said, that when we turned round, arms in hand, the Indian stopped short. He stood our rapid scrutiny with perfect calmness, and with steady and unflinching eye. When he saw that we had no hostile intentions, he smiled: probably he perceived that we had been alarmed.

I never before had remarked how completely a mirthful expression changes the savage physiognomy; I have a hundred times since had occasion to notice it. An Indian grave and an Indian smiling are different men. In the motionless aspect of the former there is a savage majesty which inspires involuntary fear. But, if the same man smiles, his countenance takes an expression of simplicity and benevolence, which is really captivating.

When we saw our Indian thus unbend, we addressed him in English. He allowed us to talk as long as we liked, and then made signs that he did not understand us. We offered him brandy, which he readily accepted without thanking us. Still making signs, we asked him for the birds which he carried; he gave them to us for a little piece of money. Having made acquaintance, we bade him adieu, and trotted off.

A wilderness of forty miles separates Flint River from Saginaw, and the road is a narrow pathway, hardly perceivable. Our host* approved of our plan, and shortly brought us two Indians whom he assured us that we could perfectly trust. One was a boy of twelve or fourteen; the other a young man of eighteen. The frame of the latter, though it had not yet attained the vigor of maturity, gave the idea of agility united with strength. He was of middle height; his figure was tall and slender, his limbs flexible and well-proportioned. Long tresses fell from his bare head. He had also taken care to paint his face with black and red in symmetrical lines; a ring was passed through his nose, and a necklace and ear-rings completed his attire. His weapons were no less remarkable. At one side hung the celebrated tomahawk; on the other, a long sharp knife, with which the savages scalp their victims. Round his neck hung a cow-horn, containing his powder; and in his right hand he held a rifle. As is the case with most Indians, his eye was wild, and his smile benevolent. At his side, to complete the picture, trotted a dog, with upright ears and long nose, more like a fox than any other animal, with a look so savage as to be in perfect harmony with the countenance of his master.

After examining our new companion with an attention which he did not seem to notice, we asked him his price for the service that he was about to render to us. The Indian replied in a few words of his native tongue; and the American immediately informed us that what he asked was about equivalent to two dollars.

"As these poor Indians," charitably added our host, "do not understand the value of money, you will give the dollars to me, and I will willingly give him what they represent."

I was curious to see what this worthy man considered to be equal

---

*A trader located on the Flint River, or approximately half the distance between Pontiac and Saginaw.

to two dollars, and I followed him quietly to the place where the bargain was struck. I saw him give to our guide a pair of moccasins and a pocket-handkerchief, that certainly together did not amount to half the sum.

. . . .

As we proceeded, we gradually lost sight of the traces of man. Soon all proofs even of savage life disappeared, and before us was the scene that we had so long been seeking—a virgin forest.

Growing in the middle of the thin brushwood, through which objects are perceived at a considerable distance, was a single clump of full-grown trees, almost all pines or oaks. Confined to so narrow a space, and deprived of sunshine, each of these trees had run up rapidly, in search of air and light. As straight as the mast of a ship, the most rapid grower had overtopped every surrounding object; only when it had attained a higher region did it venture to spread out its branches, and clothe itself with leaves. Others followed quickly in this elevated sphere; and the whole group, interlacing their boughs, formed a sort of immense canopy. Underneath this damp, motionless vault, the scene is different.

Majesty and order are overhead—near the ground, all is chaos and confusion: aged trunks, incapable of supporting any longer their branches, are shattered in the middle, and present nothing but a sharp jagged point. Others, long loosened by the wind, have been thrown unbroken on the ground. Torn up from the earth, their roots form a natural barricade, behind which several men might easily find shelter. Huge trees, sustained by the surrounding branches, hang in mid-air, and fall into dust, without reaching the ground.

. . . .

We had been riding for five hours in complete ignorance of our whereabouts, when our Indians stopped short, and the elder, whose name was Sagan-Cuisco, traced a line in the sand. He showed us one end, exclaiming, *Michi, Conte-ouinque* (the Indian name for Flint River), and pointing to the other, pronounced the name of *Saginaw*. Then, marking a point in the middle, he signed to us that we had achieved half the distance, and that we must rest a little.

The sun was already high, and we should gladly have accepted his invitation, if we could have seen water within reach; but as none was near we motioned to the Indian that we wished to halt where we could eat and drink. He understood us directly, and set off with the same rapidity as before. An hour later he stopped again, and showed us a spot where we might find water about thirty paces off in the forest.

Without waiting for us to answer, or helping us to unsaddle our horses, he went to it himself; we followed as fast as we could. A little while before the wind had thrown down a large tree in this place; in the hollow that had been filled by the root was a little reservoir of rain-water. This was the fountain to which our guide conducted us, without the thought apparently having occurred to him that we should hesitate to partake of such a draught. We opened our bag. Another misfortune! The heat had entirely spoilt our provisions, and we found our dinner reduced to the small piece of bread, which was all that we had been able to procure at Flint River.

Add to this, a cloud of mosquitoes, attracted by the vicinity of water, which we were forced to fight with one hand while we carried our bread to our mouths with the other, and an idea may be formed of a rustic dinner in a virgin forest.

. . . .

At last night came. The air under the trees became damp, and icy cold. In the dark the forest assumed a new and terrible aspect. Our eyes could distinguish nothing but confused masses without shape or order; strange and disproportioned forms; the sort of fantastic images which haunt the imagination in fever. The echo of our steps had never seemed so loud, nor the silence of the forest so awful. The only sign of life in this sleeping world was the humming of the mosquito.

As we advanced the gloom became still deeper. Now and then a fire-fly traced a luminous line upon the darkness. Too late we acknowledged the wisdom of the Indian's advice; but it was no longer possible to recede.

We therefore pushed on as rapidly as our strength and the night permitted. At the end of an hour we left the woods, and entered a vast prairie. Our guides uttered three times a savage cry, that vibrated like the discordant notes of the *tam-tam*. It was answered in the distance. Five minutes afterwards we reached a stream; but it was too dark to see the opposite bank.

The Indians halted here. They wrapped their blankets round them, to escape the stings of mosquitoes; and hiding in the long grass, looked like balls of wool, that one might pass by without remarking and could not possibly suppose to be men.

We ourselves dismounted, and waited patiently for what was to follow. In a few minutes we heard a faint noise, and something approached the bank. It was an Indian canoe, about ten feet long, formed out of a single tree. The man who was curled up in the bottom of this frail bark wore the dress and had the appearance of an Indian. He spoke to our guides, who, by his direction, took the saddles from our horses, and placed them in the canoe.

As I was preparing to get into it, the supposed Indian touched me on the shoulder, and said, with a Norman accent which made me start,—

"Ah, you come from Old France! . . . stop—don't be in a hurry— people sometimes get drowned here."

If my horse had addressed me, I should not, I think, have been more astonished.

I looked at the speaker, whose face shone in the moonlight like a copper ball. "Who are you, then?" I said. "You speak French, but you look like an Indian." He replied, that he was a "Bois-brulé," which means the son of a Canadian and an Indian woman.

I shall often have occasion to mention this singular race of half-castes, which extends over all the frontiers of Canada, and, in fact, over the borders of the United States. At that time I felt only the pleasure of conversing in my mother-tongue.

Following the advice of my countryman, the savage, I seated myself in the bottom of the canoe, and kept as steady as possible; my horse, whose bridle I held, plunged into the water, and swam by my side, meanwhile the Canadian sculled the bark, singing in an undertone to an old French tune some verses, of which I caught only the first couplet,—

> "Between Paris and Saint Denis
> There lived a maid," &c.

We reached the opposite bank without any accident; the canoe immediately returned, to bring over my companion. All my life I shall remember the second time that it neared the shore. The moon, which was full, was just then rising over the prairie behind us, half the disk only appeared above the horizon; it looked like a mysterious door, through which we could catch a glimpse of the light of another world. Its rays were reflected in the stream, and touched the place where I stood. Along the line of their pale, tremulous light, the Indian canoe was advancing. We could not see any sculls, or hear the sound of rowlocks. The bark glided rapidly and smoothly—long, narrow, and black, resembling an alligator in pursuit of his prey. Crouching at the prow, Sagan-Cuisco, with his head between his knees, showed only his shiny tresses. Farther back, the Canadian was silently sculling, while behind followed Beaumont's horse, with his powerful chest throwing up the waters of the Saginaw in glittering streams.

In the whole scene there was a wild grandeur which made an impression upon us which has never been effaced.

. . . .

The village of Saginaw is the farthest point inhabited by Europeans to the north-west of the vast peninsula of Michigan. It may be considered as an advanced post; a sort of watch-tower, placed by the whites in the midst of the Indian nations.

European revolutions, the continual noisy clamor of politics, reach this spot only at rare intervals and as the echoes of a sound, the source of which the ear can no longer distinguish nor comprehend.

Sometimes an Indian stops on his journey to relate, in the poetical language of the desert, some of the sad realities of social life; sometimes a newspaper dropped out of a hunter's knapsack, or only the sort of indistinct rumor which spreads, one knows not how, and which seldom fails to tell that something strange is passing in the world.

Once a year a vessel steams up the Saginaw to join this stray link to the great European chain which now binds together the world. She carries to the new settlement the products of human industry, and in return takes away the fruits of the soil.

Thirty persons, men, women, old people, and children, at the time of our visit composed this little society, as yet scarcely formed—an opening seed thrown upon the desert, there to germinate.

Chance, interest, or inclination, had collected them in this narrow space. No common link existed between them, and they differed widely. Among them were Canadians, Americans, Indians, and half-castes.

Our New Home in the West

CAROLINE KIRKLAND

> *Mrs. Hardcastle.* I wish we were at home again. I never met so many

From *Our New Home in the West; or Early Glimpses of Life Among the Early Settlers* (New York: James Miller, 1872), pp. 53-58, 69-71, 107-109, 201-206.

accidents in so short a journey. Drenched in the mud, overturned in the ditch, jolted to a jelly, and at last to lose our way.

At length came the joyful news that our moveables had arrived in port; and provision was at once made for their transportation to the banks of the Turnip. But many and dire were the vexatious delays, thrust by the cruel Fates between us and the accomplishment of our plans; and it was not till after the lapse of several days that the most needful articles were selected and bestowed in a large wagon which was to pioneer the grand body. In this wagon had been reserved a seat for myself, since I had far too great an affection for my chairs and tables, to omit being present at their debarkation at Montacute, in order to insure their undisturbed possession of the usual complement of legs. And there were the children to be packed this time,—little roley-poley things, whom it would have been in vain to have marked, 'this side up,' like the rest of the baggage.

A convenient space must be contrived for my plants, among which were two or three tall geraniums, and an enormous calla ethiopica. Then D'Orsay must be accommodated, of course; and, to crown all, a large basket of live fowls; for we had been told that there were none to be purchased in the vicinity of Montacute. Besides these, there were all our travelling trunks; and an enormous square box crammed with articles which we then, in our greenness, considered indispensable. We have since learned better.

After this enumeration, which yet is only partial, it will not seem strange that the guide and director of our omnibus was to ride

'On horseback after we.'

He acted as a sort of adjutant—galloping forward to spy out the way, or provide accommodations for the troop—pacing close to the wheels to modify our arrangements, to console one of the imps who had bumped his pate, or to give D'Orsay a gentle hint with the riding-whip, when he made demonstrations of mutiny—and occasionally falling behind to pick up a stray handkerchief or parasol.

The roads near Detroit were inexpressibly bad. Many were the chances against our toppling load's preserving its equilibrium. To our inexperience, the risks seemed nothing less than tremendous—but the driver so often reiterated, 'that a'n't nothin',' in reply to our despairing exclamations, and, what was better, so constantly proved his words by passing the most frightful inequalities (Michiganicé, 'sidlings') in safety, that we soon became more confident, and ventured to think of something else besides the ruts and mud-holes.

Our stopping-places after the first day were of the ordinary new country class—the very coarsest accommodations by night and by day, and all at the dearest rate. When every body is buying land, and scarce anybody cultivating it, one must not expect to find living either good or cheap: but, I confess, I was surprised at the dearth of comforts which we observed everywhere. Neither milk, eggs, nor vegetables were to be had, and those who could not live on hard salt ham, stewed dried apples, and bread raised with 'salt risin,' would necessarily run some risk of starvation.

. . . .

The last two days of our slow journey were agreeably diversified with sudden and heavy showers, and intervals of overpowering sunshine. The weather had all the changefulness of April, with the torrid heat of July. Scarcely would we find shelter from the rain which had drenched us completely—when the sunshine would tempt us forth: and by the time all the outward gear was dried, and matters in readiness for a continuation of our progress, another threatening cloud would drive us back, though it never really rained till we started.

We had taken a newly-opened and somewhat lonely route this time, in deference to the opinion of those who ought to have known better, that this road from having been less travelled, would not be quite so *deep* as the other. As we went farther into the wilderness, the difficulties increased. The road had been but little 'worked,' (the expression in such cases,) and in some parts was almost in a state of nature. Where it wound around the edge of a marsh, where in future times there will be a bridge or drain, the wheels on one side would be on the dry ground, while the others were sinking in the long wet grass of the marsh—and in such places it was impossible to discern inequalities which yet might overturn us in an instant. In one case of this sort, we were obliged to dismount the 'live lumber'—as the man who helped us through phrased it, and let the loaded wagon pass on, while we followed in an empty one which was fortunately at hand—and it was, in my eyes, little short of a miracle that our skilful friend succeeded in piloting safely the top-heavy thing which seemed thrown completely off its centre half a dozen times.

At length we came to a dead stand. . . . There is but one resource in such cases. You must mount your remaining horse, if you have one, and ride on till you can find a farmer and one, two, or three pairs of oxen—and all this accomplished, you may generally hope for a release in time.

The interval seemed a *leetle* tedious, I confess. To sit for three mortal hours in an open wagon, under a hot sun, in the midst of a swamp, is not pleasant. The expanse of inky mud which spread around us, was hopeless, as to any attempt at getting ashore. I crept cautiously down the tongue, and tried one or two of the tempting green tufts, which looked as if they *might* afford foothold; but alas! they sank under the slightest pressure. So I was fain to regain my low chair, with its abundant cushions, and lose myself in a book. The children thought it fine fun for a little while, but then they began to want a drink. I never knew children who did not, when there was no water to be had.

There ran through the very midst of all this black pudding, as clear a stream as ever rippled, and the wagon stood almost in it!—but how to get at it? The basket which had contained, when we left the city, a store of cakes and oranges, which the children thought inexhaustible, held now nothing but the napkins, which had enveloped those departed joys, and those napkins, suspended corner-wise, and soaken long and often in the crystal water, served for business and pleasure, till papa came back.

'They're coming! They're coming!' was the cry, and with one word, over went Miss Alice, who had been reaching as far as she could, trying how large a portion of her napkin she could let float in the water.

Oh, the shrieks and the exclamations! how hard papa rode, and how hard mamma scolded! but the little witch got no harm beyond a thorough wetting, and a few streaks of black mud, and felt herself a heroine for the rest of the day.

. . . .

Behold me then seated on a box, in the midst of as anomalous a congregation of household goods as ever met under one roof in the backwoods, engaged in the seemingly hopeless task of calling order out of chaos, attempting occasionally to throw out a hint for the instruction of Mrs. Jennings, who uniformly replied by requesting me not to fret, as she knew what she was about.

Mr. Jennings, with the aid of his sons, undertook the release of the pent-up myriads of articles which crammed the boxes, many of which though ranked when they were put in as absolutely essential, seemed ridiculously superfluous when they came out. The many observations made by the spectators as each new wonder made its appearance, though at first rather amusing, became after a while quite vexatious; for the truth began to dawn upon me that the common sense was all on their side.

'What on airth's them gimcracks for?' said my lady, as a nest of delicate japanned tables were set out upon the uneven floor.

I tried to explain to her the various convenient uses to which they were applicable; but she looked very scornfully after all and said, 'I guess they'll do better for kindlins than any thing else, here.'

And I began to cast a disrespectful glance upon them myself, and forthwith ordered them up stairs, and wondering in my own mind how I could have thought a log house would afford space for such superfluities.

All this time there was a blazing fire in the chimney to accommodate Mrs. Jennings in her operations, and while the doors and windows were open we were not sensible of much discomfort from it. Supper was prepared and eaten—beds spread on the floor, and the children stowed away. Mrs. Jennings and our other 'helps' had departed, and I prepared to rest from my unutterable weariness, when I began to be sensible of the suffocating heat of the place. I tried to think it would grow cooler in a little while, but it was absolutely unsufferable to the children as well as myself, and I was fain to set both doors open, and in this exposed situation passed the first night in my western home, alone with my children and far from any neighbor.

If I could live a century, I think that night will never fade from my memory. Excessive fatigue made it impossible to avoid falling asleep, yet the fear of being devoured by wild beasts, or poisoned by rattlesnakes, caused me to start up after every nap with sensations of horror and alarm, which could hardly have been increased by the actual occurrence of all I dreaded. Many wretched hours passed in this manner. At length sleep fairly overcame fear, and we were awakened only by a wild storm of wind and rain which drove in upon us and completely wetted every thing within reach.

A doleful morning was this—no fire on the hearth—streams of water on the floor—and three hungry children to get breakfast for. I tried to kindle a blaze with matches, but alas, even the straw from the packing-boxes was soaked with the cruel rain; and I was distributing bread to the hungry, hopeless of any thing more, when Mr. Jennings made his appearance.

'I was thinking you'd begin to be sick o' your bargain by this time,' said the good man, 'and so I thought I'd come and help you a spell. I reckon you'd ha' done better to have waited till the old man got back.'

'What old man?' asked I, in perfect astonishment. 'Why, *your* old man to be sure,' said he laughing. I had yet to learn that in Michigan, as soon as a man marries he becomes 'the old man,' though he may yet be in his minority. Not long since I gave a young bride the how d' do in passing, and the reply was, 'I'm pretty well, but my old man's sick a-bed.'

But to return. Mr. Jennings kindled a fire which I took care should be a moderate one; and I managed to make a cup of tea to dip our bread in, and then prodeeded to find places for the various articles which strewed the floor. Some auger-holes bored in the logs received large and long pegs, and these served to support boards which were made to answer the purpose of shelves. It was soon found that the multiplicity of articles which were to be accommodated on these shelves would fill them a dozen times.

'Now to my thinkin,' said my good genius, Mr. Jennings, 'that 'ere soup t'reen, as you call it, and them little ones, and these here great glass-dishes, and all *sich,* might jist as well go up chamber for all the good they'll ever do you here.'

This could not be gainsaid; and the good man proceeded to exalt them to another set of extempore shelves in the upper story; and so many articles were included in the same category, that I began to congratulate myself on the increase of clear space below, and to fancy we should soon begin to look very comfortable.

My ideas of comfort were by this time narrowed down to a well-swept room with a bed in one corner, and cooking apparatus in another—and this in some fourteen days from the city! I can scarcely, myself, credit the reality of the change.

. . . .

'Mother wants your sifter,' said Miss Ianthe Howard, a young lady of six years' standing, attired in a tattered calico, thickened with dirt; her unkempt locks straggling from under that hideous substitute for a bonnet, so universal in the western country, a dirty cotton handkerchief, which is used, *ad nauseam,* for all sorts of purposes.

'Mother wants your sifter, and she says she guesses you can let her have some sugar and tea, 'cause you've got plenty.'

This excellent reason, ''cause you've got plenty,' is conclusive as to sharing with your neighbors. Whoever comes into Michigan with nothing, will be sure to better his condition; but woe to him that brings with him anything like an appearance of abundance, whether of money or mere household conveniences. To have them, and not be willing to share them in some sort with the whole community, is an unpardonable crime. You must lend your best horse *qui que ce soit* to go ten miles over hill and marsh, in the darkest night, for a doctor; or your team to travel twenty after a 'gal;' your wheelbarrows, your shovels, your untensils of all sorts, belong, not to yourself, but to the public, who do not think it necessary even to *ask* a loan, but take it for granted. The two saddles and bridles of Montacute spend most of their time travelling from house to house a-man-back; and I have actually known a stray martingale to be traced to four dwellings two miles apart, having been lent from one to another, without a word to the original proprietor, who sat waiting, not very patiently, to commence a journey.

Then within doors, an inventory of your plenishing of all sorts, would scarcely more than include the articles which you are solicited to lend. Not only are all kitchen utensils as much your neighbor's as your own, but bedsteads, beds, blankets, sheets, travel from house to house, a pleasant and effectual mode of securing the perpetuity of certain efflorescent peculiarities of the skin, for which Michigan is becoming almost as famous as the land "twixt Maidenkirk and John o' Groat's.' Sieves, smoothing irons, and churns, run about as if they had legs; one brass kettle is enough for a whole neighborhood; and I could point to a cradle which has rocked half the babies in Montacute. For my own part, I have lent my broom, my thread, my tape, my spoons, my cat, my thimble, my scissors, my shawl, my shoes; and have been asked for my combs and brushes: and my husband for his shaving apparatus and his pantaloons.

But the cream of the joke lies in the manner of the thing. It is so straight-forward and honest, none of your hypocritical civility and servile gratitude! Your true republican, when he finds that you possess anything which would contribute to his convenience, walks in with, 'Are you going to use your horses *to-day?*' if horses happen to be the thing he needs.

'Yes, I shall probably want them.'

'O, well; if you want them—I was thinking to get 'em to go up north a piece.'

Or perhaps the desired article comes within the female department.

'Mother wants to get some butter: that 'ere butter you bought of Miss Barton this mornin'.'

And away goes your golden store, to be repaid perhaps with some cheesy, greasy stuff, brought in a dirty pail, with, 'Here's your butter!'

A girl came in to borrow a 'wash-dish,' 'because we've got company.' Presently she came back: 'Mother says you've forgot to send a towel.'

'The pen and ink, and a sheet o' paper and a wafer,' is no unusual request; and when the pen is returned, you are generally informed that you sent 'an awful bad pen.'

I have been frequently reminded of one of Johnson's humorous sketches. A man returning a broken wheel-barrow to a Quaker, with, 'Here, I've broke your rotten wheel-barrow usin' on't. I wish you'd get it mended right off, 'cause I want to borrow it again this afternoon.' The Quaker is made to reply, 'Friend, it shall be done:' and I wish I possessed more of his spirit.

. . . .

One of the greatest deficiencies and disadvantages of the settler in the new world, is the lack of the ordinary means of public religious instruction. This is felt, not only when the Sabbath morn recurs without its call for public worship, and children ask longingly for that mild and pleasing form of religious and moral training, to which they are all attached as if by intuition of nature; but it makes itself but too evident throughout the entire structure and condition of society. Those who consider Religion a gloom and a burden, have only to reside for a while where Religion is habitually forgotten or wilfully set aside. They will soon learn at least to appreciate the practical value of the injunction, 'Forsake not the assembling of yourselves together.'

We have never indeed been entirely destitute for any length of time of the semblance of public worship. Preachers belonging to various denominations have, from the beginning, occasionally called meetings in the little log school-house, and many of the neighbors always make a point of being present, although a far greater proportion reserve the Sunday for fishing and gunning. And it must be confessed that there has generally been but little that was attractive in the attempts at public service. A bare cold room, the wind whistling through a thousand crevices in the unplastered walls, and pouring down through as many more in the shrunken roof, seats formed by laying rough boards on rougher blocks, and the whole covered thick with the week's dirt of the district school; these are scarcely the appliances which draw the indolent, the careless, the indifferent, the self-indulgent, to the house of worship. And the preacher, 'the messenger of Heaven,' 'the legate of the skies,'—Alas! I dare not trust my pen to draw the portraits of *some* of these well-meaning, but most incompetent persons. I can only say that a large part of them seem to me grievously to have mistaken their vocation.

'All are not such.' We have occasionally a preacher whose language and manner, though plain, are far from being either coarse or vulgar, and whose sermons, though generally quite curious in their way, have nothing that is either ridiculous or disgusting. If we suffer ourselves to be driven from the humble meeting-house by one preacher with the dress and air of a horse-jockey, who will rant and scream till he is obliged to have incessant recourse to his handkerchief to dry the tears which are the natural result of the excitement into which he has lashed himself, we may perhaps lose a good plain practical discourse from another, who with only tolerable worldly advantages, has yet studied his Bible with profit, and offers with gentle persuasiveness its message of mercy. Yet to sit from two to three hours trying to listen to the blubberer, is a trial of one's nerves and patience which is almost too much to ask; greater, I confess, than I am often willing to endure, well convinced as I am, that the best good of all, requires the support of some form of public worship.

· ·

It was some little time before we could learn the rules of etiquette which are observed among these itinerant or voluntary preachers. We supposed that if a meeting was given out for Sunday morning at the school-house by a Baptist, any other room might be obtained and occupied at the same hour by a Presbyterian or Methodist, leaving it to the people to choose which they would hear. But this is considered a most ungenerous usurpation, and such things are indignantly frowned upon by all the meeting-goers in the community. If a minister of any denomination has appointed a meeting, no other must preach at the same hour in the neighbor- hood; and this singular notion gives rise to much of the petty squabbling and ill-will which torments Montacute as well as other small places.

This is one of the many cases wherein it is easier to waive one's rights than to quarrel for them. I hope, as our numbers increase rapidly, the evil will soon cure itself, since one room will not long be elastic enough to contain all the church-goers.

· ·

Ministers who cannot or will not conform themselves to the manners of the country, do more harm than good. Pride is, as I have elsewhere observed, the bugbear of the western country; and the appearance of it, or a suspicion of it, in a clergyman, not only destroys his personal influence, but depreciates his office.

It takes one a long while to become accustomed to the uncere- monious manner in which the meetings of all sorts are conducted. Many people go in and out whenever they feel disposed; and the young men, who soon tire, give unequivocal symptoms of their weariness, and generally walk off with a *nonchalant* air, at any time during the exercises. Women usually carry their babies, and some- times two or three who can scarcely walk; and the restlessness of these youthful members, together with an occasional display of their musical talents, sometimes interrupts in no small measure the progress of the speaker. The stove is always in the centre of the room, with benches arranged in a hollow square around it; and the area thus formed is the scene of infantile operations. I have seen a dozen people kept on a stretch during a whole long sermon, by a little, tottering, rosy-cheeked urchin, who chose to approach within a few inches of the stove every minute or two, and to fall at every third step, at the imminent danger of lodging against the hot iron. And the mamma sat looking on with an air of entire complacency, picking up the chubby rogue occasionally, and varying the scene by the performance of the maternal office.

I fancy it would somewhat disconcert a city clergyman, on ascending his sumptuous pulpit, to find it already occupied by a deaf old man, with his tin ear-trumpet ready to catch every word. This I have seen again and again; and however embarrassing to the preacher, an objection or remonstrance on the subject would be very ill-received. And after all, I must confess, I have heard sermons preached in such circumstances, which would have reflected no disgrace on certain gorgeous draperies of velvet and gold.

Large numbers of Dutch and German immigrants settled in Michigan before the Civil War. The Germans came from diverse backgrounds, and although the "Forty-Eighters" (exiled German revolutionaries) scattered themselves across the state, the typical newcomer joined ethnic enclaves near Ann Arbor, Frankenmuth, or in the Saginaw Valley. The Dutch came from varied Netherlandic provinces but settled almost exclusively in Western Michigan. Zeelanders, South Hollanders, and even Frisians drew close to each other either in Albertus Van Raalte's emigrant colony or in small communities scattered around its fringes.

The selections below, chosen to illustrate immigrant pioneer life, emphasize the conflicting urges that motivated their aspirations. Hoping to retain their Old World cultures, they sought isolation, but economic success required a measure of cultural adaptation in their new homes. Desiring both money and their native ways, the Dutch in Western Michigan and the Germans in Eastern Michigan clung to their natural tongues and traditional churches while quickly adopting the economic methods and perspectives of their Yankee neighbors.

Although eventually Americanized, they were not molded totally by the frequently honored American melting pot. The Dutch in Holland or Grand Rapids, and the Germans in Frankenmuth or Westphalia remain deeply loyal to their churches and many have sought to educate their youth in schools controlled by officials who sympathize with their peculiar religious and cultural preferences.

Henry Lucas' *Netherlanders in America* (Ann Arbor, 1955) is, without question, the best overall treatment of the Dutch-Americans. For the

Germans, Johan Russell has provided an authoritative analysis in his *Germanic Influences in the Making of Michigan* (Detroit, 1927). As a general study, Henry A. Pochmann's *German Culture in America, 1600-1900* (Madison, 1957) provides a broad cultural approach to the study of German-Americans. More specific studies on the Dutch include Albert Hyma's *Albertus Van Raalte and His Dutch Settlement in the United States* (Grand Rapids, 1947), and Aleida L. Pieters' *A Dutch Settlement in Michigan* (Grand Rapids, 1923). A recent study of Michigan's immigrants, *Settling the Great Lakes Frontier: Immigration to Michigan, 1837-1924* (Lansing, 1970), by Warren Vander Hill is also available.

Albertus Van Raalte Advises
Paulus Den Bleyker About the Americans

ALBERTUS VAN RAALTE

Friend Bleeker:

A sense of prudence, as well as the confinement of a woman, prevented me from coming along with Neerink. While conversing with Ds. Kleyn yesterday, I came to know about your character, which up till then was unknown to me. After calm reflection, I've concluded that since I failed to visit you at Kalamazoo, I am constrained to write more openly to you. *I earnestly request you, however, not to take undue advantage of this disclosure of my heart and affairs, but to keep everything to yourself.* I should have visited Kalamazoo months ago, but after you had just arrived I have purposely evaded you. I did not wish to assume any special responsibilities concerning you. I have moreover experienced that recent "arrivals" from the Netherlands usually profit more by way of their own experiences than by advice on the part of others.

Next I can not interfere with matters in Kalamazoo, since I consider it strictly unsafe, even destructive for you to mix and intermingle with Kalamazoo people. My reasons are these: Americans usually do not possess that certain open heartiness and mutual understanding of each other, which the Dutch possess. An impassable chasm of *language, character, custom* separates you from the Americans. Among them you will be as helpless as a child in its mother's arms. They shall carry you wherever they choose, and you will not even understand the reason why. You'll constantly be

Letter from Albertus Van Raalte in Holland, Michigan, to Paulus Den Bleyker in Kalamazoo, Michigan, Jan. 9, 1851. From the Paulus Den Bleyker *Papers,* Michigan Historical Collections, Bentley Historical Library, University of Michigan. Translated by Effa Zwier.

subject to a feeling of the most painful insecurity, for every new intermingling from your side will lead you into another labyrinth. My chief counsel is this: Don't enter a business which you cannot probe. You yourself can certainly not attain a social level in which you can safely move among Americans. Only your children *after you* will become capable of doing this. If you choose to disregard my advice, your future will be constantly subject to uncertainty and suspicion. You'll be compelled to trust these people blindly. You'll tempt them to do the wrong. Just recall the proverb, "Opportunity makes a thief."

Above all—Americans are disposed to despise Hollanders, and we Hollanders naturally become embittered against them because of their cold selfishness. They may approach us with bold flatteries, but in reality they are after our money and influence, yes, they actually despise us. They take us for a dull, slow, uncultured people, and boldly boast of their own superior intelligence. You'll never be able to move with a feeling of sincere, mutual trust and openness among them, like a friend among friends. Much of this I have learned either by close personal experience, or by profiting by the experiences of others. I myself can't bear being despised. At times, very true, I am burdened by numerous miseries, nevertheless I thank God that I may dwell in the midst of my own people.

Social Life, School and Church

R. T. KUIPER

For someone who is considering leaving his fatherland and settling in the New World, it cannot be a matter of indifference what the situation is in society, the education of the young, and the church. Before I write about this, however, let it be stated once more that I speak only about the Dutch settlement in Michigan and from personal experience, so that I do not guarantee that the conditions described will be found everywhere. Others may have

From *A Voice from America about America*, pp. 64-69. Originally published in 1881 and translated by E. R. Post. Copyright © 1970 by Wm. B. Eerdmans Publishing Company. Reprinted by permission.

found things to be different; I merely give my own impressions and observations, and let them count for what they may.

(A) As far as *social life* is concerned, in many respects there is much to be desired. The freedom of speech and action that is enjoyed does at times result in licentiousness. Still it strikes me that on the whole there is much in its favor, compared to that of the Old World. For that reason surely, very little homesickness is encountered among the thousands, yes millions of immigrants. It is of course natural that all are not equally satisfied, and many, especially at first, might wish to return. But, as a rule, it does not take long before there is improvement, and seldom does one find people who have been here one or two years and who would gladly go back. Experience has taught abundantly that one who has been here for some time and goes back to the old fatherland, really is not happy there. Life is more roomy here, freer, easier, more common; there is more open-heartedness. Here there are fewer restricting and oppressive laws, rules, regulations and orders. There are far fewer formalities and rules of conduct. Everyone associates on a more equal level. True, everyone is called "mister," but no one "sir," with the exception of the preacher, who is still addressed as "Dominie." But no one removes his hat for him. One who is somewhat ahead of others, because of intelligence and education, possessions and income, profession or position, does not allow himself to be very prominent; and whoever is less endowed in one or in all of these respects does not need to stand back on that account. Already at the time of the trip over here, at least if one travels on the regular trains, he becomes aware of this. Here there are no waiting rooms and coaches with first, second, and third class, as in the Netherlands; but the Yankee (American) and the immigrant, the boss and the workman get their tickets at the same window, remain in the same waiting room and sit in the coaches next to or immediately behind one another on similarly covered, and even upholstered seats. Only those who wish to smoke must leave the waiting room or must seat themselves in the coaches where smoking is permitted, to avoid giving offense to the ladies. I think that the social life is not worse because of this. During the time that I have been here, I have traveled more than in my whole life in the Netherlands; but I have seen and heard more in the way of lack of decency on a short trip from Zuidbroek to Leeuwarden, from Groningen to Meppel or from Zwolle to Utrecht than on my longest trip here. Still that is not because of close supervision; because one sees very little of policemen, and as far as I can recall, I have seen no soldiers at all. It seems that the public conscience serves as a policing supervision that prevents the indecencies.

Most of the immigrants experience this immediately upon their arrival. Otherwise, how would the ten thousands who have arrived this year, with the lack of housing here and with much shortage of money, have been able to get shelter and food so soon? I have heard it said by more than one of them: "People do seem to be much different and better than they were back home." Now that is not actually the case. Ah, no, people are certainly very nearly alike all over; but here they are somewhat more considerate, and circumstances have brought that about. Most of them know from their own experience what it means to be a stranger, and what a joy it is to find friends in a strange place and to receive good advice and assistance. Anyone then who still possesses any human feeling will wish to show the same acts of kindness, also because of the pleasure that can be enjoyed in the doing, in return to those newly arrived. Since the latter do not expect this from total strangers they think at first that this country and people are so much better than those they have left. Later, however, they become aware that just as they themselves were not improved by their immigration, and have also brought their selfishness with them, so too their helpers have the ordinary human weaknesses and faults. Eventually, and sometimes before long, they discover that the American slogan—Help yourself—is not without significance here. Fortunately, here the situation is such that anyone with a healthy body, with a good mind and a good will, can with the Lord's blessing soon help himself and is no longer in need of help from strangers.

Those, however, who are really helpless, for example the widows and orphans and cripples, are cared for much better here than in many places in the old fatherland. As a rule those in need of help are much more fortunate here. Whether the care of the poor here is always in harmony with the Scriptures and our Reformed confession, I have my doubts; but the poor are not the worse off as a result, as town, county and state, as well as the church, assume the responsibility for the care of the indigent.

It is hardly necessary to say that the social life in the cities differs a great deal from that in the country; and that this affects and determines the lot and situation of the immigrant, speaks for itself.

The Hollander can get along in the cities; but it is necessary for him to learn the American language if he really wishes to belong. In the country and especially in our Holland settlements, many weeks pass by for some without hearing a single word spoken in English; so that he can hardly imagine that he is no longer in the Netherlands.

In the cities there are Hollanders who with effort, practice, diligence and good behavior have attained to a good position in society with the Lord's blessing and do not have to stand back for the Yankees by any means. The present mayor of Grand Rapids, Mr. Steketee, is a Hollander, and many of our fellow countrymen are very successful. But in contrast to a hundred who have a somewhat independent position there are a thousand who must seek a subordinate position to make a living in factories, mills, in stores, or other employment.

In the country it is different. There everyone is more his own master and in the long run is better off, but not without application and hard work; at least so it appears to me.

In the cities one sees many children of Hollanders already drifting away from the life of their parents in the American world; so that they are soon almost ashamed of their background and no longer speak the Dutch language. In the country our national character is better preserved along with the Dutch language, and it will doubtless be some time before our Holland colony in Michigan is Americanized.

As a result of such social conditions, two immigrants from the same place, traveling together as far as Kalamazoo and parting there, the one going to Chicago and the other to our area, after a few years will have had quite a different history. It is even very well possible that their children after ten or twelve years will not be able to understand one another. A mother living in my neighborhood can no longer speak a word with her son. As a lad he went to live among the English and has completely forgotten the Holland language. Still he is a good man.

I thought I should tell about these things so that they can be taken into account. Everyone does not agree on these matters. Some seem to be concerned only about where the most dollars can be earned. What becomes of their language, religion, and children appears to be nothing for them to worry about. Others, and many of them, pride themselves on being the only ones who know what is right. They think that an immigrant must push himself into the American world as soon as possible and lay aside everything that is Dutch as quickly as he can, even though he is ridiculed by both Americans and Hollanders in his endeavors. There is no danger, they think, that later benefit will not doubly repay him. There are Hollanders who set to work in this way, and who will sometimes even disguise their descent and pretend that they no longer understand the Holland language.

Still, there is no want of intelligent people who view the matter very differently. They do agree that it would be foolish to set themselves against the trend of Americanization adamantly and to try to establish a little Netherlands in Michigan and to keep it going.

But they consider it to be equally foolish to make of our people at once what they can become after a long period of gradual development. They do not wish to discard anything of their Dutch ways for which the American cannot offer something better. They are willing to train themselves to learn and become accustomed to the language, manners, laws, and customs of the land, and choose the best English schools and teachers for their children; but they understand that they need not for that reason neglect the Holland language. Therefore they continue to preserve their nationality in the midst of the peoples. Do they because of this reason have to stand back for the others? As I look about in the county I find many of them, in the church as well as in society, in the front ranks, and I hear that they are respected not less but more by intelligent Americans as a result. In my immediate neighborhood I notice that those who do the most business, or in their vocation and profession associate most with Americans, are especially the strongest advocates for the preservation of the language, religion, and morals. One would possibly ask whether it is not a nuisance to have to live in a country and not to be able to understand its language. It certainly is; but prompted by necessity one soon learns enough of it to be able to get along. And as a rule the Americans are very ready to be helpful to the strangers, and involuntarily one adjusts to the circumstances, more easily here than in the old fatherland. Generally, it is better than had been expected, but still it can also be extremely disappointing here.

America is a wonderful country and wonderful things happen. One finds many farmers and merchants here who were laborers in the Netherlands and most likely would have advanced to a good position, but here they are included in the front ranks. There are also on the other hand those who in the Netherlands did amount to something and came here with a goodly sum of money and are now in unfavorable circumstances, or who must spend their days in a strange country on a small farm with a great deal of toil and drudgery. People who come here with money have a good chance of losing it, especially if they are quite conscious of their riches and allow themselves to depend upon them. Such a one can find a partner very easily in the cities to begin some kind of business. The partner is a professional, who knows everything in connection with it, and has experience. The immigrant has money, a necessary requirement. But before very long the man of experience has the money and the man of money has the experience, but not of the most pleasant kind. Also in the country it is possible to make bad deals, and a person can be grievously cheated in the purchase of a farm.

Karl Neidhard's Reise Nach Michigan

FRANK X. BRAUN

The little town of Ann Arbor looks freshly carved and painted, as if it had stepped out of a Nuremberg toyshop only yesterday. By far the greater part of the town is situated on a knoll practically surrounded by woods. There the doctors and lawyers, the clergy-men and teachers have their "temples," and everybody, be he sailor or weaver, carpenter or blacksmith, has his shop and dwelling there. Down near the Huron River there are about twenty beautiful houses, mostly brick, and there, too, is the noisy world of the merchants and millers. Ann Arbor is only six years old. Its founder, a planter who met with a fatal accident in Virginia, gave the town its name in honor of his wife. At the time I entered this embryo metropolis there were four good taverns, several churches, ten shops, five doctors, and tradespeople of all sorts, all in all about eight hundred souls. The inhabitants are mostly Americans from New York state and Englishmen from Canada. A courthouse had been completed only a few days before, and I saw three judges, simple but honorable men, sitting on the elevated bench, their faces intelligent and serious. To their right, on separate seats, were the jurymen, and down in the bar were half a dozen lawyers.

. . . .

Once here, I was, in a manner of speaking, at the goal of my journey. Ann Arbor is the principal city of Washtenaw County, and in its neighborhood is the German settlement, which now consists of about sixty families. Here in Ann Arbor lives Mr. Mann, their patriarch, an honorable and pious citizen from Stuttgart. About five years ago he and his family moved here from the interior of Pennsylvania and drew after them, on the basis of a true and faithful description of the country, a considerable number of their countrymen. There were also some Rhenish people, Saxons, and Prussians, as well as Pennsylvania Germans. I had become acquainted with the Mann family in Pennsylvania, and great was their joy when I unexpectedly appeared. They had believed that I had returned to Germany long before. Mr. Mann and his busy wife had aged somewhat, but the cares of resettlement had not deprived them of their old gaiety. They had a bright future. Mann's daughters had grown to be young women. The eldest was even engaged to

From *Michigan History*, XXV (Spring, 1951), 46-49, 55-58. Reprinted by permission of the History Division, Michigan Department of State. Footnotes in the original have been omitted.

the pastor recently arrived from Germany. His son, a mechanical genius, was by now a sturdy man, and had built houses, constructed implements, and set up fulling and tanning mills for his father. Mr. Mann was in the tannery business. With a great deal of satisfaction, they showed me the various parts of their property, which was small, but which nevertheless satisfied their needs. The whole family lived in a house with two main rooms, a kitchen, and attic rooms. A small barn gave shelter to a horse and a cow, while a tract of land surrounding the house and extending down the slope of a hill furnished feed for the animals and supplied the family with vegetables and, presently, with fruit. A wild plum tree had already been transplanted into the garden. In the lower part of the garden, a small creek drove a mill wheel, and on top of the hill Mr. Mann was engaged in building a pleasant little house for his son-in-law.

Instead of bringing them tidings from the eastern parts, I listened to news about Swabian countrymen, some of them relatives of Mr. Mann, who had arrived just recently and who had lived with Mr. Mann until they were established. The unselfish hospitality which Mr. Mann extends to all German newcomers and the care which he gives them is astonishing, especially if one knows that he himself has only a moderate income, and that food prices are fairly high due to the demand created by the masses of emigrants. His attic rooms and barn are often full of such guests, who are always welcome at a table which may not abound in delicacies, but which has plenty of good and simple food. On the other hand, one must realize that in this manner Mr. Mann invests a capital in the hearts of his countrymen, a capital which one day will pay high dividends. This is evident even now. Without being asked, they brought him all the material for his new house, helped him build it, and presented him with a share of their first crop.

A few days later, after we had "talked ourselves empty," I expressed a wish to visit the whole Swabian settlement, and Mr. Mann offered to act as my guide on this first trip.

On a beautiful August morning he pocketed his compass, that indispensable guide in the wilderness, and, well provided with food for emergency use, we set out. For the first few miles we passed through woods and only here and there saw a log house surrounded by cleared land. Soon we reached the so-called oak openings, where the trees stand a few paces apart and where the ground is overgrown with luxurious grass. Passage is obstructed neither by bushes nor by fallen trees. Small knolls alternate with lovely little valleys, each more charming than the last. No park laid out by human hands could compare with this natural setting.

Fifteen miles from Ann Arbor we reached Pleasant Lake, one of the innumerable lovely lakes so characteristic of Michigan Territory. This lake, although only two miles long and half a mile wide, is nevertheless one of the larger ones. Some of them measure but a few acres. Small hills adorned with oak openings line its shores. Up to now only one settler had showed enough good sense to settle in this neighborhood. Greedy for only the best arable land, the barbarians rush past these small paradises which have their own advantages. These lakes owe their origin to natural springs, and they always have an outlet, which, to be sure, is often difficult to find. Therefore, living conditions near them are healthy, especially if the shores are of sandy soil. The fact that they abound in fish is not to be despised either. If these lakes have an area of only a few acres, they are counted as part of the land; however, if they are larger, they are subtracted from the total acreage. In this case, they become the common property of all the riparian land owners. Only log houses are in evidence, since hardly anyone has been in the country more than two or three years.

. . . .

The settlement of the Germans, for the most part Swabians from the neighborhood of Stuttgart, is located on the southeastern slope of these hills. Approximately sixty families are living here, only short distances apart, and each family owns from 160 to 240 acres of land.

Mr. Stadtmann turned back after driving us about ten miles and we continued our journey on foot. When we reached the first log house, it was already dark and Mr. Stolz, the owner, and his family were already fast asleep. The barking of his dog and our calls soon awakened the whole house. The little window was opened with the question: "Wear ischt doh?" ["Who is there?"].

"Friends," answered Mr. Mann. "Your burgomaster from Ann Arbor, and a commissioner from Europe who wants to investigate you."

"Ah, it's you, Mr. Mann," replied Stolz, laughing. "In that case I'd better open up; I have a clear conscience."

We entered and found the whole family up already and half dressed.

"Wife," called out Mr. Stolz, "cook and bake and serve the very best; we must treat the gentlemen well, so they won't be too severe."

In two minutes flames were roaring in the fireplace, for the settler never lets his fire go out. The glowing embers are covered with ashes in the evening, and in the morning one needs only to remove the ashes and to lay on more wood in order to have a fresh fire. The roughly hewn table was neatly set in a short time, and on it were placed fresh pancakes, ham, the most beautiful wheat bread, butter, honey, and several pitchers of milk.

"Sit down, gentlemen," said Mr. Stolz. "Excuse the rough benches and table, commissioner; at least you will be able to convince yourself that there is no lack of food!"

We did full justice to Mrs. Stolz' cooking and amidst much joking went to bed. The next day we went through the whole settlement from house to house, always accompanied by a crowd, and everywhere we found the same hearty reception. Mr. Mann was greeted by all just like a beloved father and everyone wanted to do him favors. Wherever we entered, they wanted us to stay as their guests. At least, we had to have bread, butter, and milk with them.

"We have no wine," said the good people with regret, "but if you come back when our trees have grown bigger, we will have some good cider for you."

Thus we wandered around in the settlement for three days, taking a meal here and a night's shelter there, especially with the Laubegayer, Gross, and Beck families, all of them from the "Filder," a district near Stuttgart. Mr. Beck is, to the best of my knowledge, the wealthiest man in the whole settlement. He arrived here only a year ago from New York, bought a well-established farm of 240 acres, three horses, a nice herd of cattle, sheep, pigs, and chickens, all for $2,000. This year he had a very fine harvest, and I am convinced that ten years from now he will be one of the richest farmers in Michigan. I was glad to see in him an example of how quickly our German countrymen learn to imitate the methods of the Americans and to handle their farm equipment. I had to laugh, however, when the old man complained of how carelessly his people bound and threshed the grain and of how little they valued this gift of God in this country. The good man had not calculated that here labor is worth three times as much as that which might be gained by excessive carefulness, and that after all, whatever is left in the straw or out in the fields is not actually lost. Chickens and pigs are much cheaper gleaners than people, and any grain left in the straw is found by the cattle. It is difficult for newcomers to understand this principle of economy. There were times when I observed people practically in tears when they saw pigs eating the most beautiful apples because the owners had no other use for them. One time I happened to pass by as a group of Americans were admiring a German farmer and his wife who were cutting wheat with sickles.

"They are actually shaving it," remarked an American with a smile.

Both of these good people cut the wheat close to the roots, in the old-country fashion, and by doing so accomplished less than a quarter as much work as an American would have without bending over. He knows that he has sufficient straw anyway and, after all, the straw remaining in the stubble is not lost to the field.

As to our Swabians, I have to admit that they know how to adapt themselves quickly to the new conditions. I have not met a single one among them who did not employ the better farming methods of this country. They rapidly lose one of their old habits too, namely, the saving of wood. I saw an old farmer stand in front of a big fire which he had built out of logs. He never uttered a word, but his eyes expressed only too plainly how happy he was in not suffering from a shortage of wood. Mr. Mann, who from the very beginning assisted all of his countrymen with good advice, rendered great services to the settlement in respect to farming methods.

3: Natural Resources

Copper mining in Michigan dates from at least 1771, but continuous mining, beginning with the 1844 copper boom, hastened the exploration and settlement of the Upper Peninsula, while giving Michigan an early stake in the nation's industrial interests. But, as the following selections demonstrate, copper mining depended on investments from Boston and the industry that copper encouraged centered in isolated company towns.

The most scholarly discussion of Michigan's copper mining is *Michigan Copper and Boston Dollars* (Cambridge, 1951), by William B. Gates, while Angus Murdoch's *Boom Copper* is a more popularized account. The *Michigan History Magazine* has published good memoir selections and articles treating several special topics connected with copper mining. Among them are Robert T. Hybel's "Lake Superior Copper Fever," XXXIV (1950), and "Michigan's Cornish People," XXIX (1945), by James Fisher.

Opening the Michigan Lodes, 1845-1866

WILLIAM B. GATES

The Michigan Copper Country is located on Keweenaw Peninsula, which reaches out like an index finger from the southern shore line of Lake Superior. . . . All of the known copper deposits lie along a mineral range which runs a hundred miles through what today are the Upper Peninsula counties of Ontonagon, Houghton, and Keweenaw.

Discovery and Exploration

Early exploration. The deposits were known to the Indians at the time the French began to explore the Lake Superior region and had

From *Michigan Copper and Boston Dollars* (Cambridge, Mass.: Harvard University Press, 1951), pp. 1-10, 18-20. Copyright,1951, by the President and Fellows of Harvard College. Reprinted by permission of the publishers. Footnotes in the original have been omitted.

been worked by a forgotten race of miners long before Columbus discovered America. The Indian tales were passed along with embellishments by the early French explorers and missionaries, but it was not until 1771 that an Englishman, Alexander Henry, organized the first mining expedition of modern times to reach the Copper Country. The enterprise failed after a long winter spent in the southern section of the Peninsula, and interest in the district lapsed until 1800 when the United States Congress directed the President to appoint an agent to investigate the copper deposits of Lake Superior. No action was taken under the bill, and the next authentic report of the existence of copper on the shores of the lake came from Henry R. Schoolcraft in 1820, who found the indications so promising that he suggested the government should work the deposits. Twenty years more elapsed before scientific exploration was undertaken by Douglass Houghton, first geologist of the newly admitted state of Michigan.

The surveys and land laws. In 1840 Houghton began a careful examination of the district and by late 1841 had issued two reports to the State Legislature in which he gave a cautious but encouraging appraisal of copper mining potentialities of the Peninsula. Congress showed sufficient interest in 1841 to appropriate funds for the purchase of the lands from the Indians, and in the summer of 1842 a treaty was negotiated with the Chippewas by which they ceded some 25,000 square miles of territory to the Federal government. Shortly thereafter an agreement was concluded with Houghton to take charge of a linear survey for the United States in addition to the topographical and geographical survey upon which he was already engaged for the state of Michigan. Work on the surveys went forward rapidly, and by 1843, when the first mining permit was issued, locations and boundaries could be designated in something resembling an orderly fashion.

By that year interest in the district had become intense, particularly in the East, and the federal government was under pressure to throw the area open and designate rules under which the deposits might be worked. Following the precedent set in leasing early western lead lands, permits were issued by the War Department—first for nine square miles, and, later, in March, 1845, reduced to one square mile. After a location had been made the permit holder was to apply to Washington for a lease and forward surety bonds amounting to $20,000. The lessee was "allowed one year for exploration, and three more years to mine, with the privilege of two renewals of three years each, making the whole term ten years." He was required to send in returns to the Mineral Agency giving the amount of copper raised and to pay the government 6 per cent royalties for the first three-year mining period and 10 per cent thereafter.

The first major United States mining boom. A few hardy souls came overland into the district from the Wisconsin lead lands as early as the summer of 1843, but it was not until the spring of 1844 that the real boom began. Several schooners owned by the fur companies were operating on Superior at that time, and during the following two years, a half dozen more, including the propeller *Independence* and the sidewheeler *Julia Palmer*, were hauled over the portage at Sault Ste. Marie to carry explorers, miners, speculators, and their supplies up to Keweenaw, and small quantities of copper and hundreds of disillusioned failures back.

Twenty to twenty-five days were required to send mineral from the mines to Buffalo and thence to Boston—the cost running from $18 to $20 per long ton. (At about this same period the rate on a long ton of ore from Chile to Boston was $15; from Cuba to Boston, $6.) Cargoes had to be hauled by human or animal labor almost a mile across the portage at the Soo and then reshipped on the other side. Even worse, navigation was impossible for at least five months of the year as a result of winter storms and ice formations along the shore of Lake Superior, and was apt to be risky even during the summer season. Although there were a number of harbors at the Peninsula, most were blocked by sand bars to all but the smallest vessels, and passengers and supplies often had to be transferred to lighters before shore could be reached. Finally, the phrase bandied about among returning prospectors of "a howling wilderness" was perhaps a harsh generalization but was, nonetheless, a fitting description for some of the conditions encountered once the Copper Country had been reached. The Peninsula was heavily wooded, swampy in many places, and cut off by land from the outside world by over 200 miles of virtually uninhabited wilderness. Only experienced woodsmen or those fortunate enough to have at their command a sleigh and dog team could reach civilization once the snows began in November.

During the first two years of prospecting and mineral land speculation, there was little that could be dignified by the term "mining." Hundreds of men tramped the wilderness, each equipped with a pick and a few pounds of gunpowder, and with one eye on speculation in land permits where the real money lay. What little copper they found was lying on the surface or easily blown loose from outcropping rocks. But even in these early days there were a few beginnings at real mining, and by 1847 the main outlines of prevailing technology are discernible.

In general discarded methods drawn from the earlier history of other mining fields of the world, particularly Cornwall, were employed. Drilling was by hand, one man holding the drill and one or two others driving it into the rock with sledges. Blasting was done with ordinary gunpowder, and both processes required much skill to get effective results. As the shaft went down into the vein, rock and copper masses were hauled to the surface in an iron bucket, known as a "kibble," which was attached to a heavy chain and powered by men at a windlass or by one or more horses at a whim. The whim was a seventeenth-century Cornish invention, used for both hoisting and pumping, which had been very largely replaced in England by steam power. Copper rock was transported underground to the shafts by wheelbarrows rolled along boards, in contrast with the carts pushed along wooden or iron rails which had been adopted in older fields of the world. Finally, Michigan miners, trammers, and laborers climbed in and out of the shafts by ladders, whereas their Cornish counterparts were already beginning to use man-engines as early as 1841.

The main items of surface equipment usually consisted of a small farm, a blacksmith shop, a carpenter shop or small sawmill, a log bunkhouse or two, a storehouse, a rockhouse, and sometimes a stamp mill. The early prospectors searched for lodes made up of copper masses, almost pure chunks of metal, often weighing ten tons or more, which were laboriously cut up underground and usually shipped directly to the smelter. Barrelwork, copper in very small masses which was detached from its rock matrix by hammering at the rockhouse, was also valued, in part because it did not require milling. But even in 1847 a certain amount of stamp work, or low copper content rock, was considered worth treating. During the summer and fall of 1845, a stamp mill operated by an overshot water wheel was working at Eagle River. These early stamps were of Cornish design with wooden stems and iron heads weighing around 200 pounds, which dropped on the rock some twenty-odd times per minute. Copper mineral was extracted from the resultant sands by hand treatment—the washing and jiggling on boards being about the same technique as that used in the early gold fields. Mass copper was often roasted in kilns or small ovens in order to eliminate waste rock. The rock was piled upon a layer of crossed cordwood, allowed to burn for several days, and then cooled by water which helped to complete the splintering of the matrix.

. . . .

Internal problems involved in opening up the Michigan lodes. Internal problems were quite serious enough without the complication of a world copper glut. The Peninsula comprised approximately 3,000 square miles of territory within which were scattered some 400 lava flows and conglomerate and sandstone beds which the early prospectors might have discovered. And of these 400 possible locations, not more than a dozen or so were destined to yield copper in commercial quantities. Careful exploration of the range had barely begun, and it was still not known that the mass deposits, which, in the forties, had been considered the only lodes worth mining, were geological freaks representing little more than icing of the main copper cake. The really significant deposits were of finely disseminated metal in amygdaloid and conglomerate rock, running to great depth, and seldom outcropping in a fashion which would make proving of potentialities rapid or inexpensive. Past mining and metallurgical experience of the world had little to offer in the way of adequate methods for handling these new problems, and tremendous uncertainty, springing from technical and geological ignorance, was the greatest handicap to be overcome.

Only a little less important were transportation difficulties, which were closely associated with those of obtaining an adequate labor supply. For many years the problem of getting copper out and supplies in at something less than prohibitive cost was too much for many of the infant companies and a severe handicap for all except the two or three with bonanza finds. Copper content of all shipments had to be high; in 1847 the trustees of the Copper Falls Company were advising their agent that his first consignment of some 7,000 pounds of mineral had not paid costs. As a result of high transportation charges, nothing yielding less than 40 per cent metal should be shipped.

The industry approached these problems with a number of factors in its favor. Bad as the transportation problem was, the Great Lakes waterway represented an incalculably great asset, as did the fact that the copper discoveries were of pure metal, uncontaminated by sulphur or other undesirable elements which greatly complicated the refining of copper ore found in other parts of the world. In addition the corporate form of enterprise was available from the beginning, as well as stock exchanges in the East which tapped the meager store of speculative capital available in the young nation. Finally, there came to the district a steady stream of high-class labor from older mining and industrial centers of the world. The immigrants brought to Michigan not only their youth and skill, but a highly favorable incentive wage system and the best mining knowledge the world had to offer.

The accomplishment by 1866. From a production standpoint the accomplishment in this first period of 22 years was an impressive one. By the early 1860's the new district was producing about 14 million pounds of copper per annum, an amount equivalent to 60 per cent of domestic requirements, which had tripled since the early forties. Actually, since 1855 the United States had become an exporter as well as an importer of refined copper. The Lake product was of particular value for military and artistic purposes and sold at a premium in foreign markets. From 1855 to 1861, 30 to 80 per cent of annual Michigan output was shipped abroad. The less expensive fire refined metal from Chilean and other foreign and domestic mines continued to be good enough for the requirements of most domestic manufacturers.

The most rapid increases in output were made between 1854, when production stood at about four million pounds, and 1861, when it topped 15 million. By the peak inflationary year of the Civil War, some $5.8 million worth of copper was flowing Eastward from the distant shores of Lake Superior where five thousand men worked for the mining companies in a community which now numbered 19 thousand.

. . . .

Roads and Canals or Bust

Although the industry's output had grown substantially since the early fifties and proved adequate to meet the wartime needs of the North, the most significant accomplishments were those laying groundwork for the future. First among these was the development of a cheap transportation system from the Copper Country to the metal markets and sources of labor and material supply of the East. The waterway system, as completed during these years, not only gave the Michigan mines a competitive advantage over the California copper mining industry (which boomed in consequence of high Civil War prices) and even over isolated districts in the East, such as Ducktown, Tennessee, but assured Michigan preëminence over potential competitors in the West, until the railroads opened up that country in the early eighties. Even after that date it continued to represent an asset which compensated, in some part, for western advantages, such as precious metal content in copper lodes.

Development of the Lake transportation system. It was immediately apparent that the worst link in the transportation system was at Sault Ste. Marie. Not only was it necessary to unload all cargoes, consign them to one of the two forwarding houses, and reload them on the other side of the portage, but the vessels operating on Superior were enabled to charge monopolistic prices in consequence of their small number and of the expense involved in hauling ships over from the Lower Lakes. A few more were brought across between 1846 and 1854, including another sidewheeler and another propeller, but the operating fleet remained small. An improvement was made in the early fifties by the laying of a railroad across the portage, but this was nothing more than a palliative; the Copper Country had to have a canal.

About this time Congress granted Michigan 750,000 acres of land to be disposed of in defraying the cost of such a project, and work was begun by contractors in June, 1853. Two years later the canal was completed at a total cost of $875,000, and on June 18, 1855, the first boat went through the locks. The impact of the opening of the canal was just as substantial as had been anticipated. For a year or more before 1855 purely developmental work had been under way on a large number of locations whose owners now felt able to ship their product eastward. Lower Lake vessels were attracted to the trade, and rates fell by 1860 to $11 per ton to Boston and $9 to New York. Charges of monopoly were still rife since all of the tonnage was owned by a few Cleveland and Detroit shipping firms, but rate reduction was substantial enough to represent real progress.

The second major improvement was made shortly after the Portage Lake district was opened up. Until 1862 the channel from Superior to Portage Lake was so shallow that vessels drawing more than 4.5 feet were obliged to anchor off the entry and transfer their cargoes to lighters, which were towed to and from the mine landings some 14 miles away. In 1859 and 1860 the mines of the district joined together and spent $30,000 dredging the mouth of the entry. Later, in 1862, they formed a company to deepen the 14,000-foot channel and to collect tolls on all outgoing and incoming cargoes.

Thus, by the end of the Civil War it was possible to ship copper and copper mineral direct from the mining company docks at Portage Lake to the Lower Lake wharves. The port of Ontonagon was still handicapped by sand bars, necessitating flat boats to load and unload the larger vessels outside the harbor and run the 12 miles up the river to the mine landings. But the Federal government had begun work on the harbor entrance, and real improvements were expected within a year. Even the Detroit and Cleveland shipping monopoly seemed to be weakening, partially as a result of the competition of a Chicago line. In April, 1866, the *Portage Lake Mining Gazaette* reported that the steamship companies were offering contracts for the full season. Formerly the fall rate had been more than twice the summer rate, in part because shipping risks were greater at that time of year. The *Lac La Belle* was lost in 1866 with a heavy load .of copper aboard, and three vessels were lost in

1865, two by fire and one by collision, but most of the mining companies carried insurance against such contingencies and had a great deal of explaining to do to stockholders when they lost shipments which had not been covered. As far as water transportation went, the main battle was over. Future improvements were to be refinements and enlargements of the already existing system.

Benevolent Octopus

ANGUS MURDOCH

A man who lived for years in the shadow of Calumet & Hecla says the company always made him think of that time-honored advertisement of some forgotten furniture concern: "We Stand Behind Every One of Our Beds." The wife of an ex-trammer explains, "The company was wonderful—a man always came and fixed the toilet." Strike an average between these two statements, and you have a fair idea of what life in Calumet Township was like.

If you lived on company property you rented one of the twelve hundred company houses and paid only six to eight dollars a month in rent. You could build your own house if you preferred, but only on rented land with penalizing clauses in your lease. You could buy land outright in Red Jacket or Laurium and build the house of your choice, but your independence amounted to little more than a gesture. Your home was heated with coal brought on company boats, you washed in water from company pumps, had your dinner under company-made electric light. Even your garbage was carried off in company wagons. The books you read were from among the sixteen thousand volumes of the $50,000 company library. The company penetrated your most private life: more than likely your wife would have your children at the company hospital.

No one could deny that, for the most part, company infiltration into your life was good and most economical. The schools in which your children were educated were among the best in the United

From *Boom Copper: The Story of the First U.S. Mining Boom* (New York: The Macmillan Company, 1943), pp. 153-159.

States. The Froebel system of kindergarten teaching was adopted by the Calumet schools long before it was accepted by the school systems of great cities, and even the youngest pupils were cosmopolites, for they imbibed progressive education together with Italians, Poles, Swedes, and Finns. Sundays, you went to the church of your choice; twelve denominations and thirty churches flourished in Calumet Township. The company stood ready to give, rent-free, ground for a house of worship for any reasonable faith. Sunday afternoon the menfolk could bowl, play billiards, or talk in company-owned clubrooms. The young bloods could drill with the Calumet Light Guards in the $33,000, company-built Armory.

If you died underground, if you were sick or your family ailed, there was an employee benefit fund which provided for such contingencies. If your family birth rate got out of hand a company nurse called and made suggestions. If you were hopelessly improvident the company did what it could to teach you to keep your share of the $6,000,000 in wages it paid out every year. You couldn't expect to grow rich, but your monthly stipend was more than ample in a community where living was simple and the company made a business of keeping your expenses down.

Your wife shopped for groceries in either Red Jacket or Laurium and, notably, at independently owned stores. She could take advantage of week-end sales and so spread the budget as far as it would go. One of the pioneer cooperative meat and grocery stores in the United States was located at Tamarack. It was financed with mine money, but mine officials had no part in its operation. It was founded in 1890 and was so successful that the *Saturday Evening Post* devoted an article to it, and the whole country marveled at such progressive economies. The Calumet & Hecla and its independent neighbors never countenanced that curse of most mining communities—the racketeering, employee-bleeding "company store." When Henry Ford was still thinking "Model T" thoughts, the Lake magnates were encouraging their employees to raise their own vegetables and keep their own cow, and provided land free for the purpose.

Alexander Agassiz discovered, long before other corporation heads, that a well housed, well doctored, and diverted employee roll shows up in production figures. Back in 1868, before it had paid a single dividend, the Calumet & Hecla Mining Company had a company hospital, perhaps the first industrial hospital in the United States. Other corporations of the time said this interest in employee health was foolish pampering, but Agassiz was not one to let others mind his business. C. & H. and its neighbors looked after their children, and if the children sometimes grew rebellious at this paternalism there wasn't much they could do about it.

The simpler lives were good ones, but the white-collar workers, living a more complicated social existence, were inclined to resent the Boston caste system, superimposed on Calumet Township. A clerk was a clerk all twenty-four hours a day, and his wife couldn't expect to be included in the afternoon whist parties of ladies whose husbands bore such titles as Assistant Geologist, Associate Metallurgist, or Mill Engineer. And these ladies, in turn, draped by Red Jacket couturiers, were apt to feel uncomfortable as they passed down the reception line at Calumet's yearly balls. This impressive line was invariably made up of transplanted Bostonians who brought the airs and graces of an older world to what they considered frontier functions. Those in the upper reaches of the company mingled, in their social lives, with only the merchants, bankers, and lawyers of the community. Even these leading lights, they considered rather quaint.

This tight little world lived by virtue of the twenty-one prolific shafts of the Calumet & Hecla Mining Company. These fabulous underground highways kept C. & H. production on a par with that of any other mine on earth, and one year outdid them all. A billion feet of timber supported the endless miles of levels, stopes, and drifts. Another forest of dressed pine went underground to line the shafts; and huge steel skips, big as freight cars, sped up and down them at forty miles an hour. Double-decked man cars hurried six thousand miners to and from work as rapidly and nearly as comfortably as the speedy passenger elevators of the Flatiron Building in New York City. The greatest, deepest shaft of them all was the Red Jacket—man's nearest approach to the center of the earth. All the way along its 6,000 feet of vertical depth it was wider and broader than your living room. The Red Jacket shaft was so deep and arrow-straight that a pebble dropped down its mouth would bounce against the pine-paneled sides as the earth rotated.

Reverberations of the Calumet & Hecla's whirring hoists were heard plainest a thousand miles to the east on the Charles River. The twenty-one shafts were financing a copper élite in Back Bay Boston, as rich and haughty as the East India aristocracy once had been. Shares Quincy Shaw had begged friends and relatives to buy for a dollar in the 1860's were worth a round thousand dollars in 1907. C. & H. dividends were building mansions for families to whom Upper Peninsula Michigan was still, in the words of the seventeenth century explorer Baron L'Hontan, "the fag end of creation." Names dating from the *Mayflower* and Plymouth Rock were commonplace on the roll of C. & H. stockholders—Putnam, Frothingham, Bowditch, Hunnewell, Sargent, Thayer. Such early American immortals as Paul Revere, John Alden, and Miles Standish may have been missing, but their cousins were prominent among those listed. Brahms and Beethoven were beneficiaries of C. & H. largess, for Colonel Henry Higginson met the Boston Symphony Orchestra deficits, at least in part, with Michigan copper dividends. Literature, too, owes a debt to Calumet & Hecla—633 of its shares reputedly kept a Miss Amy Lowell in long black cigars.

With a lavish Boston aristocracy and the well-being of 66,000 Keweenawans resting on their shoulders, Alexander Agassiz and his board of directors may be pardoned if they occasionally forgot some of the democratic principles their forefathers fought for in the American Revolution.

Critics accuse the company of running politics to suit itself. Its connivings, detractors say, began in Calumet Township, and extended through county and state to the very halls of Congress. The company, had it bothered to reply, could have pointed to the neighboring Iron Country, where politicians taxed the mining corporations unmercifully. The Calumet & Hecla preferred to spend as it chose, and would go to great lengths to retain this privilege.

Oldsters say election fixing in Houghton County was accomplished by pure psychology and seldom, if ever, by thuggery or ballot-box stuffing. The company simply saw to it that election judges were friendly and could be trusted to remember who buttered their bread; a C. & H. straw boss or two invariably sat among them. A voter entering the polling place was asked whether he wanted a red or blue ballot, though the question was unnecessary. The blue ballot was Republican, while the red, even then, had its present-day connotation; it was left-wing, low-tariff, it was Democratic. Only God Himself, it is said, could help a miner who faced the election judges and said, "Red, please." Each day, thereafter, he was put to meaner and harder tasks so that he was finally driven to depart of his own accord or became so openly rebellious that he could be fired with justification. Election returns in Houghton County seldom surprised anyone.

The company, keeping a weather eye on the polls, usually managed to put down any advanced ideas occurring to the Michigan solons at Lansing. Patriots in the state legislature gagged every time they read the C. & H. stockholders list. Hardly more than 10 per cent were residents of Michigan. Seldom did a session pass without proposed taxation on copper dividends rolling out of the state. Keweenawans understood why such bills never went through. The company also found it advantageous to have a friendly senator or representative in Washington. One of the nation's greatest producers of copper, it liked to see tariff walls built high.

Once Calumet Township reached 66,000 population, it could have become a city. But this was not to company liking. Red Jacket and Laurium could be run more cheaply as villages, and the company, of course, ran Calumet as its chattel. The township government ran the villages, the Houghton County board ran the townships, and the Calumet & Hecla ran all of them. Once the company, tired of the continuous squabbling over the fee office of township treasurer (it was probably the fattest plum in Michigan), suggested that state legislators alter the existing laws. After this, all the township treasurers of Michigan worked on fixed salaries. Yet the only recorded criticism of company high-handedness is that it made election nights so dull.

Calumet Township, grown tall and sturdy on its diet of copper rock, was undoubtedly a regimented domain; but it was this very regimentation that lined its streets with homy, though liver-colored houses (the company was partial to this uninspiring pigment) and its broad parkways with tall shade trees. The houses were not the crude bachelor hovels of the Keweenaw's earlier days. Their windows were curtained, and their front stoops swept immaculate. They bore the face of home and children, and every chimney smoked cheerfully, as if to say, "This is a community of regular pay days."

In the first decade of the new century, all of Europe seemingly poured through America's front door. And the thousands who found their way to the Keweenaw couldn't believe their eyes when they saw the comforts their compatriots enjoyed every day in the week. To these newcomers, Calumet Township was paradise and, in their eyes at least, the company was justified in regarding itself as God. They gratefully adopted the Keweenaw as their own, their native land, and the day on which they became United States citizens was only an incident compared to the day they moved into a company house. Those who had stopped off in the squalid industrial centers of the eastern states were even more thankful for the benevolence of the company. They had a standard of comparison.

Sweetness and light, however, didn't reign universal in the middle of the Keweenaw thumb. There were individualists with a holy hate for the company's domination. Men who had grown up in free and easy copper camps, from one end of the range to the other, bitterly resented the industrialization of their beloved frontier country. Cornish shift bosses often threw up steady jobs under the aegis of C. & H. for precarious employment of one of the prospect mines some new company was always developing. Finnish trammers worked for the company only in between their meager potato crops, and the Irish willingly risked their jobs to run for public office against a company man. Old-time Germans saved every penny

until they could go into business and so call themselves independent.

New arrivals, although they may not have realized their motives,
gathered their children together and went off on the steam train to
Houghton or Hancock. On a Saturday these thriving lake ports were
crowded with miners and their families who could have shopped as
well if not better right at home. The twin cities somehow gave them
a feeling of being on their own. Single miners found escape in the
saloons of Red Jacket hard by company property. Company or no
company, Red Jacket was an old-fashioned boom town on Saturday
night.

Directly after church, on summer Sundays, Calumet Township
moved into the surrounding pine forests. Some took the trolley cars
and rode out to the Ferris wheel at Electric Park. Some saved up,
hired a horse and rig, and drove out to the Cornish community at
the Allouez Mine, four miles away. Young bloods made a day of it,
and went on horseback all the way to Copper Harbor and Fort
Wilkins. It was an historical journey, for all along the road they
could see abandoned shaft houses and listen to the reminiscences of
old folk who refused to move from their near-by homes.

Fact is, the Keweenaw had changed its face. The day of the
pioneer mines was largely past, and life on the range was centered
around Ontonagon, Portage Lake, and Calumet Township. The
mines to the west were producing plenty of copper, but they, like
the Osceola, Tamarack, and Kearsarge, were overshadowed by the
Colossus of the range. From here on in, the people of the Keweenaw, as well as the outside world, thought of the Copper Country as
the Calumet & Hecla.

The discovery and exploitation of Michigan's iron ore deposits occurred shortly after Douglas Houghton's report (1841) suggested that the
Upper Peninsula contained iron ore as well as copper. The iron range
developed more slowly than the copper region, but after 1855, when the
St. Mary's Falls Ship Canal Company completed the Sault Canal, iron ore
became the main cargo of lake transportation. Before that time considerable effort went toward the establishment of a regional pig iron industry,
and while it did not flourish consistently, the local blast furnaces did
continue on into the 1870s and '80s. Ultimately iron ore became the
nearly exclusive commercial product of the iron range, which in sheer

volume has amounted to a staggering output. It continues to be a major economic mainstay for the Upper Peninsula.

The best general source of information about the Upper Peninsula's early pig iron and iron ore productions is A. P. Swineford's *History and Review of the Copper, Iron, . . .* (Marquette, 1876). Other general accounts include Harlan Hatcher's *A Century of Iron and Men* (Indianapolis, 1950), and Walter Havighurst's *Vein of Iron: The Pichands-Mather Story* (New York, 1958). For an examination of Peter White there is a biography by Herbert Brinks published by Eerdmans in 1970 as part of that publisher's *Great Men of Michigan* series. Articles concerned with specific aspects of the iron industry include Ray Brotherden, "The Discovery of Iron Ore," *Michigan History*, XXVII (1944), and Clint Dunathan, "Fayette," *Michigan History*, XLI (1957).

The Iron Region of Lake Superior

PETER WHITE

The existence of valuable copper mines along Lake Superior had long been known. The narratives of the Jesuit Fathers during the seventeenth century make frequent mention of them, and they have also been noticed by several travelers in the last century. The copper of Lake Superior occurs in the form of metallic copper, which can be hammered, sharpened and hardened, and hundreds of years before our period, extensive mining developments had been made at many points along the range by rude races whose metallurgical knowledge did not extend to the smelting of iron from its ores. With their stone hammers they beat out pieces of copper for arrow heads and knives from the rocky veins, which they softened by building fires over or against them, but the iron ores were no more interesting or valuable to them than any of the other rocks of the country. Thus it happened that there was no antecedent knowledge of the iron deposits of the upper peninsula derived from Indian traditions or the observation of early travelers. The first knowledge of them was obtained from the U. S. government surveyors in 1844. In the summer of that year the late Dr. Douglass Houghton, whose memory is deeply reverenced throughout the region, where were his latest labors and where he lost his life, was engaged in the linear survey of this portion of the upper peninsula. The late Mr. William A. Burt, deputy surveyor under him, was

From *Michigan Pioneer and Historical Collections* (Lansing: Robert Smith Printing Company, 1885), VIII, 146-161.

running the township lines in Marquette county, and on the 18th of September encamped, with his party, at the east end of Teal Lake. Mr. Jacob Houghton was a member of that party, and gives the following account of the first discovery of Lake Superior iron ore:

"On the morning of the 19th of September, 1844, we started to run the line south between ranges 26 and 27. As soon as we reached the hill to the south of the lake, the compassman began to notice the fluctuation in the variation of the magnetic needle. We were of course using the solar compass, of which Mr. Burt was the inventor, and I shall never forget the excitement of the old gentleman, when viewing the changes of the variation, the needle not actually traversing alike in any two places. He kept changing his position to take observations, all the time saying: 'How would they survey this country without my compass?' 'What could be done here without my compass?' It was the full and complete realization of what he had foreseen when struggling through the first stages of his invention. At length the compassman called for us all to 'come and see a variation which will beat them all.' As we looked at the instrument, to our astonishment, the north end of the needle was traversing a few degrees to the south of west. Mr. Burt called out, 'Boys, look around and see what you can find!' We all left the line, some going to the east, some going to the west, and all of us returned with specimens of iron ore, mostly gathered from out-crops. This was along the first mile from Teal Lake. We carried out all the specimens we could conveniently. Hon. J. N. Mellen, of Romeo, Michigan, who was one of the party, has still in his possession one of the specimens found that day."

The ores to-day make nearly one-third of all the iron produced in the United States. This was eleven years before the building of the first canal at Sault Ste. Marie. The transportation of the iron ore to the coal fields of Ohio and Pennsylvania would then have been impracticable, and had not yet occurred to anybody. Thus it happened that the first attempt to utilize these deposits was by making blooms from the ore in forges with charcoal. The first of these forges was built by the Jackson Iron Company on the Carp river, three miles east of Negaunee, in 1847. This company was organized at Jackson, Michigan, in June, 1845, for the purpose of exploring the mineral regions on the south shore of Lake Superior, and dispatched an expedition to Lake Superior, under the charge of Mr. P. M. Everett, during the summer of that year. They located a War Department permit on section 1, town 47 N., range 27 W., which they subsequently purchased of the United States government. This was the first iron location to be developed, and it became an exceedingly valuable and productive mine. The following extract of a letter from Mr. Everett, written after his return to Jackson in the autumn of 1845, may be of interest:

"I took four men with me from Jackson, and hired a guide at the Sault, where I bought a boat and coasted up the lake to Copper Harbor, which is over three hundred miles from Sault Ste. Marie. There are no white men on Lake Superior except those who go there for mining purposes. We incurred many dangers and hardships; we made several locations, one of which we called Iron at the time. It is a mountain of solid iron ore, one hundred and fifty feet high. The ore looks as bright as a bar of iron just broken. Since coming home we have had some of it smelted, and find that it produces iron and something resembling gold; some say it is gold and copper. Our location is one mile square, and we shall send a company of men up in the spring to begin operations. Our company is called the Jackson mining company."

In the following year, 1846, another expedition was fitted out by the Jackson Iron Company, in charge of Mr. A. V. Berry, to make further explorations. The following extract from a letter from Mr. Berry describes his experience, and its conclusion relates a fate which has befallen many another pioneer. He says: "I found our location much beyond what I had anticipated. After spending twelve days in the woods exploring the surrounding country, including what was afterwards known as the Cleveland location, and building what was called a house, we returned to the mouth of the Carp with three hundred pounds of ore on our backs. We there divided—one party was left to keep possession of the location and another went farther up the lake to use the remaining permits, while I returned to the Sault with the ore. On arriving at Jackson we endeavored on two occasions to smelt the ore which I had brought down, in our common cupola furnaces, but failed entirely. In August of the same year Mr. Olds of Coo Cush Prairie, who owned a forge, succeeded in making a fine bar of iron from our ore in a blacksmith's fire—the first iron ever made from Lake Superior ore. In the winter of 1846-7 we began to get up at Jackson a bellows and other machinery for constructing a forge at the Carp; and in the summer of 1847 a company of men commenced building the same and continued until March, 1848, when a freshet carried away the dam. The association was then (1848) merged into an incorporated company—by some means the pioneers in the enterprise are now all out."

The first iron made in the first forge was on the 10th of February, 1848, by forgeman Ariel N. Barney, who also established the first hotel in the village of Marquette, and was one of its first justices of the peace. The forge was a primitive affair. The power was supplied by the Carp river across which a dam eighteen feet high was built. There were eight fires, from each of which a lump was taken every six hours, placed under the hammer, and forged into blooms, four inches square and two feet long, the daily product being about three tons. It required two six-horse teams to draw this product to the lake shore, over a wretched road. The Jackson forge was finally abandoned in 1854, after steadily having lost its owners and several successive lessees. The next forge to be built was that of the Marquette Iron Company. Its building was the beginning of the city of Marquette. In the winter of 1848 the late Robert J. Graveraet, who had acquired some iron lands and leases, visited Worcester, Mass., and in connection with Mr. Edward Clark, enlisted Mr. Amos R. Harlow in the enterprise. Mr. Harlow, who was the owner of a machine shop, constructed and purchased the necessary machinery for the projected works, and in the spring of 1849 shipped the whole to Lake Superior, following with his family a few months later. That spring, where is now Marquette, there was no sign of a human habitation, save one or two Indian huts and a small log warehouse belonging to the Jackson Iron Company.

Your narrator, then a boy of nineteen, had landed on the beach a few weeks before Mr. Harlow's arrival. I had made one ineffectual attempt, shortly after the first excitement over the discoveries of copper in 1845, to go up to Lake Superior, which had gained a great hold on the imagination of the boys of that day. I got as far as the Sault, and endeavored, without success, to get passage by the little schooner "Merchant," which was the only craft just then going up the lake. I had no money, and they would not let me work my way. Had I got passage, it is safe to say, some one else would be giving you this narrative to-day. The schooner was never heard of afterwards; she went to the bottom, with all on board. The second time I had better luck. I joined a party, under the lead of the late Robert J. Graveraet, which set out from Mackinac in April, 1849, on the old steamer, "Tecumseh," with the intention of claiming and developing all the iron mountains which had then been, or should subsequently be, discovered in that region. At Sault Ste. Marie, we succeeded in crowding our large Mackinac barge up the rapids, and after eight days' rowing, towing, poling and sailing, we landed at what was then called Indian town, near the present site of the freight station of the Detroit, Mackinac & Marquette Railroad in the city of Marquette. The next morning we started for the much-talked-of iron hills. At the Cleveland mountain we found Capt. Samuel Moody and John H. Mann, who had spent the previous summer and winter there. I well remember how astonished I was the next morning, when Captain Moody asked me to go with him to dig some potatoes for breakfast. He had half an acre on the summit of the hill, since known as the Marquette Company's Mountain, partially cleared and planted with potatoes. This was in the month of May, and the winter's snow had preserved them. He opened one or two hills and filled his pail with large and perfectly sound potatoes. He then said: "I may as well pull up a few parsnips and carrots for dinner, to save coming up again;" and sure enough he had them in abundance. From this time till the 10th of July we kept possession of all the iron mountains then known west of the Jackson, fighting mosquitoes at night and black flies through the day. On the 10th of July we returned to the lake shore.

Mr. Harlow had arrived with mechanics, goods, lots of money, and what was better than all, we got a glimpse of some female faces. At one o'clock of that day we commenced clearing the site of the present city of Marquette. We began by chopping off the trees and brush at the point of the rocks just south of the Cleveland ore docks. We cut the trees close to the ground and threw them over the bank onto the lake shore; then, under the direction of Captain Moody, we began the construction of a dock, which we thought would stand like the pyramids. We did this by carrying these whole trees into the water and piling them in tiers crosswise, until the pile was even with the surface of the water. Then we wheeled sand and gravel upon it, and by the end of the second day had completed the structure upon which we looked with no little pride. The eastward, or outer, end was solid rock and all inside that was solid dirt, brush and leaves. We thought it would last as long as the adjacent beach itself. On the third day we continued to improve it by corduroying the surface, and by night of that day it was, in our eyes, a thing of beauty to behold. Our chagrin may be imagined when, on rising the next morning, we found that a gentle sea had come in during the night and wafted our dock to parts unknown. The sand of the beach was as clean and smooth as if it had never been disturbed by the hand of man. It was a long time before anyone had the hardihood to attempt the building of another dock. The propellers would come to anchor sometimes as far as two miles from shore, and freight and passengers were landed in small boats. Cattle and horses were pitched overboard and made to swim ashore.

The boiler for the Marquette forge was plugged, heaved over-board three miles out, and towed ashore. Your narrator has a vivid recollection of that boiler, which he took a contract to fill, after it was placed, for a dollar and a half. It required nearly four days' hard work with two pails and a yoke. This was the first steam boiler introduced into Marquette county. During the ensuing winter and spring (of 1850) the original Jackson Company had exhausted both its capital and credit, the Marquette Company's forge was now finished, and the Marquette Company entered upon the process of exhausting theirs. Their forge was burned early in 1853. These early developments in Marquette county were never stimulated or encouraged, by any return upon any capital invested, in any single instance until 1863. It was all a work of faith and perseverance, founded upon intuitions which were sound and sure, but which it took twenty years to realize. Meanwhile man after man and company after company cast all they had into the gulf which time only could fill. Those days were days of hardships to the early settlers.

Marquette, in 1851-3, consisted of a few houses, a stumpy road winding along the lake shore; a forge which burned up after impoverishing its first owners; a trail westward, just passable for wagons, leading to another forge (still more unfortunate in that it did not burn), and to the developed iron hills beyond, with two or three hundred people uncertain of the future,—they had fallen into the march of the century and were building better than they knew.

. . . .

But better times were in store for us. A ship canal at Sault Ste. Marie and a railroad to the mines were in the near future. The shipping or exportation of iron ore in either large or small quantities had not entered into the ideas or plans of the earliest settlers in the country; their only thought was to manufacture either bar or bloom iron which could bear the cost of many handlings— particularly the very costly transportation over the portage at Sault Ste. Marie. The realization of the ship canal project at the Sault transformed the existing dream of a railroad from Marquette to the iron mountains into a certainty. In August, 1852, Congress passed an act granting to the State of Michigan 750,000 acres of land, to be located within the State, for the purpose of aiding in the construction and completion of a ship canal around the falls of Ste. Marie. This was largely due to the persevering efforts of Mr. John Burt, of Detroit. At this juncture Mr. Charles T. Harvey rendered valuable service in inducing the right men to go in and furnish the capital to carry out what was universally considered to be a work of enormous magnitude, surrounded by unfavorable circumstances, and in the way of whose successful termination and inauguration almost insuperable obstacles lay. The names of the men who backed Mr. Harvey with capital and encouragement in the construction of the canal deserve to be enrolled in the archives of this association, and I am proud to mention them here for that purpose. They were: John F. Seymour, Erastus Corning, James F. Joy, J. W. Brooks, J. V. L. Pruyn, Joseph P. Fairbanks, and John M. Forbes. These names are well known and have been recognized in very many large and honest enterprises in different quarters of the United States during the past forty years. The land was selected about one-third in the upper and two-thirds in the lower peninsula. The total cost of the construction of the canal was $1,000,000. Mr. John Burt, of Detroit, who had rendered important services in various ways during the construction of the canal, was, at its completion, appointed its first superintendent.

Many other persons, all of whose names I cannot recall, were personally instrumental in promoting the building of the canal, among whom these should be mentioned: Judge Wm. A. Burt, the father of Mr. John Burt; Captain Canfield, of the United States Topographical Corps; Mr. J. W. Brooks, Dr. Morgan L. Hewitt, and the late Heman B. Ely. The canal proved equal to all expectations in its workings for several years, but later on the vast increase of commerce made it necessary to use larger lake craft, drawing a greater depth of water than this canal would accommodate, and the State of Michigan was induced to spend some part of the earnings of the canal on its enlargement, but all that was done in this way was so manifestly inadequate that Congress was again successfully appealed to and asked to make a cash appropriation on the score of its being a great national work on the national frontier. The general government has made repeated appropriations which have been expended under the skillful direction of General Weitzel and General O. M. Poe, until the locks are now the largest and most perfect and durable structures of the kind in the world. I might say in closing my reference to the canal that the State of Michigan, under the advice of Governor Jerome, very wisely transferred its title and interest, with the care and management of the canal, to the United States. Congress has by public act accepted the trust and has since made this great national highway free to the commerce of the world.

The first railroad projected and completed in all the vast domain known as the upper peninsula was the Iron Mountain Railroad, from Marquette to the iron mines, whose first terminus was on the present site of the city of Ishpeming. In 1852 the late Mr. Heman B. Ely caused a preliminary survey to be made for this road. At that time there was no general railroad law, and at the request of the people of the district, Mr. Ely accepted the office of representative in the State Legislature in order that he might procure the enactment of such a law. The original general Railroad Act, which was passed by the Legislature and approved February 5, 1855, was drawn, introduced and its passage advocated by Hon. Heman B. Ely. This accomplished, Mr. Ely at once organized a railroad company and commenced the construction in the early spring of 1855. His brothers, George H. and Samuel P. Ely, had given him material aid up to 1855, when he prosecuted the work as an individual enterprise, now joined with other friends, among whom were Jos. S. Fay, Lewis H. Morgan, Edward Parsons, and John Burt, in the organization of the Iron Mountain Railroad Company. The starting and carrying on of an enterprise of such magnitude at that early day, so far from a base of supplies, together with a scarcity of labor and the many other difficulties, was a work requiring more pluck, skill and capital than the canal which I have just described to you. The grades were heavy—rock cutting very extensive, bottomless swamps to cross, with fills numerous and difficult to make. And to add to the numberless obstacles and annoyances, the severe winters of those days came with deep snows and extreme frosts, while the summer season brought overwhelming swarms of black flies, gnats and mosquitoes. The road was not fully completed and equipped for business until the year 1857.

Mr. H. B. Ely, to whose clear foresight and indefatigable energy the origin and success of this railroad enterprise was almost wholly due, and to whom the general interest of the Lake Superior country, as well as the State of Michigan at large, became in many ways greatly indebted, died in Marquette, in October, 1856, half a year before the work he had so zealously labored upon was fully completed. Mr. Heman B. Ely was a man of prophetic insight, who saw even at that early day the future growth and greatness of the iron region. All the development and prosperity of the present day is but the realization of his confident expectations and predictions.

. . . .

The first mining superintendent in the iron region was Captain Henry Merry, who opened the Jackson mine, and has ever since remained in charge of it. These old companies have not been prone to change their superintendents. Captain F. P. Mills remained in charge of the Cleveland mine for twenty-two years, and Captain G. D. Johnson, who opened the Lake Superior mine, remained in charge of it for eighteen years. All three were men of unusual energy and capacity, and made their mark in the successful development of a kind of mining in which there was no former experience. If the time at our command and the proper restrictions of an occasion devoted to strictly pioneer history admitted, it would be interesting to trace in detail the subsequent large development of iron mining on Lake Superior.

But the limitations, both of time and our subject, will allow only mention of some of the more noted of the later mines, and such a brief survey of the later important developments of the business as may serve to connect its beginnings, which have been described to you, with the present enlargement. The Lake Angeline, the Barnum, and the New York mines were opened soon after at Ishpeming, and a few years later the Champion mine, which was become distinguished as a large producer. In 1872, a branch from the Marquette & Ontonagon Railroad was completed to the now well known Republic mine, which was opened in that year. This location was discovered as far back as 1852, by the veteran explorer, Mr. S. C. Smith, and it had been known as the Smith Mountain for twenty years before it had been reached with railroad facilities. The Michigamme and various other mines were opened at the same time, along the extension of the iron range westward. Active explorations for iron ore on the Menominee range commenced about this time, and many promising deposits were discovered, which began to be developed in 1877, after the completion of a branch of the Chicago & Northwestern Railroad gave them an outlet at Escanaba. The Menominee range has proved to be of very great productive capacity, and has been developed with great rapidity.

Among many other well-known mines, the Chapin has become conspicuous as a very large producer. I do not intend to burden you with statistics, but it may interest you to compare the shipments of the three "old mines" in 1858, which were 25,067 tons, with the total shipments in 1884, of both the Marquette and the Menominee iron ranges, from the ports of Marquette, Escanaba, L'Anse and St. Ignace. Seventy-two mines on the Marquette range had shipped 19,502,069 tons, and twelve mines on the Menominee range had shipped 3,452,174 tons, making a total of 22,954,243 tons.

Mining Becomes Big Business

HARLAN HATCHER

The consolidations, highly publicized by the names of Rockefeller, Carnegie and Morgan, caused some anxiety on the part of the American public and their representatives in the Government and the press. Brought up in the era of small private business, they feared the specter of monopoly. They attempted to cope with the potential evil by governmental regulation. The controls which were set up did aid, perhaps, in preventing their worst apprehensions

From *A Century of Iron and Men,* pp. 193-197. Copyright,1950, by The Bobbs-Merrill Company, Inc. Reprinted by permission of the publisher.

from materializing. Actually the iron-ore industry remained strongly competitive. And under the given conditions, the movement toward a few strong companies was inevitable. By no other means could an industry requiring such heavy financial obligations and such a delicate balance between raw materials and transportation and the processing plants be successfully managed. The mills had to have a guaranteed supply of various grades of ore to keep them running regularly and without interruption. Since the Great Lakes are open to navigation only seven to eight months of the year between the melting of the ice in the spring and the first heavy freeze in the early winter, the mining, shipping and stockpiling of a year's supply must be planned for with close precision.

The amount of capital necessary to sustain such a far-flung and expensive operation steadily increased. Even on the Mesabi, where the ore could be scooped up from open pits, the outlay was still great. Consider simply the demand for machinery. In the early open-pit days, when each little company operated a mine or two on slender capital, horses or mules were used as a matter of initial economy. But as the scale of operations enlarged, this form of power became the most expensive and the most wasteful. Major Brooks, writing a classical report in the Geological Survey of Michigan in 1873, said flatly: "If ever there comes a period when our mines do not pay it may be due largely to horses." What he meant was that horses had been introduced when only a little power was needed, and more had been added as the demand increased. Now the mines were involving costs too great to be borne and yet they did not have enough capital to make the transition to steam. At one time 350 horses were employed at the mines, with the expense for all their work reaching $250,000 a year. It cost $650 to work one horse for one year. This investment, Major Brooks pointed out, was "sufficient in itself to supply all the mines in the region with all the additional steam-hoisting and pumping machinery and small locomotives required to do the work now done by horses and at a very much less yearly cost." The day of "pick-and-shovel, hammer-and-drill, horse-and-cart business," he said, was over. He was correct. But the only way the change-over could be effected was by consolidation, because the small operator could neither stand the loss of production during the transition nor provide the capital with which to buy the machinery.

The situation was no different in principle on the Mesabi Range. Little or no blasting or drilling was required. But the overburden had to be stripped off and moved out of the way. Steam shovels were the only practical tools for such massive duty. They, too, cost a lot of money. They had to be manufactured down below, transported to the Upper Lake port, and hauled back to the mines. They broke down frequently and were repaired with difficulty and delay. Steam engines and ore cars were needed for the pits, and the track construction along the cut-away shelves, involving switches at each level, was expensive in material and in labor. Once again, only the strongest companies could engage in this operation, and they needed not one but several mines to make it profitable.

As the competition increased, every penny that went into the cost of a ton of ore became of vital importance. The price of ore declined steadily, driven down by forces outside the control of the individual mine operators. They had to get out more ore at less cost. The only method by which they could accomplish this was a vastly increased capital outlay to provide machinery that would ultimately reduce these costs. Steam and electric power got rid of the horses and increased the output per man in the mines. The power drill could replace the three-man team—one to hold and turn the drill and two to swing the sledge hammers—and it could make a hole more quickly. Machinery could also reduce the burden of all the dead work, i.e., uncovering the ore, or removing dirt and rock and preparing the face for mining. Royalty rates were an important item. They were fixed charges generally covering long terms. Many of them, contracted for during speculative booms, were very high. This was especially true on the Gogebic where some of the properties were saddled with rates up to 75 cents per ton. Oliver had leased Missabe Mountain at what was considered the exorbitant rate of 65 cents per ton, but Rockefeller had secured his at 25 cents.

Every mile of haulage entered into the calculations and the cost. Rail haulage, as compared with water transportation, is exceedingly costly because of the huge outlay for rolling equipment, the relatively small loads on each train, the upkeep of the road and the wages of the men who operate it. Compared to rail costs, shipping by water is cheap, and the distances over which the ore must be transported are great. The water route from Duluth-Superior to Cleveland is 834 miles; from Two Harbors to the same port it is 810 miles; from Ashland, the chief outlet port for the Gogebic Range, it is 789 miles; from Marquette, 598 miles; and from Escanaba, the port for the Menominee mines, 540 miles. The fact that water transportation was available for the shipment of iron ore from these ranges has been of great importance in the development of the Lake Superior district mines. It is even more economical to dump coal out of rail cars into a freighter at Toledo and float the cargo to Detroit than to take the train itself the additional 70 miles overland.

The mines on the Marquette Range, although having the disadvantage of being mostly underground mines as compared to the open pit operations on the Mesabi Range, have the advantage of a short rail haul to the loading docks at Marquette. This, coupled with the lower lake freight rates from Marquette as compared with those from the head of Lake Superior, has served as an offset to the higher costs of underground mining, making possible the continued large movement of ore from this range.

In attempting to understand Michigan's history, some knowledge of the significance of the Great Lakes is crucial. They have virtually dictated the importance of some cities—Detroit, Marquette, and Saginaw—while also supplying transportation, food, and recreation. Our inland seas have supplied interesting lore for historians, novelists, and that large army of nautical talebearers who follow the fortunes of ships, ships' captains, and shipwrecks. The selections given below touch on only two aspects of Great Lakes history, but they suggest interesting possibilities for further reading and research.

Milo M. Quaife edited his *American Lakes Series* in the 1940s, and contributed his own volume, *Lake Michigan*, in 1944. Others published that same year in Indianapolis include Fred Landon's *Lake Huron*, Grace Lee Nute's *Lake Superior*, and Harlan Hatcher's *Lake Erie*. General studies of the Great Lakes vary from the pictorial and impressionistic to those with solid scholarly content. Among the better ones are J. H. Beers' *History of the Great Lakes*, two vols. (Chicago, 1899); George Culbertson's *Freshwater: A History of the Great Lakes* (New York, 1932), and Walter Havighurst's *The Long Ship's Passing* (New York, 1942). One journal, *Inland Seas*, directs its content almost exclusively to topics relating to Great Lakes history.

Fish and Fishing

BELA HUBBARD

The largest and best white-fish are taken further up the lakes, the ordinary weight of those from our river being about four or five pounds. In lakes Huron and Michigan they average five or six

From *Memorials of a Half-Century* (New York: G. P. Putnam's Sons, 1887), pp. 268-277.

pounds, and in Lake Superior attain to ten pounds, and even more. The largest I ever saw was estimated to weigh twelve to fifteen pounds, and had been pulled ashore by an otter out of the cold waters of our great lake. The creature made off on the approach of our boat, relinquishing his prey to our superior claims—the right of the strongest.

The seine, of course, catches all kinds of fish that come within its sweep, and are not too small to escape through its two-and-a-half-inch meshes. Among these is occasionally a hugh sturgeon, often of forty pounds weight. And more rarely . . . the muskallonge. The latter is also taken by hook and line in our river and in Lake Ste. Claire.

Another fish of the salmon family is caught in great numbers in the lakes above, and is an article of commerce only second in importance to the white-fish—the salmon trout. It is much larger than its white cousin, attaining to forty pounds. Though a hard fleshed and admirable fish, it lacks the delicate flavor which makes the white-fish so dainty a dish for the epicure.

. . . .

Before concluding my "angling" experiences, I must relate a yet more novel method of fish capture, of which I was witness, "et quorum pars fui," in one of my wanderings upon our great inland waters. Our party, landing at a rocky island in Lake Huron, came suddenly upon a shoal of fish, that were gambolling in the light surf that broke among the boulders which lined the shore. They were not porpoises, as you might suppose had it been an ocean shore, but sturgeon, better known in a distant part of the country as "Albany beef." So engaged were they in their sport as to be unconscious of our presence, while we stripped and waded in among them. We thus succeeded in nabbing several with our hands alone, and after a pretty hard tussle one fine fellow was safely landed. It kept our larder in beef and chicken for several days.

On the flats of Lake Ste. Claire a novel scene may be witnessed from a boat floating over the shallows; namely, sturgeon in the act of *pumping*. This is their mode of supplying themselves with craw-fish. These burrow in the sand, leaving holes behind them. Here the fish stations himself, with his mouth over the hole, and by a strong effort of suction produces a current in the water, which is drawn violently into his mouth. Considerable sand accompanies, which is ejected by the gills, and settles in piles or ridges on either side. Whether or not the craw-fish comes out from his retreat to see what all the commotion is about, or whether he comes because he cannot help it, certain it is that up he comes, the torrent carrying him directly into the mouth of the wily fish; but he does not pass out through the gills.

. . . .

The vast increase of our fisheries during the last ten years, and the repeated observations of intelligent fishermen, as well as of a few scientific observers, have elicited many curious facts in the life history of the white-fish, which are of great interest.

The following facts seem to be well established:

The white-fish is short lived, and of very rapid growth, maturing the second year, and ending its life with the third.

The spawn is deposited in the fall (October and November), in shallow water, and the hatching takes place in the spring, or first month of summer, according to locality.

Soon after hatching, the young fry withdraw into deep, cold water, where they remain until the summer of the following year.

They then commence their return to the hatching grounds, for the purpose of spawning. And it is well attested,—incredible as the fact may seem,—that during the three months succeeding, or between June and September, they increase in size from about two and a half ounces to from four to nine or ten pounds weight. In other words, from mere minnows of one year they attain maturity.

Early in the summer of the third year they retire again into deep waters, and are seen no more. The white-fish is a bottom-feeder, and lives upon the young, or aquatic larvae of the ephemera, which are found in the river mud.

These fish do not migrate, as was formerly supposed, from the lower to the higher lakes, the superior size of those found in the latter being due to the local breed, and not to age. Fish of the same locality are of remarkably uniform size.

During the summer months, it will be observed, the fish of the second year are making their way up from the deep waters to the spawning grounds, while the old fishes are returning to the deep water to die. The fishing season is therefore confined to the spring and fall,—from the time the ice leaves until about the middle of June, and from September to the end of November.

At these seasons only full-grown fish are liable to be taken.

It is contended by advocates of the exclusive use of the seine that the stock of fish is being needlessly diminished by the use of the pound, which takes the fish indiscriminately, the small with the large, whole schools being taken at once.

On the other hand, it is maintained that the pound-net cannot so operate, for the reason that the minnows and half-grown fish escape through the meshes of the lead. And further, that by the constant capture of the sturgeon and long-lived fishes of the sucker tribe, which live upon the spawn of the white-fish, the annual stock of the latter is on the increase wherever these nets are in constant use.

It is also said that it is impossible to diminish the number, no matter how many are taken, because only those are caught which have matured and never propagate again. Some further time and observation must yet be had before these questions can be fully settled.

. . . .

Since the above was written, forty years ago, fisheries have not only been largely extended, but stringent laws have been enacted for their regulation. Active measures are also being taken by both the general and State governments, for stocking our streams and lakes with young fry, artificially hatched, of the kinds most suitable.

In 1841 about 30,000 barrels of white-fish only were packed annually. Probably not less than 50,000 are now sold annually by Detroit merchants alone.

In 1868 half a million of white-fish were captured by Detroit River fisheries, as many as 20,000 being sometimes secured in a single haul of the seine.

Though the fishing season proper is in the spring and fall, modern luxury, at the time when this note is being recorded, has invented methods for bringing to our tables at all times of the year this estimable food. Not only are the finer sorts brought from the cold waters of the upper lakes, packed in ice, and with their firmness and delicacy little impaired, but they are transported in the same frozen condition to the most distant markets.

In 1855, Mr. George Clark, of Detroit, inaugurated a method of impounding the fish, at the time of the fall fishing, by dragging them by means of the nets into large pens, where they are kept alive and sound for the winter supply. There is a very large demand, and the trade is carried on in Detroit chiefly. Probably not less than half a million are sent from here annually, the produce of these winter pens.

How well I remember the time when the fishing season—at which time alone could this dainty fare be obtained—was looked forward to by the old residents with pleasure and impatience, and one of the hardships of a removal to other parts of the country was experienced in the longing after this favorite dish. Now this "deer of the lakes"—par excellence—is not only universally known, but is procurable cheaply, at all seasons, both fresh and salted, from the lakes to the Gulf, and from the Mississippi to Cape Cod. It has even overleaped these bounds, and is shipped direct to Liverpool.

But this constant drain has of late years, in spite of all precautions, tended to constantly diminish the annual catch. The gill-net has superseded the seine, necessity having withdrawn the operations into deeper waters. The greed of trade outruns all sober precautions. And it is to be feared that the time is rapidly approaching when the inhabitants of our lakes and rivers, like the wild animals which were once so abundant and are now so few, will be in like manner exterminated, and this great industry of Michigan will cease to be remunerative.

Perils of the Deep

MILO M. QUAIFE

Probably the most constant single cause of disasters on Lake Michigan throughout the centuries has been the tempests, which often develop suddenly and rage with appalling fury. The Indian canoe was always at their mercy, and legends are not wanting of large-scale tragedies which resulted when fleets of canoes ventured too far from land. At one time the Wisconsin Winnebago, at war with the Foxes on the Michigan side of the lake, sent an army of 500 braves against them, but a tempest arising, they perished to the last man. "Their enemies were moved by this disaster," the chronicle continues, "and said that the gods ought to be satisfied with so many punishments; so they ceased making war on those who remained."

The absence of natural harbors made the navigation of Lake Michigan particularly hazardous for the early mariner. From Green Bay and the Manitous southward there was not a single place of refuge, so that vessels were compelled to anchor in the open lake to receive and discharge passengers and cargo and in case of storm to flee 200 miles or more before shelter could be found.

The story of the loss of the *Hercules* illustrates the peril to which

From *Lake Michigan*, pp. 252-258. Copyright, 1944, by The Bobbs-Merrill Company, Inc. Reprinted by permission of the publisher. Footnotes in the original have been omitted.

all ships which ventured into Lake Michigan were exposed. The little schooner sailed from Chicago homeward bound to Detroit on the evening of October 2, 1818. On the morning of the third, one of the worst gales the oldest inhabitant could remember developed, and raged for two days. No tidings of the *Hercules* came to the anxious watchers at Chicago until on October 9 a party of Indians from Grand River arrived, bringing with them some objects they had picked up along the shore at the south end of the lake. Among them was a scale which belonged to Lieutenant Eveleth, a promising young West Pointer attached to the Engineer Corps of the Army, who was returning on the *Hercules* from a tour of observation of the military defenses in the Northwest. A rescue party dispatched from Fort Dearborn returned three days later with the report that they had found the lake shore near what is now Michigan City strewn with fragments of the ship for a distance of twelve or fifteen miles. Only one body had been found and that in an unrecognizable condition. The hull of the ship had vanished completely, although portions of the masts had blown ashore. Before the arrival of the searching party the neighboring Potawatomi Indians had appropriated and carried off every article of value which had come ashore.

One of the seamen on the *Hercules* was a young Vermonter named Luke Sherwin, who had recently come to the lakes, and who a few weeks before her destruction had proudly written his brother in Vermont, "I am now a sailor," adding that when the season of navigation closed he might accompany a friend upon a journey to New Orleans. A few weeks later his corpse was battered to nothingness amid the breakers which dashed themselves upon the shore at the head of Lake Michigan.

The fate of those aboard the *Hercules* is still braved by all who embark upon the Inland Seas, despite all the improved resources of modern scientific and mechanical skill. The tempest of November 9, 1913, in which a dozen vessels and over two hundred lives were lost, remains the greatest destruction of life and property by a single storm. But almost a century earlier, in November 1842, when Great Lakes shipping was still in its infancy, about a hundred lives were lost and almost fifty vessels wrecked in a single tempest. Eighteen ships were wrecked on the north shore of Lake Erie alone and many more on the shores of Michigan and Ontario. Again in 1869 a three-day tempest raged from November 16 to 19. Almost a hundred vessels were driven ashore or foundered, and thirty-five of them were total losses.

That the strength of the gale still laughs to scorn the puny devices of men is illustrated by a storm, described in the press as the greatest of a decade, which broke over Lake Michigan on November

11-12, 1940. Several great freighters were lost or driven ashore and over sixty lives were reported lost. Off Pentwater the pulpwood carrier *Novadoc*, running between Chicago and Fort William, went aground, its back broken by the fury of the November gale; all but two of its crew of nineteen men were saved from impending death by the small fishing tug *Three Brothers*, which braved the stormy sea to bring them ashore.

. . . .

Among the most distressing tragedies ever enacted on Lake Michigan were the destruction of the *Phoenix* by fire in 1847 and the *Lady Elgin* by collision in 1860. In both cases scenes of horror which could scarcely be excelled were relieved by displays of heroism which thrill the heart of the reader even after the lapse of a century.

The *Phoenix* was a propeller of 302 tons, built in 1845, which plied between Buffalo and Chicago. On November 11, 1847, she began her westward run, heavily laden with merchandise consigned to Chicago and with a capacity load of passengers, almost all of them emigrants from Holland coming to join relatives and friends who had already found homes in Michigan or other states of the Middle West. The route of the *Phoenix*, like that of most other ships, ran down the Wisconsin shore of Lake Michigan, since there were no important towns on the eastern coast. Leaving Manitowoc in stormy weather after midnight of November 21, the vessel strained under her load and the firemen fed her boilers furiously. About four o'clock in the morning smoke began pouring from the engine room and the alarm of fire was given. Although a bucket brigade was formed, it soon became apparent that efforts to subdue the fire were vain and the vessel's two small lifeboats were launched with forty-three passengers and crew, all of whom reached the shore in safety.

Left behind on the doomed *Phoenix* were some 200 souls, including passengers and crew, most of them the Dutch emigrants who were hopefully nearing the end of their 4,000-mile pilgrimage. Two hours passed by, while the fire continued to rage and they desperately awaited the return of the lifeboats or the arrival of other rescuers. They came, but too late. Many of the passengers had sought refuge from the fire and smoke by retreating to the rigging, where they perished one by one as the flames mounted the tarred ropes and fired the sails. Others leaped into the lake, to sink at once in the icy water or to cling precariously to pieces of floating wreckage from which they eventually slipped to their watery graves; some remained on their floats and perished from the cold.

Meanwhile at near-by Sheboygan the alarm had been given and the work of rescue was set in motion. The lifeboat of the schooner *Liberty* was manned and started for the scene, followed by many small boats launched by civilians, while the propeller *Delaware*, which chanced to be in the harbor, began raising steam to join in the work. As it turned out she arrived first, about seven o'clock, to find but three persons, all men, still alive. Two hundred had perished in the flames or in the icy water.

Amid the murky hell of the burning *Phoenix* looms forever the heroic figure of David Blish, a Southport merchant. Only thirty-three years of age and the father of four small children, he had every reason to wish to live, yet he cheerfully gave his life to ease the agony of a crowd of alien immigrants. Offered a place in one of the lifeboats, he declined, preferring "to take my chances with the rest," and while the boats were being loaded he stood at the gangplank to prevent them from swamping. During the voyage he had made friends with the Hollanders, paying particular attention to the children, and in their last agony he did not fail them. One story represents that when the fire was far advanced he took in his arms a lost and terror-stricken little girl, shielding her body from the flames by interposing his own. So he moved through the inferno, a veritable angel of mercy; at the end he contrived to launch a little raft and with two children still in his arms clung to it until overcome by the cold. "Greater love hath no man than this."

Fortunately for those who found places in the lifeboats, the lake was now calm after the storm which had prevailed. Although an effort had been made not to swamp the boats, they were loaded to capacity, and some who had plunged into the water endeavored to cling to them. One woman thus held on all the way to shore. Another passenger, a girl who had got her hands on one of the boats, was forcibly thrust off and sent to her death by those inside. In such an extremity necessity knows no other law. The second boat was launched with only one oar and had to be sculled all the way to shore. It dipped a good deal of water and the Hollanders baled this out with their wooden shoes.

Although there was no wholesale absence of discipline on the part of the crew, only three of whom manned each of the lifeboats, it is significant of the changing standards of the sea which have since come about that among them were the captain and the first mate of the *Phoenix*. Today such officers remain with their ship, while "women and children first" is the universal rule.

4: Social Reform

Michigan's involvement in social reform prior to the Civil War has been the concern of much research and writing, but the material is scattered. No author has synthesized this topic in a single monograph similar to *Freedom's Ferment* in which Alice Felt Tyler surveyed the reform movements that swept across the nation between the Revolutionary and Civil Wars. Recently published general histories, Willis F. Dunbar's *Michigan* and F. Clever Bald's *Michigan in Four Centuries,* do brush lightly over Michigan's role in the reform era, but these two authors concentrated heavily on the anti-slavery movement and the Civil War. Michigan's proximity to Canada, coupled with a heavy influx of New Englanders, made it an enthusiastic proponent of anti-slavery. Thus, it is not a distortion to emphasize the importance of the state's anti-slavery sentiment. Still, there were other reform urges in Michigan such as the agitation for co-educational opportunities at the University of Michigan, which stirred controversy as early as 1855.

Social communitarians, temperance advocates, and revivalists preached their messages or practiced their convictions in many corners of the state. Elijah Pilcher's *Protestantism in Michigan* (Detroit, 1878) explores some aspects of revivalism, but the basic research on this topic remains incomplete. The health food movement, frequently combined with medical quackery or bizarre religious tenets, came to clear expression in the career of Doctor John Kellogg. Gerald Carson's *Corn Flake Crusade* (New York, 1957) explores the origins and growth of the breakfast cereal industry in Battle Creek.

Other aspects of the reform movement are discussed in Floyd B. Streeter's "History of Prohibition Legislation in Michigan," *Michigan History Magazine,* II (1917); David C. Byers' "Utopia in Upper Michigan," *Michigan Alumnus Quarterly Review,* LXIII (1957), and Carl Wittke's "Ora Labora, A German Methodist Utopia," *Ohio Historical Quarterly,* LXVII (1958).

A Dangerous Experiment Begins

DOROTHY G. McGUIGAN

It was against this background in the 1850's—the rising momentum of the anti-slavery movement and the first agitation of woman's rights activists—that the debate over whether the University of Michigan should be opened to women began.

In Michigan boys and girls had always gone to grade school together, as they had in other parts of the country; simple economy dictated it. More often than not they had gone on together to the high schools, academies and seminaries. Girls had even been admitted to the University's "branches"—preparatory schools set up in towns throughout the state to ready students for the University, since the high schools were by no means of even quality.

Now families with daughters and no sons, or families with daughters as well as sons, began to wonder why, if they paid taxes, their daughters might not go on the the publicly-supported University.

The original statute of the University establishing it in 1837 simply declared that "the University shall be open *to all persons* who possess the requisite literary and moral qualifications."

A few colleges had accepted women in their classes from their founding—notably Oberlin and Antioch in Ohio, Hillsdale in Michigan, the University of Desaret in Utah, and the University of Iowa. And a few women's colleges had already been chartered; Georgia Female College and Mary Sharp College in Tennessee were probably the first.

The first salvo of the battle over coeducation at Michigan was fired in May of 1855, when the liberal-minded State Teachers' Association held their annual meeting in Ann Arbor, "the most interesting and important ever held by this body." Accounts of the lively debates at that meeting—which counted many women secondary school teachers among its members—were carried in *The Detroit Tribune* and *The Michigan Argus.*

Nearly all the speakers who followed Putnam favored the admission of women to the University.

Professor D. Putnam of Kalamazoo presented all the arguments against coeducation, which he proceeded to refute one by one, concluding with a ringing recommendation that "the system . . . be allowed to have a fair and impartial trial in the highest institution of the State," namely at the University.

University of Michigan Professor Erastus Haven, who would later become President, claimed long after in his autobiography that he had at this early date supported coeducation:

> So far as I know [he wrote of the Teachers' Convention debate] the subject had not been suggested before. It was considered wild and insane. Not a member of either Faculty approved it, but usually it was regarded as a rather dangerous joke on my part.

In actual fact, according to the report of the proceedings, Haven talked all around the point:

> "If the young women of the country were rising *en masse*, and demanding a college education, why do they not go to [Antioch, Oberlin] where the doors are open? It would not seem that there was so great a demand after all."

Furthermore, he said:

> "If we educate mind simply as mind, this would be right. But if our Colleges in their course of education, look to the preparation of young men for the profession of law, medicine and theology, then women would be necessarily excluded, as she would not choose to follow these professions."

What Haven really favored, both at the Teachers' Conference and later as President of the University, was not the admission of women on an equal basis, but rather a separate and not necessarily equal facility: "a Female Seminary . . . right across the street from our State University."

On the final day of their meeting the state teachers did adopt a resolution "that the coeducation of the sexes is in accordance with true philosophy, and is practically expedient."

If any women applied for admission to the University in the early 1850's, no record remains.

But in March of 1858, according to the Regents' Proceedings, a Miss Sarah Burger of Ann Arbor wrote the Board, informing them that "a class of twelve young ladies would present themselves for admission as students in June next." The Regents hastily tabled that letter, as if it were a combustible substance.

When the Regents met next, at Commencement time in June, one of the chief problems on the agenda was to act on the applications now in hand of Misses Sarah J. Burger and Harriet Ada Patton, of Ann Arbor, and of Miss Augusta J. Chapin of Lansing.

The Regents applied that classical device for handling knotty problems: a committee was appointed to study the matter, and report back in two days.

The next day, June 23, was Commencement—and Commencement in that day was a ceremony designed to be remembered all one's life. Attendance of graduates was compulsory; the solemn procession formed at 9 o'clock in the morning in 94° heat, and marched to the newly-built high school: the Governor, the State Superintendent of Public Instruction and the President of the University, the Board of Visitors, the Board of Regents, the entire faculty, the graduating class, and finally any students who wanted to participate. According to the *Detroit Free Press* reporter, who followed the events of those three days closely, the high school auditorium was jammed to capacity, the ceremony itself took eleven long hours in scorching heat and included no fewer than 13 full-length orations by members of the graduating class including one in Greek and one in Latin, a speech by President Henry P. Tappan, an address by an honored alumnus, and the conferring of degrees. In the evening the President held a levee at his house "for faculty, Regents, alumni and friends."

Exactly when the committee deliberated on the admission of women is not clear, but their report was ready the following morning of June 24 when the Regents again met. Two of the three members declared themselves in favor of admitting women; one member, Benjamin Baxter, former principal of the University's Tecumseh branch, dissented.

"Active and stormy session," the *Free Press* reported of the bitter argument that ensued. No doubt everyone was worn out by Commencement, but President Tappan was not too exhausted to oppose the admission of women with all the force he could muster—and even to take on the governor of the state. Governor Bingham had been invited to give his views on the subject and declared himself "favoring the admission of the ladies"; apparently he added a few remarks about the high-handed and authoritative stance the President and the faculty were taking. President Tappan replied saying "he should call on the Governor to sustain certain charges made by him in the course of his remarks against the University." Tappan then proceeded with all the arguments at his command to persuade the Board to postpone a decision.

He knew that his faculty, almost to a man, bitterly opposed opening the doors to women.

And he himself, who had set about remodelling Michigan along the lines of the German universities, viewed the admission of women as an unbearable threat to his whole concept of what a university should be.

A few years later, when he was no longer President and in self-exile in Europe, Tappan wrote his friend, German Professor E. P. Evans (1867):

> After [the admission of women] no advancement is possible. . . . The standard of education must now be accommodated to the wants of girls who finish their education at 16–20, very properly, in order to get married, at the very age when young men begin their education.

Tappan harked back to the anxieties expressed in the seventeenth-century pamphlet, *The Ladies Calling*:

> I sometimes fear we shall have no more women in America. If the Women's Rights sect triumphs, women will try to do the work of men—they will cease to be women while they will fail to become men—they will be something mongrel, hermaphroditic. The men will lose as the women advance, we shall have a community of *defeminated* women and *demasculated* men. When we attempt to disturb God's order we produce monstrosities.

The afternoon of June 24, 1858, ended with the question recommitted to the same committee for study over the summer. In the meantime that afternoon, "a petition from some young ladies of Lansing asking admission as students was received and referred to the committee on the subject."

On September 28, 1858, the Regents again gathered in Ann Arbor, but they did not reach the matter of women until their second day of business. After a favorable vote had been taken to appropriate $12.63 to buy twenty feet of Atlantic Cable for the University Museum, Regent McIntyre rose to read aloud his 14-page report, "On the Admission of Females," which would decide whether Sarah Burger and the other applicants would be the first women at Michigan.

. . . .

The committee had written during the summer to leading educators all over the country, asking their opinion on the question of coeducating the sexes. It need hardly be said that no women were consulted; such noted educators as Catherine Beecher, Emma Willard were passed over, for this was a decision to be made by men only.

The replies were, on the whole, scarcely astonishing.

President Woolsey of Yale declared that he "is averse to mingling the sexes in any place of education above the school for the elements." For, he adds, "Of what use degrees are to be to girls I don't see, unless they addict themselves to professional life, and I should expect the introduction of such a plan would be met with ridicule."

President Walker of Harvard averred that "there is an immense preponderance of enlightened public opinion against this experiment,"—in which opinion he entirely concurred, and that "its decision must turn in no small measure, on the question whether we propose to educate females for public or private life."

Dr. Nott of Union College was certain the whole matter had "already been decided by the common consent of mankind. . . . A difference of sex and of destination through the entire life has in the judgment of mankind been thought to require a difference in the distinctive attributes to be called into exercise. . . . Delicacy of sentiment, a feeling of dependence and shrinking from the public view, are attributes sought for in the one sex, in the other decision of character, self-reliance, a feeling of personal independence, and a willingness to meet opposition and encounter difficulties. . . ." He could not see how they could be educated together "without endangering alike their virtue and their happiness."

And finally Regent McIntyre read aloud letters from the presidents of two colleges where coeducation had actually been tried: Oberlin and Antioch.

Horace Mann, president of Antioch, had watched the experiment closely for five years. His reply could scarcely have been more cautious:

> The advantages of a joint education are *very great*. The dangers of it are *terrible*. Unless those dangers can be excluded with a degree of probability *amounting almost to certainty*, I must say that I should rather forego the advantages than incur the dangers.

Mann then proceeded to name the grave dangers that lay in wait for the unwary who tried the experiment:

> These dangers consist in their opportunities for association together *without supervision*, or *privately*. . . . If, for instance, women students must be permitted in a city like yours to board promiscuously among the inhabitants, I should prefer that the young women of the age should lose the advantages of an education rather than incur the moral danger of obtaining it in that way.

Mann suggested the Regents ask themselves such questions as:

> Can you make yourselves secure against *clandestine* meetings [of the sexes]? And also against clandestine correspondence—reasonably so, for absolute security is impossible. Are your President and Faculty in a state of mind to exercise vigilance over the girls committed to their care as conscientiously as they would over their own daughters or sisters?

If Horace Mann's letter did not thoroughly dampen any enthu-

siasm for coeducation among the Regents, the letter from President
C. G. Finney of Oberlin most certainly did:

> With us the results are quite satisfactory and even, we think, admirable.
> You will need a wise and pious matron with such lady assistants as to
> keep up sufficient supervision. You will need a powerful religious influ-
> ence to act upon the whole mass of students. You will need a surround-
> ing community who are united in sustaining the regulations and laws of
> the University in their details, so far as the moral conduct of the young is
> concerned.

The gentlemen listening to these grave words must surely have
blanched.

Some years before, dormitories for men had been abolished in
order to reduce the chores of discipline and regulation. Even so,
there had been quite enough troublesome problems involving young
male students—and frequently friction between town and gown; the
thought of maintaining the kind of monastic atmosphere President
Finney described at Oberlin was enough to shake the resolution of
the staunchest defender of coeducation—and there were none of
these in any case on the Board of Regents.

. . . .

In conclusion the committee, while protesting they were certain
the application of the young ladies for admission had nothing to do
with the unpopular woman's rights movement, managed to leave a
strong impression that in fact these applications very likely did. In a
final paragraph they tossed in the hair-raising phrase "Free Love," a
phrase to frighten any good Victorian family man concerned with
upholding honor, purity and motherhood:

> We give no heed to those who attempt to connect or identify the
> application of the young ladies which we are now considering with the
> political or social movements known as "Women's Rights," "Free Love,"
> etc. etc. This application has no such connection in our minds, and we
> would not have the question prejudiced or the request of these young
> ladies spurned because some persons who advocate the Free Love move-
> ment or attend Women's Rights conventions may also advocate the
> coeducation of the sexes.

In view of all the dangers involved, it was obviously inexpedient
to admit young ladies to attend the University. A suggestion was
made that perhaps at some future date, some suitable provision
might be made for their further education—a female seminary, no
doubt, that would educate young ladies, as Dr. Nott advised, for
their special sphere in life.

The findings of the University Board of Regents on the question of coeducation were duly published. The problem did not, however, go away.

In June of the following year, 1859, a petition signed by 1,476 citizens of the state was presented to the Regents, pleading that women be admitted.

And apparently not at all dashed by the tone of negative finality in that Regent's report, Sarah J. Burger of Ann Arbor again asked to be admitted, along with three other young ladies.

The Regents' response was to appropriate money to have 2,000 copies of their report printed and circulated throughout the State.

The next year the Civil War broke out. For the moment the question of admitting women was laid aside.

A Station on the Underground Railroad

PAMELA THOMAS
edited by Alexis Praus

I came to Schoolcraft in 1833, when sixteen years of age. We left Vermont May 23d, arriving here June 15th. The last time that I was in New England we were twenty-six hours making the journey.

When I reached Prairie Ronde, most of the land was in its natural state, the tall grass and wild flowers gave beauty to the landscape. This was four and a half years after the first settlement in this county. The fields, already under cultivation, gave promise of bountiful harvests, which were more than realized.

. . . .

A school house was built in 1834 and I taught the first public school on Prairie Ronde in the summer of that year. I had twenty-five or thirty pupils. Those recently from New England were bright scholars. Others, whose parents had always lived on the border of civilization, scarcely knew the alphabet. The latter were perhaps only the more eager to tread the paths of learning. I remember,

From *Michigan History*, XXXVII (Summer, 1953), 178-182. Reprinted by permission of the History Division, Michigan Department of State.

especially, the surprising progress made by a brother and sister aged ten and twelve years respectively.

The malaria arising from the decaying vegetation of the newly-turned prairie sod, together with crowded, ill-ventilated apartments, caused much sickness. We were among the sufferers. My sister was sick many weeks with fever and we all had ague.

The attending physician in our family, Dr. N. M. Thomas, whom I afterwards married, was an ardent antislavery advocate. He was a birthright member of the Society of Friends and from youth had been taught to abhor slavery. I thought him fanatical, when he asserted, "Slavery cannot continue to exist under our government. If it is not put down by the ballot, it will go down in blood." That was many years before William H. Seward wrote of "The Irrepressible Conflict."

Through my marriage with Dr. Thomas in 1840, I became connected with "The Underground Railroad." His antislavery views were so well known, that, while he was a bachelor boarding at the hotel, fugitives from slavery had called on him for assistance and protection on their way to the Queen's Dominion and freedom.

After we began housekeeping they came singly and by twos and threes. The first was a woman advanced in years, who had made her way on foot and alone from Missouri. At first she was helped by people of her own color, then by the Friends, or Quakers, who were always ready to aid the fleeing slaves. This woman was an eloquent talker. She told me what some women had to endure from cruel, licentious masters. From that time I felt it my duty to do the little I could for those attempting to escape from bondage.

About the year 1843 a Mr. Cross stopped with us. He was arranging for safe and speedy conveyance for fugitives from slavery to Canada. This was "The Underground Railroad" and our house was to be a station. Zachariah Shugart, a Quaker on Young's Prairie, in Cass County, was to bring the cargoes here and my husband was to have them taken to Mr. Erastus Hussey, a Quaker in Battle Creek. They soon began to arrive in loads of from six to twelve. This brought much hard work to me and great expense to my husband. Often after my little ones were asleep and I thought the labor of the day over, Friend Shugart would drive up with a load of hungry people to be fed and housed for the night.

My husband's extensive acquaintance with the antislavery men in this state frequently gave us the pleasure of entertaining genial, cultivated gentlemen. At the time the Presbyterian Church was organized in Schoolcraft—it was Congregational, I believe, at first— two elderly clergymen, who had often visited us, came to our house, accompanied by a young man, a recent graduate from the

Andover Theological School. He was sent by the Home Missionary Society to form a church in the West. And they decided upon Prairie Ronde. They came Saturday afternoon and we had an agreeable social visit. About dark, Friend Shugart drove up with a lumber wagon filled with colored people, whom I soon fed and ushered into my husband's office where couches were to be prepared for their rest until morning. The young candidate for the ministry asked if I was willing to have him pray with them. I assured him I had no objection.

Soon after his return to the sitting room, one of the elderly clergymen inquired, "Where is the Doctor this evening?" I answered, "He has gone to engage a man and team to take these colored people to Mr. Erastus Hussey's in Battle Creek in the morning." The youth turned a censorious glance toward me saying, "It does seem, when the Lord has protected them thus far on the road to freedom, that they ought to be allowed to rest on the Sabbath day." "Sir," said I, "How would my Sabbath be passed, if I had all of these colored folks to cook for?" The older minister laughed heartily, adding, "And the ministers too?" I echoed, "And the ministers too!" Long before the clergymen had arisen the next morning, the fugitives had eaten their breakfast and were on their way. Friend Shugart, too, had left for his own home.

When visiting relatives in Ann Arbor in 1844, we told of the aid we gave to the fugitive slaves. Our hostess, who was a member of the Baptist Church and whose husband was a deacon in the same church, remarked, "I think it right and am glad to have them escape, but I could not take them into my home." I told her that when overburdened with work, I often had occasion to recall the words, "Even as you have done it unto one of the least of these, you have done it unto Me." It also occurred to me that she never could have read James Montgomery's, "The Stranger and His Friend" with the same feelings with which I had perused that little poem when scarcely more than a child.

One of the most intelligent of escaping fugitives, Henry Bibb, came to our house with Mr. Treadwell in Jackson. My husband invited a houseful of friends and neighbors to hear him tell of his life in slavery. He also sang some of Whittier's antislavery songs with a voice and feeling that were very affecting.

In 1847 slave hunters came to Cass County, claiming men, women, and children as their property. The people rescued some of the bondsmen from their clutches and sent them posthaste on to Canada. A courier came to us with some of the fugitives, telling us of the danger, adding, "The slave hunters will soon be here." He asked us only to get food as they could halt but for a few moments.

I hastened to prepare what I could and asked for help from a kind neighbor, who often so accommodated me. They soon arrived, took the provisions without alighting and passed in safety to Canada. Their rescuers in Cass County were heavy losers financially, as they had resisted officers of the law. Friends subscribed generously for their relief, yet several were obliged to sell their farms. Many, as a result, moved to Oregon.

After the passage of the fugitive slave law of 1850, greater precaution was observed and fewer passed on the regular route through southwest Michigan. Yet, during the next ten years, many came to us. It has been estimated that during the twenty years that our house was a station, between one thousand and fifteen hundred received our aid.

At the close of the Civil War, a colored man, George Harris, who had lived in this county several years after escaping from bondage, came to see us and told of his experience as a soldier. He said he offered to enlist in this state, when the first troops were called for, but was refused on account of his color. Later he learned his name was on the roll for drafting. Preferring to go as a volunteer, he went to Boston, where he enlisted in a colored regiment and was at the taking of Charleston. He said he knew many in the same regiment who had been in Canada and came to help fight for the freedom of their brethren. They told him of being aided by my husband when escaping from slavery. Then he turned toward him, saying, "Doctor, that is the way you helped take Charleston."

It is now between thirty and forty years since the last of that long line of fugitives stopped at our house on the road to freedom. And I, an old lady of seventy-six years, feel glad and proud of my small share in the glorious emancipation, consummated by our Martyr President in his proclamation of 1863.

Letters to the Front:
A Distaff View of the Civil War

SOPHIA BINGHAM BUCHANAN
edited by George M. Blackburn

One hundred years after the Civil War ended, it would seem that every conceivable phase of that great conflict has been thoroughly studied and exhaustively narrated. Yet there are two broad areas of the Civil War about which final statements have not been made. One is the ultimate meaning of the war. Since the sectional strife was caused by differences of opinion over the most fundamental aspects of human life, such as freedom and government, and since each person has different standards or values, no amount of analysis will enable a historian to reduce the significance of the Civil War to a simple generalization. Obviously today the war has a different meaning to the governor of Mississippi and to an official of the National Association for the Advancement of Colored People. Likewise, contemporaries differed sharply on the meaning of the war. Some of them wrote extensively on the subject, but with divergent conclusions, depending upon whether an individual was a northerner or a southerner, a farmer or a plantation owner, a soldier or a civilian.

The articulate contemporary who wrote extensively on the war, however, was definitely in the minority. We just do not know what great numbers of the people thought. Some, like illiterate Negro slaves, left no written records, and their attitudes can be inferred largely by oral tradition. Others, such as soldiers' wives, were certainly literate, but left few records. While some kept diaries, the letters of wives to their soldier husbands seldom survived.

Fortunately, a collection of over sixty letters from Sophia Bingham Buchanan to her husband, Captain John Claude Buchanan, of the Eighth Michigan Infantry, has been preserved in the Clarke Historical Library at Central Michigan University. Highly literate, warm, and expressive, Sophia embodied the anxieties and trials suffered by women left behind as men fought the war.

. . . .

She wrote to her husband, Claude, as she called him, about all sorts of things. Naturally she was much interested in the war, and,

From *Michigan History*, XLIX (March, 1965), 53-67. Partially reprinted by permission of the History Division, Michigan Department of State. Footnotes in the original have been omitted.

true to her feminine nature, frequently viewed the war in highly personal terms.

> Why must we be separated? I often ask myself. Some one must go, you would say, & why not I! but oh! the loneliness & sadness that so often fills my soul, when I think of you, my cherished one, enduring toil & hardship for your country. Sometimes I cannot feel reconciled to it at all. But I try to keep up or I never could get along at all.

Sophia especially agonized after reading reports of battles.

> I am always delighted of course to get your letters, but after a battle, in which I know you are engaged, such anxiety & suspense is so great, I more than ever welcome them, as almost coming from one . . . near death's door. Oh, my dear husband, what great cause for thankfulness . . . that God has . . . spared your life. . . .

Sophie, as her husband called her, remembered when they had parted at Detroit on

> that beautiful, but to me sad moonlight night, [you said] . . . keep up good courage Sophie, the war will be over soon, & I'll come home all right, in a little while. How little did we think then, that you had scarce tasted of war. . . . God grant [that] we may meet again & be permitted to spend the remainder of our days, at our own fireside, in peace & happiness. What thrilling tales you will then have to tell your dear children—but I dare not anticipate, for . . . [who knows] How many lives, must still be sacrificed. . . .

She also remembered when the regiment left Grand Rapids.

> I shall never forget how you looked, as you turned the corner by Squire Moore's, the whole Reg. marching on the double quick, & you ran across the road, to us, gave [our son] Claudie a kiss, & hurried on. . . . Mr. Churche's tall, noble form, rises to view, as he stood among the men—all these sad scenes are past, & many who marched forth with that Regiment a year ago this pleasant morning, are no more among the living.

Often Sophie wondered whether Claude "regretted giving up all, & fighting nearly one year & a half . . . with apparently so very slight success?" Yet she saw the cause of the war quite clearly:

> this accursed sin slavery, which is at the root of all our trouble . . . , the South fighting to maintain slavery forever, & if possible to extend it over the whole land & re-establish . . . one of the barbarities of the dark ages, the abominable slave trade. . . . [Why would] part of our own loved America . . . ever become so perverted, & degraded as to try to ruin so wise & good a government, as our's has ever been. God grant [that] his righteous retribution, may fall upon the heads of those, who have attempted this, sown the seed of secession, & brought on this most cruel and senseless of wars.

She apologized after this outburst, but excused herself by saying "when I get to thinking of the state of our country, I at times can hardly contain myself." She never minimized the importance of the war. It was "no slight struggle, [but] a matter of life & death, to the most glorious nation, the sun ever shone upon."

With such views, it is not surprising that she took an unequivocal position on political matters, and that this position was staunchly Republican. After the fall elections of 1863, she wrote:

> you cannot think how we are rejoicing over the election's. A death blow to copperheadism, surely, & those against the Gov, & Union. . . . [We all trust] that "Honest old Abe" will be our next President. . . . Down with the traitor [Clement L.] Vallandigham & up with the stars & stripes of the good old Union forever.

Vallandigham was not the only copperhead she disliked. While visiting in Buffalo, New York, she rode past the home of Millard Fillmore, the former president. Her hostess charged that he was "a miserable copperhead, & she says no respectable or decent man, will have any conversation with him hardly."

The death of Abraham Lincoln dismayed Sophie.

> What times we are living in, plots, conspiracies, assassinations &c—glad Booth's dead—none to easy for so great a villain, how he must have suffered with his broken leg, & wound in the head. Shall soon be having fuller developments—but Gods ways are just our country will be saved.

This gentle, loving, Christian wife also developed some stern Old Testament ideas of conducting the war against traitors.

> I do hope [she wrote in September, 1862, that Thomas B. "Stone-wall"] Jackson and his horde will be cornered at last. I'de [sic] be almost willing to have you one of the number, to help string him up. I am getting very fierce in my feelings toward the rebels. It is too bad you are not allowed to subsist on them as you pass through their coun-try. . . . I often feel as if I ought never to laugh.

She had some rather fierce ideas on northern leaders, too.

> what do you think of our Gen's, & those who conduct our affairs, especially these late battles; Is it not awful? Have we no experienced officer's among us,? Is it treachery, or is it on account of the superior number's [sic] of the rebels that they seem every where to overpower us,? They are . . . better off in many respects, than they ever have been before. . . . If they can in so short a time drive our forces, from the places, which it took [George B.] McClellan so long to reach; I don't know what they can't do—.

Robert E. Lee's first invasion of the North, in September, 1862, amazed Sophie.

> The rebels are now in Maryland, & it does to us here, seem very strange, that with the large armies we have in the field, we have not been able to drive the enemy, but they us, with vastly inferior numbers. . . . God grant they may in some way, be entrapped . . . and the rebellion entirely crushed out. I cannot think of it otherwise, that our national government will fail. What would be the end of it all, I cannot look at it, in this light.

After Antietam, Sophie was disturbed at the seeming inactivity of the northern armies.

> It does seem strange that our army makes no forward movements as yet, I almost feel that more will die by exposure & suffering during the winter, than to go ahead & fight to either conquer or die, for I cannot feel that we shall be conquered, but I certainly have a great horror of any more battles, it makes me fairly sick at the thought of your going through any more.

She was pleased with the removal of General George McClellan and his replacement by Ambrose Burnside.

> We out of the army, think it the best thing that could be done. But although Little McS popularity among the soldiery seemed so great, yet I hope after a little, they will *all* see it is for the best.

A month before the catastrophe at Fredericksburg she felt "great confidence in Burnside, & hope[d] this will not prove a disastrous campaign."

On July 7, 1863, the newspapers reported a terrible fight at Gettysburg, "that the rebel army is whipped, & that they are on the retreat." With remarkable foresight, she anticipated that "a few battles gained on our side, at Vicksburg[,] Port Hudson, & one or two other places, would soon change the current affairs in our favor. . . ."

The current of affairs indeed changed after victories at Gettysburg, Vicksburg, and Port Hudson. Yet the North continued to need manpower desperately and toward the end of the war secured additional soldiers with the utmost difficulty. Sophia's observations corroborate the views of historians who hold that the quality of troops enlisted or drafted in 1863 and 1864 was far below that of those who entered service in 1861.

She believed the cavalry unit which organized at Grand Rapids in 1863 and numbered five hundred men, might

> much better be merged into another. I think their Col rather a soft man. It will never fill up here any way. They lose more by desertion than they gain by recruiting.